D1607965

Poe,
Death,
and the
Life of
Writing

Poe, Death, and the Life of Writing

J. Gerald Kennedy

Yale University Press
New Haven and London

For Sarah

Designed by Sally Harris
and set in Goudy Oldstyle type by The Composing Room of Michigan, Inc.
Printed in the United States of America

Library of Congress Cataloging-in-Publication Data

Kennedy, J. Gerald.
   Poe, death, and the life of writing.

   Bibliography: p.
   Includes index.
   1. Poe, Edgar Allan, 1809–1849—Criticism and interpretation.
2. Death in literature. I. Title.
PS2642.D35K4   1987   818'.309   86–15981
ISBN 0–300–03773–2 (alk. paper)

10 9 8 7 6 5 4 3 2 1

Contents

Preface   vii

Acknowledgments   x

1 Writing and the Problem of Death   1

2 Notes from Underground: Premature Burial   32

3 The Horrors of Translation:
The Death of a Beautiful Woman   60

4 The Rhetoric of Dread: Poe's Letters   89

5 Revenge and Silence: The Foreclosure of Language   114

6 Unreadable Books, Unspeakable Truths   145

7 Metamorphoses of the Shadow   177

Notes   215

Index   225

Death looks gigantically down. — "The City in the Sea"

Preface

I can think of no better figure for the contextual emphasis of this book
than the "great wings of flame" blazing from the bank of candles in
Henry James's "The Altar of the Dead." For Stransom's altar marks
the culmination of a relationship with death that was a distinctive
feature of Anglo-American culture in the nineteenth century. De-
voting himself so completely to the dead that he fails to recognize the
possibilities of life with the woman who shares his vigil, Stransom
participates in the celebration of death; his practice seems an extravagant last flourish of the sentimental cult of mourning. Yet his altar
becomes increasingly a tribute to death itself rather than a sign of
grief or remembrance. As the candles grow more numerous, he perceives his existence in terms of absence rather than presence; and he
fixes egotistically upon the void or gap which his own death will fill.
James implies that Stransom's practice has become a secular substitute for belief and ritual. His tale thus looks ahead to the twentieth
century, to the metaphysical darkness defining the modern condi-

tion. James sounds this note in the final sentence, as Mary Antrim feels Stransom slump against her shoulder: "But alone with him in the dusky church a great dread was on her of what might still happen, for his face had the whiteness of death."

"The Altar of the Dead" gives genteel expression to the nineteenth-century crisis of death which had already received its most intensive treatment in the writing of Edgar Allan Poe. In a dismissive critique (*New York Review of Books*, October 11, 1984), Harold Bloom remarked of Poe: "I can think of no other American writer, down to this moment, at once so inescapable and so dubious." Poe has indeed remained oddly marginal, but not for the reasons adduced by Bloom, who (reviving the argument of Aldous Huxley) associates Poe with shoddiness and vulgarity. Instead, Poe remains a problematic figure because his relentless images of violence, death, grief, and decay limn the conditions of being which in the twentieth century we have done our best to deny or forget. One tactic for deflecting the psychosymbolic content has been to consider Poe (as Bloom does) principally as a fright-merchant, a writer "best read when we are very young." James himself once wrote that to take Poe "with more than a certain degree of seriousness is to lack seriousness one's self." This aversion is a curious reflex, symptomatic of the need to keep at arm's length the disturbing material which Poe—with what some would call bad taste—insists on forcing us to contemplate. But he is and will remain inescapable for the reason that his wild texts possess (as Bloom concedes) a mythological power, a capacity to stir our most basic anxieties and desires, to project in graphic terms the fixations of modern consciousness.

Poe's responsiveness to the problem of death led to self-conscious reflection upon writing and the power of words. Virtually from the outset, he began to explore the reciprocity between death and inscription, and in a broad sense his entire oeuvre may be thought of as a manuscript-in-a-bottle, a protracted discourse on the radical silence which makes writing possible and necessary. In his contemplation of textuality, Poe anticipates many of the conceptions of writing which have come under discussion in the last thirty years. Joseph Riddel has argued that the deconstruction of logocentrism and the metaphysics of presence begins with Poe; from a similar perspective I contend that the rupture between word and world, signifier and signified, finds its origin in the semiotic impasse of mortality located by Poe.

And so this book moves from a contextual study of death in the nineteenth century to a more speculative consideration of language and metaphysics. I have tried to bring together here a variety of approaches—old and new literary history, psychobiographical criticism, literary theory, and close examination of key texts with a concern for cultural history and the anthropology of death. Rather than pursue a narrow theme or rigid thesis, I have tried to distinguish a variety of ways in which death traverses writing; hence the first and last chapters develop contrasting perspectives of this relationship, the former in largely historical terms, the latter from a more theoretical perspective. Exactly between them I have situated a chapter on Poe's letters, quite deliberately to provide a connection between writing and lived experience. The remaining four chapters explore particular texts or sets of texts in which the juxtaposition of writing and death acquires some distinctive elaboration: in relation to premature burial, the translation of a beautiful woman, the poetics of revenge, or the unreadability of death.

We now perceive that dread, the "sickness unto death," is a relatively recent phenomenon and that the sentimental cult of mourning in the nineteenth century was a last, desperate tactic to mask its horror. Poe's current importance lies precisely in his recognition of the catastrophe figured by annihilation, for he anticipated the enthronement of death in our own century and probed the origins of existential despair. Daniel Hoffman once quipped that "Edgarpoe is not, decidely not, the Samuel Smiles of American Literature." Yet Poe's engagement with the life of writing marks, in its sardonic way, a resistance to the fatality of his own vision. For in writing he found a life, both in the sense of career or vocation and in the sense of an alternate existence, a space of play. That is, the recognition of death's enormity was for Poe a vitalizing insight, enabling him to frame a new relationship to writing mindful of the uncertain status of words in what he called a "Universe of Vacancy."

Acknowledgments

The writing of this book began during the winter of 1978–79 at the Franco-American Commission on the rue Chardin in Paris, where, armed with a pen, a notebook, and my battered Modern Library edition of Poe, I worked out some ideas about death and writing (the first draft of my comments on "MS. Found in a Bottle") at a quiet table provided by Genevieve Acker. The impetus for this work came largely from a Collège de France seminar by Roland Barthes called "Préparation du roman"; his reflections had suggested a provocative way of thinking about the "desire of writing" and one's consciousness of mortality. Through those unpredictable lectures, Barthes explored his compulsion to write an autobiographical novel of memory and his presentiment of impending death. I spoke with him only once, and the conversation was simultaneously unremarkable and memorable. Rather than a theoretical framework or a critical method, he provided the example of a writer insistently pursuing the origins of his own death-defying activity.

Through the several stages of composition and revision which have produced this book, a number of friends have tendered assistance of one kind or another. James W. Gargano, Louis J. Budd, G. R. Thompson, Martha Banta, and Lewis P. Simpson kindly wrote supporting letters for grant applications. Howard Kerr asked me to write the Poe essay for *The Haunted Dusk* (University of Georgia Press, 1983) and thus enabled me to try out some of the approaches employed in the present study. Joan Dayan directed me to the work of Blanchot, and John Irwin gave counsel and encouragement at a critical juncture. Several colleagues at Louisiana State University have supplied useful information: James Olney on death in autobiography; Joseph Kronick on Heidegger; Bainard Cowan on Lacan and Derrida; Fred Schwarzbach and Richard Burke on death in Victorian England. My former colleague Max Webb first interested me in *The Denial of Death*, a book that changed the way I read Poe. And my father, John R. Kennedy, tracked down a rare copy of John J. Moran's *Defense of Edgar Allan Poe*.

I owe special thanks to Daniel Hoffman, Barton Levi St. Armand, and John Carlos Rowe for careful readings of the manuscript. I have benefited from their understanding of Poe and the nineteenth-century context. I am also appreciative of the efforts of Ellen Graham, Channing Hughes, and Stella Hackell at Yale University Press.

Louisiana State University has contributed to the completion of this book through a summer grant from the Council on Research and a sabbatical leave. The College of Arts and Sciences has provided released time for research, and the Department of English has handled much of the photocopying associated with the project.

Finally, I would like to thank my wife, Sarah, for her careful proofreading, superb editorial suggestions, boundless patience, and professional grasp of the difficulties of writing. She has made this a better book, but more important, she has opened for me a rich and happy life. At the end of *The Second Coming*, Walker Percy's Will Barrett reflects on the transformative effect of Allie Huger's love and asks himself, "Is she a gift and therefore a sign of a giver?" I understand Will Barrett's question.

1

Writing and the
Problem of Death

In the grip of death, Poe's Ligeia asks her husband to recite "certain verses composed by herself not many days before." Nineteenth-century readers must have anticipated a scene of deathbed intimacy in which the dying woman would through a consolatory rhyme signify her readiness to die. Similar scenes filled contemporary fiction and poetry and—according to memoirs and biographies of the same period—mirrored a pervasive social practice. In Victorian England as well as America, "the deathbed presented the last preserve of truth; it was a final opportunity to repent, admonish or encourage." The deathbed scene enabled writers of fiction to convey "the basic importance of the moral scheme" which underlay the popular literature of the day.[1] Dickens relied shamelessly on valedictions such as the passing of Little Johnny in *Our Mutual Friend,* and Charlotte Brontë drew upon the same convention to dispatch Helen Burns in *Jane Eyre.* For mid-century American readers, *Uncle Tom's Cabin* provided the quintessential deathbed scene, in which little Eva's "adoring Papa and a group of equally adoring slaves cluster in unspeakable grief around her bedside while she dispenses Christian wisdom and her own golden locks with profuse generosity."[2] In the ritual of farewell, all that was sacred in bourgeois, middle-class culture— innocence, love, piety, and death—commingled in a moment of idealized beauty.

As if to parody the conventional beatific parting, however, Poe ascribed to the dying Ligeia a five-stanza poem entitled "The Conqueror Worm." The lyric contains no uplifting vision, no affirmation of faith, no acceptance of death. Instead, it portrays the human condition as a "play of hopes and fears," a "motley drama" staged for "an angel throng, . . . drowned in tears," powerless to intervene in a pantomime of futility and annihilation.[3] Whereas sentimental literature emphasized the sacredness of death and insisted on the beauties of the deathbed, Ligeia sees only the physical horror personified by the intrusion of the writhing "blood-red thing," the Conqueror Worm. The narrator's recitation simply intensifies the dread Ligeia already feels; far from resigning herself to God's will, the woman springs to her feet and demands: "Shall these things be undeviatingly so?—shall this Conqueror be not once conquered?" Her challenge is both to the wisdom of Providence and to the religion of sentiment; her shocking verses overturn the prevailing image of death's loveliness and expose the hideous truth of decomposition. With Ligeia's defiant response, Poe deconstructs the idealized deathbed scene and calls into question the metaphysical assumptions upon which it was based.

Significantly, Ligeia reacts to the imminence of death through a gesture of language; she calls for a poem which allegorizes the very struggle in which she finds herself. If it does not deliver her from her creaturely predicament, the poem nevertheless voices primal anxiety and articulates the paradox that although man is created "in the form of God on high," he suffers the ignominious and revolting fate of becoming food for worms. "Are we not part and parcel in Thee?" the dying Ligeia asks her Creator, returning to the complaint of her poem. That she has recorded in writing her thoughts on dying enables the narrator to repeat her words at the hour of death. Initially, both the request and the performance seem perverse, for the poem violates the decorum of her passing: it throws into doubt the meaning of death and the survival of the soul. Indeed, the poem rigorously excludes the spirit and reduces man to "human gore." Why then has Ligeia called for the poem's recitation, and why has the narrator obeyed her? As a symbolic act, the deathbed reading inscribes a parable of the relation between language and mortality. In this crucial moment, the poem's verbal imaging of horror evokes a desperate resistance to death; its reiteration summons the woman's volcanic desire for life. Here, in the most elemental way, the word calls forth the will to be. And the narrator's presentation of the poem (in its ultimate enshrinement as a written text) marks another kind of resistance to death: language effects a symbolic transcendence of mortality. Although the poet must die, the poet's words survive as writing.

In considering the deathbed scene from "Ligeia" as a commentary on the complicity between writing and death, we arrive at a theoretical problem that pervades Poe's work and extends as well into the whole tradition of writing in Western culture. For the use of a mediating notation to signify an absent reality belongs—like death—to the legacy of man's mythic fall. In a sense the anthropological transition from oral to written culture reenacts the primal loss of an immediate and whole relationship to the created world; inscription is the sign of a transformation of consciousness.[4] The writing of Poe presents us, however, with more than a useful instance of the phenomenon we seek to probe; in ways to be developed hereafter, the modern crisis of death expresses itself most intelligibly in Poe and leaves its trace in a radical redefinition of the status of writing.

Poe's attraction to the problem of death is so conspicuous that the reticence of modern criticism on the subject seems inexplicable. Here we find a writer whose entire oeuvre is marked by a compulsive interest in the dimensionality of death: its physical signs, the phenomenology of dying, the deathbed scene, the appearance of the corpse, the effects of decomposition, the details of burial, the danger of premature interment, the reanimation of the dead, the lure of tombs and cemeteries, the nature of mourning and loss, the experience of dread, the compulsion to inflict death upon another, and the perverse desire to seek one's own death. Typically these elements have been thought to express an unsound and morbid sensibility, a neurosis rooted in traumatic early experience, a conscious exploitation of Gothic conventions to produce the effect of terror, or an esoteric symbolism for the representation of philosophical or aesthetic concepts. This summary perhaps leaves out of account other passing theories, but the general tendency—toward a critical translation of mortality—displays itself in the landmark work of Edward Davidson. While noting that Poe, "perhaps better than any other writer of his time, defined the [contemporary] idea of death," Davidson equates mortality with concealed eroticism and concludes that "death became . . . a series of seductive postures."[5] This inclination to construe death in Poe as sheer convention or as a code for other problems is itself symptomatic of a contemporary blind spot—our twentieth-century tendency (identified by Robert Jay Lifton, Ernest Becker, and others) to repress the reality of death much as the Victorians repressed references to sexuality.[6] What criticism has largely overlooked is Poe's relentless effort to probe the nature of modern death anxiety.

For Poe the imaginary was dominated by the gigantic presence of death; but death held contradictory meanings, and its tangible image changed through the course of his engagement with writing. The following chapters pursue that phantasm to elucidate the writer's ambiguous response to a phenomenon variously experienced as a physical threat, a locus of anxiety, a tantalizing opacity, a disjunction of body and spirit, an absurd predicament, and—perhaps most important—an impetus for writing. But in directing this intense gaze upon Poe's texts, we shall concern ourselves somewhat less with their originality than with their semiotic features—that is, their tendency to encode recognizable psychic patterns, popular beliefs, contemporary myths, and philosophical questions, often in response to the conventions of magazine writing. For in mapping the relationship between writing and death in Poe, we perceive that inscription and mortality possess their own distinct histories within Western experience. Insofar as these histories can be rendered intelligible, we bring to the study of Poe's texts new perspectives on the symbolic interplay between language and silence. In effect, this book explores the theory that the very strangeness of Poe's poetry and fiction is less the symptom of an occult imagination than the sign of a cultural uncertainty which manifested itself—among other ways—in destabilized conceptions of both writing and death.

Before we can disentangle this relationship, however, we must briefly examine the social history of death to clarify the dilemma which encompassed Poe's career and shaped the perception and meaning of the end of life. We approach this problem somewhat blindly, for the modern aversion to death distorts our perception of nineteenth-century customs, which treated death as an elaborate celebration and melancholy as a fashionable affect. Death was not simply more acceptable to the nineteenth century; it was a subject of quiet fascination, even (one must conclude) a source of contemplative pleasure. Mourning art—in the form of samplers, vases, and jewelry—proliferated in the early nineteenth century, generating an iconography of loss that became conventionalized and ubiquitous. The experience of dying was a public event; one's passage from this life involved extravagant preparation, both in the recording of one's parting sentiments and in the solemn deathbed gathering of family and friends. The funeral assumed major significance—indeed, it became an industry during this period—and the mounting cost of funerals even led to the creation in England of burial clubs (much like the Christmas clubs of modern banks). Spacious new cemeteries sprang up in London, Paris, New York, Philadelphia, and Boston, accommodating elaborate monuments and providing picturesque sites for increasingly pompous burials.

This was, in the apt phrase of Philippe Ariès, the "age of the Beautiful Death," a period characterized (on the surface, at least) by a romantic conception of the earthly parting, in which the prospect of an otherworldly rendezvous loomed large. In the wake of eighteenth-century rationalism, orthodox religious sentiment enjoyed a superficial resurgence in consolation literature, as the hour of death became a fetishized event. Popular literature sponsored an ethereal image of mortality, purged of gross physical detail. Ariès summarizes the pervasive attitude:

> Since death is not the end of the loved one, however bitter the grief of the survivor, death is neither ugly nor fearful. On the contrary, death is beautiful, as the dead body is beautiful. Presence

at the deathbed in the nineteenth century is more than a customary participation in a social ritual; it is an opportunity to witness a spectacle that is both comforting and exalting. . . . But this apotheosis should not blind us to the contradiction it contains, for this death is no longer death, it is an illusion of art. Death has started to hide. In spite of the apparent publicity that surrounds it in mourning, at the cemetery, in life as well as in art and literature, death is concealing itself under the mask of beauty.[7]

Lawrence Stone has also observed an undercurrent of anxiety in the sentimental response to mortality: "The fashionable preoccupation with melancholy presupposed a certain scepticism about the prospects of another and a happier world after death."[8] This contradiction carries important implications for the way we read contemporary mourning art, consolation literature, and the lugubrious tales and verses of the ladies' magazines. The illusion of lovely death and its attendant melancholy disguised troubling doubts about ultimate concerns.

How the nineteenth century arrived at this ornately artificial practice deserves closer attention. As Ariès and Stone have shown in their separate investigations, the notion of a beautiful departure itself marked a break with earlier ways of thinking about mortality. So far as one can determine from early records, wills, funerary sculpture, literature, visual art, and treatises in the *artes moriendi* tradition, the reassuring model of "familiar and tame" death prevailed throughout Europe from the Middle Ages until the end of the Renaissance. Understandably, high mortality rates made death seem a commonplace, expected phenomenon; Stone points out that during the Renaissance, "death was at the centre of life, as the cemetery was at the centre of the village." Even as late as the eighteenth century, most children died before reaching adulthood: "About half of the recorded children of French peasantry were dead by the age of ten, and between a half and two-thirds by the age of twenty. In the cities, conditions were worse still, and in London in 1764, forty-nine per cent of all recorded children were dead by the age of two, and sixty per cent by the age of five."[9]

Such high rates of mortality created the sense of death as a con-

stant, natural presence. Stone observes that "all affective relationships were thus at the mercy of sudden and unexpected death."
For adults, the hour of death involved a simple adieu without orna-
ment or sentimentality, yet it was attended by public ritual which
enabled both the dying person and his survivors to bear the parting.
Serious attention was given to the idea of the good death and to the
art of dying well, reconciled to the will of God. Loss of children,
however, carried less importance, for the likelihood of early death
obliged parents to "limit the degree of their psychological involvement with their infant children."[10] Nearly all burials were carried out
under the aegis of the Church, which provided both a theological
understanding of death and the consoling hope of a spiritual afterlife.
Ariès contends that prior to the Enlightenment, "human beings as
we are able to perceive them in the pages of history [had] never really
known the fear of death." If they felt sorrow about the inevitability of
death, "their anxiety never crossed the threshold into the unspeakable, the inexpressible. It was translated into soothing words and
channeled into familiar rites."[11] The traditional intimacy between
man and death diminished the psychological anguish of dying; the
familiar sight of dead bodies neutralized the corpse as a physical
image. These conditions enabled people to live—so far as one can
determine—without anxiety about their bodily fate. They sometimes feared the spiritual judgment associated with death, but dying
itself seems not to have aroused anticipatory dread.

By the end of the eighteenth century, however, conditions had
begun to change dramatically. Declining child mortality rates and
increasing life expectancies meant that death assumed a different
aspect: no longer a familiar presence, an expected visitor, it gradually
became a feared intruder. Revised expectations about the survival of
children (as well as spouses and friends) prompted the growth of more
affectionate relationships, which in turn altered the meaning of the
loss of a loved one: "The death of an infant or young child was no
longer shrugged off as a common event on which it would be foolish
to waste much emotion."[12] John McManners reports that "between
1700 and 1800 fully ten years were added to the average life span of
Frenchmen," creating the general impression that "death was being
defeated."[13] At the same time, the rise of rationalized religion, in

which God came to be viewed as the benign but distant maker of a harmoniously ordered world, helped to erode belief in a sacred, divinely intended death and in an edifying distinction between heaven and hell. The more "enlightened" view of death rejected the notion of eternal judgment as incompatible with divine benevolence. While the traditional concept of heaven retained some attraction, death became an increasingly secular occurrence; as Stone suggests, "the dying, as well as the survivors, were affected by the decline of confidence in the consolations of religion."[14]

Meanwhile the place of burial shifted from local churchyards to more remote public cemeteries, created to alleviate insanitary conditions in the city. As a public project, the relocation of cemeteries seems to imply a general indifference toward the dead and their burial, as if changing religious views had effected a communal devaluation of death. Yet this civic indifference stands in contrast to the private, individual experience of loss. Stone asserts: "There was an intensification of grief in the eighteenth century, and it was expressed not only more openly, and more bitterly, but also less ritually, in a more personal, more introspective manner."[15] For the bereaved, the cemetery became a focus of grief, the place of frequent visits: "Now people wanted to go to the very spot where the body had been placed, and they wanted this place to belong totally to the deceased and to his family."[16] Until this period, Ariès adds, "the pious or melancholy visit to the tomb of a dear one was an unknown act." But within a single generation, the visit to the cemetery became a significant practice; physical remains gave meaning to a plot of earth. Previously paupers and common people had been buried in open, mass graves; now even the poor desired an individual burial site and a memorial stone. This is precisely the sentiment of Gray's "Elegy Written in a Country Church-Yard," a poem which captures the idea of pleasurable melancholy while revealing the anxiety of oblivion: even if the "paths of glory" led but to the grave, the common villager as well as the hero felt the desire for remembrance.

The remarkable popularity of graveyard poetry toward the middle of the century provides the best evidence of a tendency to regard the tomb as a focus of meditation. As religion began to lose its consolatory force, death acquired a disquieting power over the imagination. Curiously, many of the poets associated with the cult of melancholy were themselves clergymen; their verses manifest an implicit attempt to recover death (which had been in a demographic sense defeated or banished) as an aid to Christian reflection. But their preoccupation with things sepulchral had quite a different general effect: popular works like Young's *Night Thoughts* and Blair's *The Grave* excited curiosity about the physical sensations of death, introduced fantasies about dead spirits, and conferred upon the tomb and the cemetery an irresistible fascination. For centuries, death had simply marked a passing, a movement toward a more important fate; with longer life expectancies, closer affective relationships, secularized funeral practices, and declining belief in an afterlife, death assumed a terrible significance in itself and was no longer familiar or tame.

Clearly the patterns of change in the later eighteenth century—notably the fetish for graveyards and melancholy—created the enabling conditions for the elaborate pageant of death that unfolded during the next century. The idealizing of death did not begin, however, with one dramatic event; rather it emerged from the nascent Romantic tendencies of the preceding era. As Enlightenment rationalism gave way to a sensibility infused with nature-worship, sentimentality, superstition, and transcendental idealism, death itself began to acquire similar attributes. One obvious development was the growing association between death and nature; death was increasingly displaced from its traditional religious context and linked to natural processes and cycles. In "Thanatopsis," William Cullen Bryant sought to efface "sad images / Of the stern agony, and shroud, and pall" with a sweeping view of natural splendors adorning "the great tomb of man." This commingling of nature and death reached its culmination in the rural cemetery movement, which endeavored to "convert the graveyard from a shunned place of horror into an enchanting place of succor and instruction."[17] For those generations raised on Rousseau, Wordsworth, and Chateaubriand, nature seemed the sign of an enfolding and consoling spiritual presence which softened the harshness of death. The inheritors of deism regarded the isolated tomb in a rural setting as the ideal site to worship God "as the author of the beauties of Nature, as [a being] supremely generous and good, and as the guarantor of the continuance of human loves and friendships beyond the grave."[18]

Interest in sustaining relationships beyond the grave reveals another aspect of change. The intensification of affective relationships, which Stone ascribes to demographic trends, led to a new emphasis in the nineteenth century on death as a separation of loved ones: "The centre of attention now shifted from the behaviour of the dying to the response of the living."[19] Ariès describes this new perspective as "the death of the other," indicating that the hour of death now found its primary meaning as social ritual—as a privileged occasion for edification and sentiment. Those who gathered to witness a death effectively enforced the decorum of dying. To manifest their involvement in the death of the other, mourners began to symbolize their sentimental attachment to the corpse through memorial jewelry which often included a lock of hair from the deceased. The proliferation of mourning art in America (said to date from the death of George Washington in 1799) testifies to a revealing vogue for commemoration.[20] Romantic emphasis on individualism, the uniqueness of the self, found its outcome in the practice of marking an individual's death with artifacts of remembrance. Commemoration became a sign of devotion, a measure of one's love for the departed Other; in this way memorializing gestures—such as wearing a mourning necklace or visiting a tomb—symbolically extended the relationship severed by death.

During the early nineteenth century social and religious practice conspired to make an edifying aesthetic spectacle out of the banal experience of death. John Reed notes that for the Victorians, the beauty of the deathbed scene required a studied avoidance of the actual physical death. He cites Dr. Dabbs's account of the death of Tennyson ("a figure of breathing marble, flooded and bathed in the light of the full moon streaming through the oriel window"), which reminds the physician not of gross physical reality but of the poet's own "Passing of Arthur."[21] This exemplary scene suggests that the nineteenth-century impression of death's beauty involved an act of communal self-delusion, a tacit refusal to see dying as a physical process. Yet the age also developed a paradoxical attachment to the dead body: death masks, portraits "in death," and locks of hair woven into floral designs all reflect this preoccupation. So too does the characteristic nineteenth-century funeral, with its ritualized attention to a corpse attired in handsome clothing, surrounded by flowers, displayed in a polished coffin, and (with growing frequency) embalmed to eliminate the possibility of odor. The funeral procession, carried out with increasing pomp, often featured an ornate, glass-sided hearse which enabled mourners to gaze upon the coffin. James Stevens Curl's description of the Victorian funeral suggests the material extremes of this "celebration of death" as practiced in England. [22] American burial customs, though less extravagant, disclose a similar attachment to the very body whose disfigurement had been largely ignored during the crisis of death.

This seemingly contradictory attitude embodies an essential dilemma in nineteenth-century culture. Death itself had become less familiar through increased life expectancy, and closer family relationships made its intrusion seem a cruel, inexplicable deprivation. In the face of these anxieties, a pious consolation literature sprang into being; as if to offset doubts about the Christian promise of eternal life, authors concocted detailed descriptions of the amenities of heaven. Ann Douglas has called attention to the necrolatry inherent in these works: "Such writings inflated the importance of dying and the dead by every possible means; they sponsored elaborate methods of burial and commemoration, communication with the next world, and microscopic viewings of a sentimentalized afterlife." [23] But the continuing erosion of Christian belief, together with the development of scientific interest in the physiology of dying (to be discussed in chapter 2) further intensified the sense of a horrible discontinuity between bodily dissolution and spiritual transcendence. Indeed, the physical signs of approaching death now presented such a powerful challenge to faith that nominal believers agreed to ignore the former in order to protect the latter. Mounting uncertainty about the survival of the soul seems in fact to underlie the conflicted strategy of the Beautiful Death. Behind this paradoxical practice, we see that the aversion to the dying flesh and the fetishization of the dead body are symptoms of the same doubts about the meaning of mortality. One cannot escape the impression that the cult of death and memory flourished precisely because it undertook to insure at least a limited, symbolic perpetuation of the deceased, a material survival in the signs and artifacts of mourning.

A long view of Western attitudes toward death—even one as diffuse as Ariès'—reveals an increasing velocity of change from the eighteenth century through the twentieth. The reassuring model of the tame death, prevalent until the late seventeenth century, disappeared with the rise of an urban, industrialized, post-Christian culture.[24] In its place emerged a multiplicity of contending beliefs and assumptions, generating pervasive anxiety about the nature and meaning of death. The Christian message of resurrection continued to be preached, although clergymen as frequently extolled the beauty of dying, outlined the spiritual benefits of grief, or portrayed heaven as a glorious family reunion. But an essential surety had been lost, and in the burgeoning cities of England and America, where capitalism had already supplanted Christianity by seeming to embrace it, a secular materialism had taken root, alienating inhabitants from each other through a subtle breakdown of communal beliefs. Perhaps in response to the obscure sense of social fragmentation and metaphysical uncertainty, believers and nonbelievers turned to death and its rituals as the last stronghold of collective values. David Stannard reaches a similar conclusion about the "overriding national treatment of death" between the Revolution and the Civil War:

> In large measure, if not entirely in response to the growing individual anonymity brought on by changes in their social world, Americans sought a return to their lost sense of community in the graveyard and the heavenly world of the dead; in the process, paradoxically, they effectively banished the reality of death from their lives by a spiritualistic and sentimentalized embracing of it.[25]

That is, the celebration of death dramatized the desire to reestablish bonds of commitment and solidarity in a decentered society, but by masking death in beauty it obscured the primal basis of community.

Many of Poe's contemporaries nevertheless participated in the effort to invest mortality with sentimentalized beauty. Displaying as much commercial acumen as craftsmanship, Washington Irving included among the materials for *The Sketch Book* a richly representative piece entitled "Rural Funerals," which expatiates on devotion to the dead: "The love which survives the tomb is one of the noblest attributes of the soul. . . . Aye, go to the grave of buried love, and meditate!" Irving also included two tales of pathos, "The Broken Heart" and "The Pride of the Village," which illustrate the sentimental association of death with young women. In the latter tale, an expiring maiden forgives the young soldier who fatally jilted her:

> He rushed into the house, and flew to clasp her to his bosom; but her wasted form—her death like countenance—so wan, yet so lovely in its desolation, smote him to the soul, and he threw himself in an agony at her feet. She was too faint to rise—she attempted to extend her trembling hand—her lips moved as if she spoke, but no word was articulated—she looked down upon him with a smile of unutterable tenderness, and closed her eyes forever.[26]

Although Irving sometimes approached the realm of terror (as in "The Adventure of the German Student"), he rarely contemplated the physical manifestations of death; he was obsessed by mutability rather than decomposition, and the tone of nostalgic melancholy struck a chord of response in a period of idealized death.

Though hardly a sentimentalist, James Fenimore Cooper also found the convention of beautiful death inescapable when he brought Leatherstocking to the bar of judgment in *The Prairie*. The aged trapper, surrounded by his Indian friends and his young protégé, Middleton, takes his leave in a ceremony of farewell which (while technically lacking a bed) incorporates the features of the standard deathbed scene. The old man's virtuous existence has enabled him to die beautifully and without suffering: "Decay, when it did occur, was rapid, but free from pain."[27] Leatherstocking declares his faith—"I die as I have lived, a Christian man"—and blesses those around him. He expresses uncertainty about meeting his Indian friends in heaven, alluding delicately to the notion of a racially segregated hereafter; but he allows that the Christian heaven and "the place of Good Spirits" may be the same: "If it should prove that the same meaning is hid under different words, we shall yet stand together." He provides for the distribution of his earthly goods, requests that his faithful dog

Hector be buried with him, and then speaks of the importance of commemoration by recalling his efforts to secure "a graven stone" for his father's resting place. The point of his story is not lost on Middleton, who promises to place a stone at the head of the trapper's grave. Even the simple woodsman betrays his desire for remembrance and specifies the inscription for his memorial stone: " 'Put no boastful words on the same, but just the name, the age, and the time of death, with something from the holy book; no more, no more. My name will then not be altogether lost on 'arth; I need no more.' "[28] Here Cooper juxtaposes the serenity of faith with the anxiety of oblivion; Leatherstocking must insure his own commemoration before he can go peacefully to his rest. The author underscores the symbolic importance of the gesture by referring in the final paragraph to the perpetuation of the trapper's memory. The grave "is often shown to the traveller and the trader as a spot where a just White man sleeps," and faithful to his word, Middleton has provided the requested stone, adding only one line dictated by a need to sanctify the burial site: " 'May no wanton hand ever disturb his remains!' " The isolated grave becomes the focus of melancholy visitation and remembrance.

One has only to compare the death of Leatherstocking with the aforementioned death of little Eva in *Uncle Tom's Cabin* to observe the consistency and durability of the idealized deathbed scene. But this model held little interest for Nathaniel Hawthorne, who made use of it only in "The Gentle Boy" and one or two minor pieces. The contemporary closest to Poe in his response to death, Hawthorne concerned himself with "the power of blackness" mainly as the source of guilt and sin. If death possessed a horror for him, that horror lay in its revelation of human weakness and imperfection. A tale like "Roger Malvin's Burial" aptly illustrates this point (and provides an implicit contrast to Cooper's handling of death in the wilderness). Roger Malvin's fatal wound creates a dilemma for Reuben Bourne, who must choose between his own survival and a proper burial of his comrade. The dying man's double messages contribute to Reuben's anguish: Malvin simultaneously urges the younger man to go on without him and laments the terrible fate of dying alone in the forest. The cruel paradox is that the intrusion of death makes it impossible for either man to do the "right" thing. The thought of abandoning Malvin to a death without burial sickens Reuben (who is endowed with a nineteenth-century fastidiousness about attending to the dying); but finally the desire to save his own life, coupled with the charge to care for Malvin's daughter, persuades Reuben to depart. However, the younger man creeps back for one last look: he wants to see how Malvin will face death. In a heavily ironic passage, Reuben imagines the terrors of the dying man and unconsciously casts himself as a figure of death: "He felt how hard was the doom of the kind and generous being whom he had deserted in his extremity. Death would come, like the slow approach of a corpse, stealing gradually toward him through the forest, and showing its ghastly and motionless features from behind a nearer, and yet a nearer tree."[29] Does the association of Reuben with approaching death imply an authorial judgment, does it mirror the younger man's guilty self-image, or does it simply reflect Reuben's own projected death anxiety? As is usually the case, Hawthorne gives us no way to cut the interpretive knot; the ambiguity of the forest scene exemplifies what Hawthorne (in *The Scarlet Letter*) called "the dark problem of this life," the inescapable enigma of suffering and death entailed by earthly existence.

In defying the muse of sentiment, Hawthorne (like Poe) risked his survival as a professional man of letters. For the American publishing scene was indeed dominated by adherents to the cult of death and memory. Perhaps the poetry of Lydia Huntley Sigourney best exemplifies the treacly treatment of mortality in all its forms. Fully half of the verses in her *Poems* (1841) pursue doleful themes, as suggested by such titles as "The Dying Mother's Prayer," "Death of a Clergyman," "Death of the Wife of a Clergyman," "Death of a Young Lady at the Retreat for the Insane," and "Death of the Principal of a Retreat for the Insane." Mrs. Sigourney was especially partial to the death of infants and small children, and in "Boy's Last Request" we observe a typical mixture of anguish and faith:

> Half-raised upon his dying couch, his head
> Drooped o'er his mother's bosom,—like a bud
> Which, broken from its parent stalk, adheres

By some attenuate fibre. His thin hand
From 'neath the downy pillow drew a book,
And slowly pressed it to his bloodless lip.

    "Mother, dear mother, see your birth-day gift,
Fresh and unsoiled. Yet have I kept your word,
And ere I slept each night, and every morn,
Did read its pages, with my humble prayer,
Until this sickness came."
                         He paused—for breath
Came scantily, and with a toilsome strife.
    "Brother or sister have I none, or else
I'd lay this Bible on their hearts, and say,
Come, read it on my grave, among the flowers:
So you who gave it must take it back again,
And love it for my sake." "My son!—my son,"
Murmured the mourner, in that tender tone
Which woman, in her sternest agony
Commands, to soothe the pang of those she loves,
"The soul! the soul!—to whose charge yield you that?"
"Mother,—to God who gave it."
                            So, that soul
With a slight shudder and a lingering smile
Left the pale clay for its Creator's arms. [30]

Here the unsoiled yet well-read Bible testifies to the spotless virtue of
the boy (he with the head precariously attached) who dies with a
smile, lamenting only the fact that he has no brother or sister to visit
his grave. To be sure, the death of a child is an incalculable loss; but
Mrs. Sigourney and her brothers and sisters in sentiment managed
not only to exhaust the literary possibilities of the subject but to turn
it into a facile cliché.

    From the 1820s until well after the Civil War, the ladies' maga-
zines and gift books promulgated an unending stream of lachrymose
lyrics, ostensibly for the sake of consolation. Ann Douglas speculates
that such writing actually enabled middle-class women and Protes-
tant ministers to capitalize on death and to recover a sense of social
purpose, since both had been dispossessed by the emergence of a post-

Christian, entrepreneurial economy.[31] Whatever its underlying intentions, this "domestication of death" (as Douglas calls it) turned grief into a commodity and dying into an increasingly unreal phenomenon. It also produced a flood of unbelievably bad writing and encouraged the likes of Emmeline Grangerford, the morose young poetess in chapter 17 of Twain's *Huckleberry Finn*: "She warn't particular, she could write about anything you choose to give her to write about, just so it was sadful. Every time a man died, or a woman died, or a child died, she would be on hand with her 'tribute' before he was cold." With respect to popular literature in the early nineteenth century, there was less exaggeration in Twain's caricature than one might suppose.

Such was the cultural environment in which Poe endeavored to sustain himself as a writer. That he found the funereal sentimentality of the day at least a valid rhetorical mode may be surmised from his approbation of Mrs. Sigourney, Mrs. E. F. Ellet, and Miss H. F. Gould, all contributors to the *Southern Literary Messenger* during Poe's editorship. In 1842 he deprecated the "namby-pamby character" of *Graham's Magazine* in a moment of pique; however, there is no evidence that he found the literary preoccupation with death unhealthy, inappropriate, or laughable. By temperament and personal bereavement, Poe was drawn into the cult of death and memory. But if he respected the fashion for sentiment, he eschewed the conventional sad-but-joyful departure, and he clearly saw through the mask of beauty that concealed the features of human dissolution. In his "Marginalia" series Poe observed trenchantly: "Who ever *really* saw anything but horror in the smile of the dead? We so earnestly *desire* to fancy it 'sweet'—that is the source of the mistake; if, indeed, there ever was a mistake in the question."[32] Unlike most of his contemporaries, he refused to soften or idealize mortality and kept its essential horror in view; but he also moved beyond the Gothic formula to explore divergent forms of death experience.

In speaking of Poe's relationship to the literature of melancholy, I have claimed that he was inclined by sensibility and personal loss to participate in the fetishizing of death. But in fact Poe's relationship to writing remains problematic, for we have as yet developed no means of gauging the fit between private contemplation and public expression. Unlike his contemporaries, Hawthorne, Thoreau, Emerson, and Melville, Poe left no journals or notebooks—no exclusive glimpses into the workings of his creative intelligence. We cannot follow (as with Hawthorne) the accretion of ideas and images seminal to a narrative; we cannot trace (as with Thoreau) the evolution of a major work from preliminary jottings in a diary through a notebook version to finished prose. Although we have been able to assemble some notions about Poe's habits of revision through comparisons of variant texts, no comprehensive view of Poe's method has yet emerged. While some of his letters refer to artistic aims and principles, these comments tend to be brief, infrequent, contrived, and patently self-serving. Similarly, his essays and reviews deliver public literary judgments but shed little light on the intimate relationship between Poe and his texts. In "The Philosophy of Composition," for example, his remarks about the death of a beautiful woman sidestep personal meanings and turn immediately to the problem of formal effects. While articulating ideas about beauty, brevity, and unity of impression, he maintained a silence about his characteristic obsessions: murder, revenge, madness, premature burial, disease, revivification, perverseness, ratiocination, mesmerism, and the like. He left no private record which might help us to understand the odd conjunctions in his work—of humor and horror, mystery and irony, passion and parody, profundity and triviality. Nowhere did Poe volunteer an explicit, privileged insight into his nightmarish vision; nowhere did he explain his commitment to the life of writing.

But Poe left traces of such a theory in the writing itself. As we have seen in "Ligeia," Poe incorporates within the tale a poetic text attributed to the dying woman; the poem allegorizes (and thus comments on) mortality within a scene which probes the relationship between language and death. Attentiveness to this self-referential element in Poe's writing enables us to construct from fragments, hints, analogies, and reflexive ironies an operative philosophy of composition that corresponds both to the broad range of his texts and to the different registers of his writing voice. Two examples of this implicit commentary, drawn from the early "Tales of the Folio Club," establish more clearly the basis of a theory of writing in the problem of death.

The abortive "Folio Club" project was implicitly an exercise in criticism, a series of fictional glosses on the modes of writing popular in Poe's day. By assigning a tale to each comically named member of the Folio Club, the author apparently intended to satirize both literary circles and parochial tastes. Most of the eleven narratives are transparently farcical, but several employ a more subtle parody in which the element of satire seems subordinate (even antithetical) to the dramatic effect.[33] Collectively the tales represent an uneven effort to mimic the forms and styles of fiction available to Poe in the early 1830s; individually, many also refer to the activity of writing or to the way that language interposes between the writer and the silence of mortality.

In the "Folio Club" collection, Poe included a surreal word painting called "Siope. A Fable," later retitled "Silence—A Fable." As A. H. Quinn has remarked, the prose-poem was probably an emulation of Bulwer's magazine tale, "Monos and Daimonos. A Legend."[34] But the haunting imagery of "Silence" seems to derive more clearly from two of Poe's early poems, "The Valley of Unrest" and "The City in the Sea," both published in 1831. These lyrics depict strange scenes of desolation which corroborate Davidson's characterization of Poe as a "verbal landscapist of death."[35] "The Valley of Unrest" portrays a remote and silent place—patently a fallen world—animated by preternatural movement; "nothing there is motionless," and "reedy grass" waves "over the old forgotten grave," while "gorgeous clouds" sail across the "terror-stricken sky" (CW, 1:192). In "The City in the Sea," one encounters an emblematic domain in which "Death looks gigantically down" from "a proud tower in the town." This is unmistakably Death's kingdom; he has "reared himself a throne" in this "strange city" of "gaping graves" and "sculptured" tombs encircled by "melancholy waters" said in a later version of the poem to be "hideously serene." The only movement occurs when the city sinks into the sea, giving the waves an infernal "redder glow" (CW, 1:201–02).

These poems anticipate the allegorized terrain of death in "Silence—A Fable," where Poe once again conjures up a weird realm agitated by "convulsive motion" (CW, 2:195). This movement is lifeless and dreamlike: the sickly waters "palpitate forever and forever"; immense lilies sigh, stretch their "ghastly necks" toward heaven, and "nod to and fro their everlasting heads"; huge "primeval" trees "rock eternally hither and thither"; "strange poisonous flowers" are seen "writhing in perturbed slumber"; gray clouds "rush westwardly forever." Motion is ineffectual (for nothing changes) yet incessant (there is "neither quiet nor silence"). Amid this scene the narrator discovers a gray rock, its surface engraved with writing that cannot initially be deciphered. The red light of the moon, however, enables the speaker to read the word DESOLATION, an inscription that refers not to the landscape (already described as desolation) but to the relationship between word and world. Immediately Poe throws into question the relationship between signifier and signified: upon the rock appears a man "longing after solitude" and filled with disgust for mankind, and when the speaker pronounces "the curse of *silence*" (presumably to admonish the seeker of solitude), the preternatural motions stop, all sounds cease, and the inscription on the rock becomes SILENCE. Patently an image of death, this vision of stillness evokes horror, and the man flees aghast. Significantly the transformation of the land occurs through an articulation of the word which literally inscribes itself upon a rock. As speech passes into inscription, the sign creates the reality that it supposedly represents. In this cryptic fable, language discloses its conspiracy with death, for its power to affect the solitary man lies in its evocation of an absolute solitude and silence. A paradox manifests itself: within the narrative, language calls forth silence; this action mirrors (and reverses) the writing of the narrative, in which the idea of silence has called forth language.

Apparently Poe changed the title of this sketch from "Siope" to "Silence" in 1840 to underscore the significance of this final transformation. But he also thereby acknowledged a relationship between the prose piece and his recently published "Sonnet—Silence," a poem which distinguishes between two kinds of silence in a way that clarifies the terror of the prose sketch. The sonnet speaks first of the silence of the body, the "corporate Silence" that "dwells in lonely places, / Newly with grass o'ergrown." This entity has been domesticated by the cult of death and memory: "some solemn graces, / Some human memories and tearful lore, / Render him terrorless: his name's

'No more'" (CW, 1:322). Physical death inspires no dread, because "no power hath he of evil in himself." Real terror resides in the nameless shadow, the silence of the soul. Here Poe exposes the anxiety underlying the Beautiful Death: if the spirit survives in an afterlife, man can endure the corporate silence, but if the soul itself also dies, there exists no hope and death is indeed evil. The shadow which personifies this latter fate is said to haunt "the lone regions where hath trod / No foot of man." Ostensibly these are the very regions depicted in the prose sketch "Silence—A Fable," for the prospect of such a silence inspires dread in the solitary observer: "his countenance was wan with terror." He has seen not simply an image of corporal death but a sign of the spirit's extinction. The latter is the source of real alarm, for as Poe observed in his preface to *Tales of the Grotesque and Arabesque*, "terror is not of Germany, but of the soul."

In casting the revelation of "Silence—A Fable" as writing which speaks in silence, Poe figured a complicity between the two. His fable permits us to contemplate the horizon of language as it circumscribes mortal experience, and it thus returns us to an inescapable theoretical problem. Walter Ong has postulated that "the connection between writing and death is very deep, so deep that it registers almost always in the unconscious or subconscious rather than in consciousness."[36] The relationship between death and writing opens upon questions of grammatology and metaphysics; it partakes of the ceaseless interplay between Eros and Thanatos, shaping the exchange between self and other in the symbolic articulation of desire. Its contemplation leads us into the domains of psychology, theology, and anthropology as well as aesthetics and literary theory. Noting that writing is often metaphorically related to death ("The letter kills but the spirit gives life," 2 Corinthians 3:6), Ong comments on this complex reciprocity:

> One of the most startling paradoxes inherent in writing is its close association with death. This association is suggested in Plato's charge that writing is inhuman, thing-like, and that it destroys memory. . . . In *Pippa Passes*, Robert Browning calls attention to the still widespread practice of pressing living flowers to death between the pages of printed books, "faded yellow blossoms / twixt

page and page." The dead flower, once alive, is the psychic equivalent of the verbal text. The paradox lies in the fact that the deadness of the text, its removal from the living human lifeworld, its rigid visual fixity, assures its endurance and its potential for being resurrected into limitless living contexts by a potentially infinite number of living readers.[37]

Indeed, we might say that the desire to write originates in the paradox that the death of writing—the fixed "body" of the text, as it were—insures the life of its spirit or sense. It is a commonplace that writing has an existence independent of its author, but Ong locates an additional truth: that writing incarnates the very principle of life in its removal from the carnal world of time, change, and death.

While the finality of death creates in the self that desire for symbolic transcendence which culminates in the temporal activity of writing, inscription must be seen—also paradoxically—as an effacement of self and an escape from the temporal order. Blanchot speaks of writing as a "surrender to the fascination of time's absence," in which the self becomes another, immersed in the solitude of "a language which no one speaks, which is addressed to no one, which has no center, and which reveals nothing." Though writing conventionally manifests an object and figures a relationship between speaker and audience, Blanchot explores the inner world of pure language, the "space of literature," in which writing consumes the writer and discloses its "incessant" demands. As an "interminable," never-to-be-completed project, writing invisibly alters the writer's relationship to death: "The fact that the writer's task ends with his life hides another fact: that, through this task, his life slides into the distress of the infinite."[38] In a sense, the writer exchanges one kind of anxiety for another; the distress of the infinite replaces the fear of human finitude. But the writer's distress at the boundlessness of his task finds its compensation in the discovery that writing transforms death into an ally. The nullity of death gives writing a means of understanding its own imperative nature; it constitutes the blank tablet upon which writing inscribes its resistance to the indifference of time. Death enforces the rule of absence which creates the need for symbolic expression; its inexorability becomes the vital insistence of writing. And so writing may be said to derive its life from death, paradoxically achieving its energy through an emulation of death—through a retreat from the formlessness of lived experience into the fixed and silent world of the unspeaking word that will always speak.

A second text from "Tales of the Folio Club" makes this complex exchange intelligible through a figuration of the writer's relationship to death. Conventionally "MS. Found in a Bottle" has been regarded as a precursor to *The Narrative of Arthur Gordon Pym* in its projection of a symbolic voyage from commonplace reality toward a fantastic realm of death. David Halliburton, however, has touched on the self-referentiality of "MS." in calling for a study of writing in Poe:

> No one seems to have noticed Poe's stages in the sequence, from oral to chirographic to typographic, of verbal expression. This is not the place to examine such a complex problem in detail. Yet we cannot help observing that here [in "MS."] . . . the narrative is in the form of a manuscript, and that a central act in the story—the drawing of the word DISCOVERY—is closely related to the act of composing in script. [39]

In his elaborate reading of *Pym* as a figurative quest for the origin of writing, John Irwin has noted that "MS." partakes of the same quest insofar as it amounts to "a fiction of its own origin as writing."[40] This may be so, but in another way "MS." also contemplates the closure of language and thus enacts a theory of textual destiny—the end of inscription. It thus affords at least a tentative model of the life of writing and the fate of the writing self.

Such a reading is invited by the fact that the tale is intrinsically a fable of composition, imaging the perils of inscription. Shortly after the narrative breaks into diary fragments, the writer refers self-consciously to the production of his text, which begins with the purloining of pen and paper: "I ventured into the captain's own private cabin, and took thence the materials with which I write, and have written." The iteration of the key verb in the present and present perfect tenses implies a continuity of activity, a sustaining of both writing and the "I" who writes. The narrator wishes to preserve both the manuscript and the self inscribed therein: "I shall from time to time continue this journal. It is true that I may not find an opportunity of transmitting it to the world, but I will not fail to make the endeavor. At the last moment I will enclose the MS. in a bottle, and cast it within the sea" (*CW*, 2:142). But even an account jettisoned at the last moment can never be complete; as Irwin observes of *Pym*: "The narrative of one's own life is always unfinished, a fragment in which meaningful closure is either a fictionalized foreshadowing or a postscript in another hand."[41] With this reference to the "transmitting" of the journal, Poe accounts for its physical existence while placing it within a new mode of coherence, as an unfinished text, literally the interrupted testimony of a doomed man. That is, Poe claims for the story the privileged status of the deathbed utterance; the authority of the discourse derives from the proximity of death, while its fascination lies in the idea that the putative writer of these lines is now already dead. The posteriority of the text reifies a truth about all writing: inscription is inherently a sign of the writer's absence; notation speaks for a self that cannot, in the moment of reading, speak to the reader.

However, in the moment of writing—at least as fictionally represented—the narrator perceives his immediate problem as revelation rather than survival. Sensing that the ship is "hurrying onwards to some exciting knowledge—some never-to-be-imparted secret, whose attainment is destruction" (145), he thinks of writing as a desperate transmission of forbidden intelligence. Because this exciting knowledge entails death, the effort of inscription is both irresistible and futile. The narrator is compelled to record his impressions by the human need to achieve coherency of experience through language, yet the very object of language, the never-to-be-imparted secret, lies beyond the reach of words.

And so Poe situates inscription between two conflicting attitudes about death. The narrator feels an eagerness for the discovery which means destruction, but he conversely registers his terror and despair and tries to describe "the horror of [his] sensations" as he moves toward extinction. His voyage is a prolonged nightmare of death anxiety, a crisis of imminent annihilation. When the trading ship of Malabar teak is wrecked by a storm, the narrator faces not only the physical threat of death but ubiquitous images of mortality as well. The sun itself seems to expire: "Just before sinking within the turgid sea, its central fires suddenly went out, as if hurriedly extinguished by some unaccountable power" (138). The narrator describes himself and his companions as "enshrouded in pitchy darkness," and he then reports: "All around were horror, and thick gloom, and a black sweltering desert of ebony" (139). The stillness of the sea is indirectly compared to death through an allusion to methods of verifying the absence of life: "The flame of a candle burned upon the poop without the least perceptible motion, and a long hair, held between the finger and thumb, hung without the possibility of detecting a vibration" (136). That the tale symbolizes a movement toward corporeal dissolution Poe makes plain in depicting the phantom ship that carries the narrator toward the vortex. Manned by spectral figures, "ghosts of buried centuries" who epitomize old age and corruption, this "terrible ship" represents a condition of death-in-life that anticipates the House of Usher. Its "worm-eaten" frame illustrates the "rottenness attendant upon age" and hence the principle of decay. The unintelligible "foreign tongue" spoken by the phantom crew reminds us that they inhabit an alien realm, Shakespeare's "undiscovered country, from whose bourne no traveller returns."

Confronted with signs of aging and death, the narrator writes and thereby deflects the primal horror of his situation by imposing the mediation of a written text. His response illustrates the truth of Ernest Becker's contention that "the idea of death, the fear of it, haunts the human animal like nothing else; it is a mainspring of human activity—activity designed largely to avoid the fatality of death, to overcome it by denying in some way that it is the final destiny for man." Recasting Freud's basic theory, Becker adds, "*Consciousness of death* is the primary repression, not sexuality. . . . *This* is what is creaturely about man, *this* is the repression on which culture is built, a repression unique to the self-conscious animal."[42] Facing annihilation, Poe's narrator buries himself (so to speak) in his writing and so reenacts the repression on which culture is built. Both participant and spectator, he is at once caught in the current of mortality and freed from it by his scribal activity, which involves both a displacement of the self (the "I" of subjective experience becoming the "I" of writing) and a subjugation of death to the conventions of discourse. As the narrator realizes, this is a temporary and perhaps illusory expedient; yet as long as he can write, he guarantees his survival. Just as his voice is literally a function of Poe's narrative, so his fictional existence coincides with the boundaries of the text he is said to inscribe. In his movement toward death, the narrator sustains himself through writing much as Scheherazade preserves herself through the telling of tales in *The Thousand and One Nights*. Each sentence is a deferral of the end of writing, a strategy of denial.[43]

The other view of death manifested in "MS." is no less pervasive in Poe's fiction—that is, the inherent longing to penetrate the *mysterium tremendum*, to satisfy the wish to die that forms the counterpart of death anxiety. Curiously, Poe's protagonists are both repulsed by putrefaction and driven to know the secret of mortality. The narrator of "MS." yearns to discover "the mysteries of these awful regions" even though the attempt may disclose "the most hideous aspect of death" (145). Like the spirit crew of the phantom ship, he approaches the great vortex with an attitude partaking "more of the eagerness of hope than of the apathy of despair." His desire perhaps stems from the urge to communicate the incommunicable or to write the impossible sentence. In effect he wishes to say with Monsieur Valdemar, one of Poe's later adventurers into the abyss, "I am dead." The will to project the life of words across the gulf of mortality, to speak the literally unspeakable, represents (as Roland Barthes has remarked) a "scandal of language" which violates both the rules of discourse and the taboos which isolate and repress the phenomenon of death.[44]

This quintessential desire to plumb the abyss—and write about it—converts the action of "MS." into an uncanny prefiguration of Poe's life as a writer. What are his subsequent texts but reformulations of the same voyage? Can we not say that Poe conceived of writing as a series of messages from the edge of silence—fragmentary glimpses of the one experience which cannot be written about in the past tense? The narrator of "MS." writes to forestall death, yet his every word carries him toward the threshold of silence. With some alarm we recognize that all inscription—including the text on this page—partakes of the same irreversible movement. Poe suggests that the desire of writing lies in the inscrutability of silence, which induces both approach and avoidance. One seeks both to defer the experience of silence and to grasp its tacit meaning. To carry out this impossible project, the narrator intends to enclose his manuscript in a bottle and cast it into the sea at the last moment, at the instant in which fate suspends the task of writing. The incompletion of the text will thereby become a sign of human finitude, a reminder of the inevitable lapse from language into silence.

As a metaphor for the project of writing, "MS." enables us to contemplate Poe's poetry and fiction as a protracted manuscript-in-a-bottle, an inexorable movement toward a final text—appropriately, in Poe's case, an unfinished manuscript called "The Light-House," that solitary tower at the margin of silence. Yet each text within this unfolding sequence also marks a resistance to silence, a defiance of the process by which the will to write is exhausted. Language performs a double role in this self-consuming quest; it provides the possibilities of discourse but also sets the bounds of disclosure. Or, to use the opposition suggested by Barthes (in terms especially relevant to the voyage metaphor), language forms a horizon, which implies both a boundary and a perspective, a limit and a looking-through.[45] The narrator of "MS." faces the intrinsic dilemma of writing: he may record his anticipations or he may plunge into the vortex, but having done the latter he cannot return to the world of words. Language carries him to the brink of insight, but he must surrender the signifier to achieve that unmediated signified which resides in silence. The mystery that he seeks to reveal cannot be placed in a bottle, which as a metaphor for language both preserves and constricts meaning. Enough of the manuscript is completed to infer the reason for its inconclusion, yet the final lines tease us with the imminence of discovery: "But little time will be left me to ponder upon my destiny! The circles rapidly grow small—we are plunging madly within the grasp of the whirlpool—and amid a roaring, and bellowing, and thundering of ocean and of tempest, the ship is quivering—oh God! and—going down!" (146). The sudden suspension of writing signals the narrator's penetration of the void beyond language, his apprehension of the never-to-be-imparted secret.

The beginning of "MS." curiously anticipates its ending. Among his asseverations about truth and imagination, the narrator notes that he has long regarded "the reveries of fancy" as "a dead letter and a nullity." As his narrative moves from mundane fact to unrepressed, primal fear, the narrator indeed approaches that nullity or nothingness in which the letter as signifier is "dead." The manuscript itself is a dead letter both in the sense of being undeliverable (it is addressed to anyone and no one) and also unreturnable (the writer's death is implied by its existence). The very act of writing is also defined as an absence (an undisclosable secret) which cancels the inscription; the writer has no way of delivering in a letter or through the system of letters the "exciting knowledge" he expects to find. The paradox of writing is analogous to the problem of describing the phantom ship that carries him along: "What she *is not*, I can easily perceive; what she *is*, I fear it is impossible to say" (142).

When he composed "MS." in 1831 or 1832, Poe had barely launched his career as a writer of magazine fiction; yet his narrative seems remarkably prophetic as an allegory of the life of writing. I do not mean to represent this figurality as a conscious forecast of his literary fate; rather it occurs as an intuitive projection of the attraction-repulsion mechanism at the crux of Poe's response to death. Writing apparently functioned for him as a diversion from melancholy, as an exploration of anxiety, and as a mode of discovery and analysis. He could simultaneously manage his dread through imaginative play—sometimes converting it to an object of satire—and construct speculative versions of death experience. Now haunted by the figure of the Red Death, now probing the spirit world through mesmeric revelation, Poe embraced the life of writing as a saving response to the consciousness of his own mortality and to disorienting changes in the contemporary meaning of death.

But when he composed "MS.," Poe had other, more immediate concerns as well: he was then in the process of devising his "Tales of the Folio Club," the collection which was to establish his place in the world of letters. Without much question, Poe conceived the sea story on one level as a tour de force, a display of his ability to blend horror and verisimilitude in the manner of popular sea narratives. He even invented a fictitious author for the piece, "Mr. Solomon Seadrift," whose name suggests parodic intent. The recognition of this satiric framework seems at first glance to undercut the idea of "MS." as an allegory of writing. Yet when we recall that the narrator's manuscript afforded an escape from the doom which constitutes its subject, the apparent contradiction resolves itself. Or, to recast our metaphorical terms one last time, we might say that the external shape of the tale (the potboiler sea story) and its conceptual message (the relationship between writing and death) exist as bottle and manuscript. The transparent form contains and preserves the record of an unfinished voyage.

Poe's own voyage extended sixteen years beyond the appearance of "MS. Found in a Bottle." Yet in some ways he never escaped its prescient metaphoricity: for Poe as for his fictive narrator, writing unfolded between dread and fascination, alternately functioning as a deferral of death and as an incursion into its domain. Significantly, in that early tale the manuscript assumes an autonomous life of its own: writing survives the writer, and set against the problematic phenomena it purports to register and inventory, it inscribes a truth that is self-revealing rather than referential. The text creates a space of discovery whose true horizon lies both beyond and within the rim of the polar sea. In a provocative essay Joseph Riddel argues that in Poe "an abyss has opened up between word and world" and that this rupture marks the origination of "a new literature, a self-critical or self-annihilating textual performance—the poem/story and even the critical essay (as performance) that deconstructs itself."[46] Poe was perhaps the first American writer to interiorize the disintegration of what Derrida has called "logocentrism and the metaphysics of presence." Through Poe's recurrent perception of a gap between phenomenal reality and meaning grounded in language—a break which finds its consummate expression in the discontinuity between death's physical horror and its putative purpose in a theological scheme—he committed himself to a relentless questioning of truth and language. Within the chasm or abyss, that insistent figure of unfathomable death, Poe located the origin of that abyss to which Riddel refers, the cleavage between sign and referent, which has itself become the sign of literary modernism.

Though we have attended more closely in this chapter to the cultural history of death than to the emergence of modernist writing (to be sketched in chapter 7), we can nevertheless begin to see that Poe's texts mark a point of convergence. Both death anxiety and the perception of death as catastrophe date from a relatively recent period in Western experience, an epoch that roughly coincides with the emergence of a new sense of writing. Derrida provides insight into the intricate process by which the crisis in Western metaphysics revealed itself in the displacement of speech by writing: he contends that inscription is the sign of a vanished presence, an originary Logos, without which the relationship between word and world falls into chaos. As writing effects a divorce from phenomenal reality, determinate meaning becomes problematic; language reveals itself as a play of differences, having reference only to itself and its textual imperatives. The apotheosis of writing coincides with the disappearance of God—and not by chance, since writing in the modern sense begins by declaring the loss of a transcendental signified and takes upon itself the task of supplanting the eternal Word with endless words. Indeed, Derrida views inscription as a violent usurpation of immanence, a killing of the spirit:

> What writing itself, in its nonphonetic moment, betrays, is life. It menaces at once the breath, the spirit, and history as the spirit's relationship with itself. It is their end, their finitude, their paralysis. Cutting breath short, sterilizing or immobilizing spiritual creation in the repetition of the letter, in the commentary or the *exegesis,* confined in a narrow space, reserved for a minority, it is the principle of death and of difference in the becoming of being.[47]

Writing carries within itself "the principle of death" in its transformation of the verbal sign from a living utterance to a fixed mark on a lifeless page.

As we shall see in the chapters ahead, the nineteenth-century crisis of death revealed to Poe both the inaccessibility of metaphysical truth and the implications of that cosmic blankness for the writing and the reading of texts. The perceived collapse of logocentrism created a strange rapprochement between writing and death, since both had previously derived their signifying power from the presence of a divine Logos. In losing its relationship to a transcendental signified, writing became more conscious of its deathlike nature (as the sign of an absence) and more uncertain of its own capacity to represent truth. Meanwhile death invaded writing as it besieged Western consciousness, manifesting its ascendancy in literature and philosophy (one thinks of Poe's contemporary, Kierkegaard), already beginning to assume the godlike proportions it would attain in the twentieth century. Oddly enough, the ascendancy of death conferred upon writing an important new function: since, as Ong observes, "writing carries within it always an element of death," it endows the writing self with a certain control over death: "Such is the virtue of texts . . . that their ability to absorb death makes death somehow less threatening. For, as already noted, the text assures a kind of life after death, which can readily be disguised as life without death."[48] As Poe perceived from the beginning—and bodied forth in "MS. Found in a Bottle"—writing held out the possibility of life, especially as it embraced the catastrophe of death.

2

Notes from Underground
Premature Burial

In Poe's fiction, the scene of writing is often perilous and problematic: perilous because writing coincides closely with catastrophe; problematic because the described horrors throw into question the survival or sanity of the putative writer (the I-narrator). As we have seen, the desperate inscription of "MS. Found in a Bottle" appears to be simultaneous with the incidents that it represents, and only the manuscript-in-a-bottle convention enables Poe to account for both the presence of the text and the absence of its writer. Other tales postulate a scene of writing in the wake of some terrible episode: the narrator of "The Pit and the Pendulum" refers to the lips of the black-robed judges who sentenced him to the torture chamber as "whiter than the sheet upon which I trace these pages" and thus situates the composition at a later moment that implicitly guarantees his survival. The narrator of "The Black Cat" places the scene of writing immediately prior to his own destruction ("to-morrow I die") in speaking of "the most wild, yet most homely narrative which I am about to pen." Likewise the supposed writer of "William Wilson" acknowledges that "death approaches" as he records the details of his crime on "the fair page now lying before [him]." In "Ligeia," however, the scene of writing remains unspecified and almost unimaginable, for the hysterical conclusion seems to preclude the possibility of future composition. We must assume, as we do in "The Fall of the House of Usher," that the narrator somehow escapes the horrific final scene to inscribe his tale.

No scene of writing could be more dire or doubtful, however, than inscription which occurs in the aftermath of the writer's burial. For readers of the early nineteenth century, such narratives had a peculiar fascination, and Poe was but one of many magazinists to exploit the predicament of writing inherent in the subgenre. In "How to Write a Blackwood Article," his fictional Mr. Blackwood cites an exemplary tale of sensation about living interment:

> There was "The Dead Alive," a capital thing!—the record of a gentleman's sensations, when entombed before the breath was out of his body—full of taste, terror, sentiment, metaphysics, and erudition. You would have sworn that the writer had been born and brought up in a coffin. [CW, 2:339]

This reference to an actual Blackwood's story (which appeared as "The Buried Alive" in October, 1821) designates a narrative type that Poe had already parodied in his 1832 farce "A Decided Loss" (later "Loss of Breath"). Mr. Blackwood's closing quip plays upon the ludicrous confusion of life and death familiar to such writing. To conceive of an author "born and brought up in a coffin" is to imagine as well a hermetic inscription delivered, beyond all expectation, from the tomb itself. In its most sensational form, the tale of premature burial created the illusion of a composition simultaneous with the terrors it recorded, presenting itself as an "inside" narrative, a communication from the coffin. Even in tales acknowledged to be the subsequent recollections of a survivor (typically rescued by a grave robber or a sexton), the verbal reenactment simulates a textual impossibility: language which seems to arrive from the other side of the grave.

That the idea of premature burial exerted a persistent hold on Poe's imagination can be demonstrated readily enough. From "A Decided Loss" to "The Cask of Amontillado" (1846), the threat of "fatal and foetal enclosure"—to borrow Daniel Hoffman's Freudian terminology—runs through his fiction like an obsessive nightmare.[1] To such a fate he consigned Berenice, Monos, and the one-eyed black cat; he caused Arthur Gordon Pym and the narrator of "The Pit and the Pendulum" to undergo symbolic burial; he sent Morella, Ligeia, and Madeline Usher to early though apparently temporary graves; and at the height of his writerly productivity he concocted an apparent case study, "The Premature Burial." Not surprisingly, the motif has generated a variety of metaphorical readings. For Marie Bonaparte, the threat of living interment symbolized "the phantasy of the return to the womb": "This it is . . . which lies at the roots of various claustrophobias and which, again, is expressed in that most fearful of all instances of morbid anxiety, fear of premature burial. It was this fear, in particular, which haunted Poe and inspired the terrible and epic vision described in "The Premature Burial," a vision in which all mankind's graves open to reveal the corpses feebly struggling in the faint phosphorescence of decay."[2] Expressing a similar understanding, D. H. Lawrence insisted that "all this underground vault business in Poe only symbolizes that which takes place beneath the consciousness." In this scheme, premature burial presumably corresponds to a penetration of the repressed by conscious intelligence. More recently G. R. Thompson has projected premature burial as the author's comprehensive figure of existential suffering: "Poe's image of man is that of a forlorn, perverse sentient being buried alive in the incomprehensible tomb of the universe."[3] Indeed, the experience of living entombment seems to a twentieth-century reader so improbable that one assumes its metaphoricity as an interpretive convention. Like myth, it seems inherently to refer to another level of intelligibility; like the story of Lazarus—that archetypal narrative of a return from the grave—it resists a literal reading and draws us obstinately toward an imaginative refiguring of the boundary between life and death.

To some extent the sheer mythopoeic force of premature burial explains the recurrence of such stories in periodicals of the early nineteenth century. But the subgenre became prevalent at a specific historical moment, its proliferation symptomatic of certain broad changes in the way Western culture had begun to understand death and burial. Ariès makes the intriguing point that fear of premature burial did not manifest itself in France until the middle of the seventeenth century; and not until well into the next century did it begin to claim attention as "one of the serious dangers of the age."[4] By the late eighteenth century, however, living interment had become a powerful obsession in Europe and America, producing new laws against hasty burial and countless publications warning of its occurrence. Particularly in times of contagion incidents of premature entombment came to public attention either through the testimony of rescued victims or through the more shocking evidence of corpses found in positions suggestive of struggle. J. H. Powell's history of the yellow fever epidemic in Philadelphia in 1793 documents the appalling conditions which made such catastrophes possible: the collapse of civil order left the collection and burial of bodies to porters with no medical training and with little regard for the formalities of interment.[5]

Surely living inhumation had occurred in earlier periods; yet not until the eighteenth century did it become an explicit threat, erupting into literary consciousness as a subject of writing. As Ariès notes, doctors sounded the first alarm; in 1740 a French physician named Jacques-Bénigne Winslow published a treatise entitled *Dissertation sur l'incertitude des signes de la mort et de l'abus des enterrements et embaumements précipités.*[6] Medical men probably learned of its occurrence through their efforts to procure corpses for dissection; and indeed the study of anatomy and physiology helped to generate anxieties about premature burial in several ways. Since the sixteenth century, surgeons in England had been granted the legal right to anatomize the bodies of executed criminals, but by the mid-eighteenth century the proliferation of medical schools created a shortage of authorized cadavers. Unclaimed bodies of the indigent dead began to appear on dissecting tables, and anatomists engaged the services of body snatchers, who under the cover of night exhumed the recently deceased. Those who lived near medical schools began to fear for the remains of their departed relatives and started to enclose grave sites with iron fences to guard against such outrages. But gangs of grave robbers nevertheless developed a profitable trade, and some even stooped to homicide to supply anatomists with fresh cadavers.[7] From these felons emerged countless stories of living corpses or of bodies bearing signs of premature inhumation.

Similarly, anatomical studies of the dead excited a powerful curiosity about the causes of death and about the phenomenon of apparent death. In 1787, a physician named Charles Kite published an *Essay on the Recovery of the Apparently Dead* in which he detailed the most frequent causes of suspended animation and advocated procedures for reviving such victims. Kite noted that galvanic experiments sometimes restored supposed corpses to perfect health.[8] While such publications may have had a practical value, they also awakened fears of living entombment. Moreover, discussions of experiments performed on the dead raised questions about residual sentience in the corpse—an anxiety carried over from earlier periods. Ariès summarizes the theories of a German doctor, Christian Friedrich Garmann, whose *De miraculis mortuorum* (1709) enunciated the idea of "the sensibility of the cadaver."[9] This same notion runs through the graveyard poetry of the eighteenth century and suggests a curious relationship between medical inquiry and imaginative literature. Uncertainty about the physiology of death extended well into the nineteenth century; Fontenelle's much-discussed work, *On the Signs of Death* (1834), described the difficulty of confirming death, and his numerous examples of premature burial seemed to indicate the scandalous frequency of such mishaps. A London reviewer scoffed that Fontenelle "seems to have persuaded himself that burial-grounds are a species of human slaughterhouse," and he assured readers that "unless by culpable recklessness and haste, there is no possibility that a single individual should be entombed before his time."[10] But as the reading public knew, recklessness and haste did in fact sometimes determine the conditions of burial.

Their suspicion was confirmed by a stream of pamphlets, treatises, and reports appearing in the early nineteenth century. Works such as Joseph Taylor's *The Dangers of Premature Burial* (1816) and J. B. Vigné's *Mémoire sur les inhumations précipitées* (1839) documented the lapses in medical and funerary practice which made possible the entombment of the living. The impact of such writings was intensified by the fact (noted in chapter 1) that interment had become an increasingly secular event, consigned to cemeteries at some remove from the church and dissociated from the spiritual consolations of the churchyard and the Christian ritual of burial. The growth of cities also had much to do with the creation of a burial "crisis." The sheer demography of death began to produce intolerable situations both within churches—where the stench of decay issuing from vaults or floor slabs caused fainting and sickness among the faithful—and in the older, centrally located cemeteries (like Les Innocents in Paris), where a teeming urban population inevitably produced shortages of burial space. Of the former problem Lawrence Stone has noted that "decomposing bodies of the rich in burial vaults beneath the church often stank out parson and congregation"; Stanley French has likewise remarked that in America, "old graveyards became so crowded that they were frequently little more than stinking quagmires— chronically offensive and occasionally serious public health hazards."[11] Custodians adopted the habit of exhuming partially decomposed bodies to create new grave sites, their excavations releasing a fetid odor thought itself to be fatal by some medical authorities. Writing of such appalling practices, a surgeon named George H. Walker observed in 1839 of London graveyards:

> Among us, in a moral and Christian country, the abode of the dead is openly violated—its deposits are sacrilegiously disturbed, and ejected—the tender solicitudes of survivors, are cruelly sported with, and the identity of relationship is destroyed,—so eager, indeed, is the haste, to dispossess previous occupants, that time is not even allowed, for the *gradual* dissipation of decaying human putrescence; this is eliminated in gaseous profusion, contaminating, as it circulates, the habitations of the living.[12]

By the early nineteenth century, the urban cemetery had become a place of scandal, making the thought of burial (premature or otherwise) more troubling and fraught with horror than it had previously been.

For Walker and his contemporaries, the very idea of violated graves often triggered the fear of living inhumation, as if such desecrations evoked sympathetic identification with the insensate corpse. Hence we find the surgeon moving from his condemnation of "the present modes of interment" to a reminder that "periods have happened, and in times not too far distant, in which persons, supposed to be dead, have been hurriedly conveyed to their long home, when, possibly, life was not extinct, and when recovery might have been effected, by the employment of judicious and persevering efforts."[13] Despite Walker's suggestion that accidental interments belonged to the past, ordinary citizens remained fearful; a writer in the London *Quarterly Review* remarked in 1844: "There exists among the poor of the metropolitan districts an inordinate dread of premature burial; and very terrible stories are told of bodies being found in coffins in positions that seemed to indicate that a struggle had taken place after the lid had been closed."[14] Ultimately the horrors of the urban public cemetery—unsupervised burials, ghastly exhumations, collapsing vaults, and noxious odors—led to the American rural cemetery movement of the 1830s and to London's spacious Kensal Green cemetery, both inspired by the pastoral dignity of Père-Lachaise in Paris.[15] Indeed, Père-Lachaise became the object of countless travel sketches and engravings in contemporary periodicals; it embodied a neoclassical conception of death in its graceful architecture and curving avenues. Impelled by a later Romantic sensibility, proponents of the rural cemetery sought to conjoin natural beauty with burial, to place death within a healthy, rustic setting, and thus to redeem it from the degrading spectacle it threatened to become in the center of the modern city.

But the rural cemetery movement, with its promise of more decorous interment, did not immediately efface anxiety about premature entombment. Fourteen years after the opening of bucolic Greenwood Cemetery in Brooklyn, a New York exhibition featured "Mr. Eisenbrant's life-preserving coffin" designed "to guard against the occurrence of burial before life is extinct."[16] Perhaps suggested by the practice in German "asylums of repose" of placing bells on the limbs of the recently dead, Eisenbrant contrived a mechanism whereby a cord attached to the hand of a corpse would at the slightest movement activate an external bell. The commercial fate of the "life-preserving coffin" is unknown, but its invention alone testifies to a continuing fear. Periodicals in England and America carried learned essays on the problem, as well as excerpts from lengthier studies. One passage from Fontenelle's *On the Signs of Death* was reprinted often during the mid-1830s, for it enumerated the medical conditions thought to render one susceptible to premature burial: "The diseases in which a partial and momentary suspension of life most often manifests itself, are Asphyxia, Hysterics, Lethargy, Hypochondria, Convulsions, Syncope, Catalepsis, excessive loss of blood, Tetanus, Apoplexy, Epilepsy and Ecstasy."[17] To what extent contemporary physicians shared Fontenelle's theories cannot be determined, but the notion that "Ecstasy" might cause a deathlike trance must have given pause to at least a few readers.

Periodicals treated the problem of premature burial in surprisingly diverse ways. For example, apart from quasi-medical or journalistic reports, the subject generated a plethora of comic anecdotes and tales, such as "Dead Alive," which appeared in the *New-York Mirror* of August 19, 1826. This piece recounts the supposed death of a nun who had been consorting with a group of monks; these "holy miscreants" had "agreed to make a dead saint of her, and bury her to all appearance, in their vaults," for the sake of convenience and discretion. But the ruse is uncovered, and an indignant youth applies a "red hot brick bat" to the feet of the recumbent "saint." Similarly, the *Casket* for November 1832 included an anecdote about an inebriate and two Irish gravediggers. Consigned mistakenly to the "dead room" of a hospital, the drunk awakens to find himself being nailed into a coffin, and when he protests that he is not dead, one Irishman retorts, "Not dead! . . . ain't that a pretty extravagant assartion now for a corpse to make? Not dead! And sure you can't be in your right mind to say so. Come, lie down, if ye plase, and we'll nail ye up and bury ye dacently." Finding himself unable to reason with the persistent Hibernians, the victim leaps from his coffin and escapes. Another sketch appeared in the *New-York Mirror* of December 10, 1836, describing the burial of a termagant who for years had bedeviled a meek country parson. The night after the interment, the minister hears a knock at the door: "There, wrapped in her winding-sheet, stood the formidable figure of his *worst* half—alive, and breathing vengeance upon her devoted lord for having prematurely consigned her to the tomb." The writer explains, "It had been a case

merely of suspended animation, and the coffin having been imper-
fectly screwed, and the door of the vault left unlocked, its rebellious
inmate had burst her cerements, and re-appeared upon the scene of
her former triumphs of temper!" When the shrew falls into another
cataleptic sleep, the parson decides to leave nothing to chance:
"Profiting from the past, her much-abused and long-suffering lord
directed the coffin to be *nailed.*" Behind the wry humor, one perceives a pattern reminiscent of such Poe tales as "Morella" and "The
Fall of the House of Usher": a willful woman returns to haunt the man
who buried her.

Through situation comedy, such writing supplied compensatory
fantasies of escape to a public disquieted by the threat of premature
burial. A return from the tomb produces the improbable confrontation between victim and survivors which forms the crux of burial
humor. This encounter, in its inevitable confusion of the living with
the dead, expresses through its crudeness the private satisfaction of
such comedy: the idea of reclaiming life by a sheer act of will. Poe's
familiarity with the comic burial tale first manifested itself in "A
Decided Loss," the 1832 "Folio Club" narrative which he repub-
lished in other versions as "Loss of Breath." His numerous emenda-
tions (documented by Mabbott) suggest that Poe tinkered for years
with a narrative which seems unworthy of such attention. Why Poe
repeatedly came back to "Loss of Breath" (his preferred title) is an
intriguing question. Surely he had no illusions about achieving subtlety, for its absurdity of plot, recondite allusiveness, and ponderous
diction remained largely intact through multiple revisions. In an
1836 letter to John Pendleton Kennedy, he spoke of "Lionizing" and
"Loss of Breath" as "satires properly speaking—at least so meant,"
with the latter piece aimed at "the extravagancies of Blackwood."[18]
That notion was insinuated in his subtitle to "Loss of Breath"—"A
Tale Neither In nor Out of 'Blackwood.'" Of this magazine, Michael
Allen has shown that while *Blackwood's* appealed to an elite audience
through its authoritative reviews, it pandered to "the less erudite
reader" through its promulgation of "blatant sensationalism" in tales
"structured around a protagonist isolated in some strange, horrific, or
morbid situation which is progressively exploited for effect."[19]

As he would later do in "A Predicament" (the outrageous sequel to

"How to Write a Blackwood Article"), Poe sought to expose the silliness of the formula for sensation by imagining an impossible calamity and then projecting a series of consequences, each marking a more absurd exaggeration of the original dilemma. And so Mr. Lackobreath, the narrator of "Loss of Breath," indeed manages to lose his breath in the midst of a tirade against his wife. Although he finds himself virtually deceased, "alive, with the qualifications of the dead—dead, with the propensities of the living" (CW, 2:63), Lackobreath's plight is marked by humiliation rather than horror. Apparent death is a matter of physical embarrassment; his body becomes alternately an object of loathing and curiosity. His misadventures enabled Poe to satirize not only the *Blackwood's* tale, but indecorous treatment of the dead and accidental entombment of the living.

Both the early and later versions of the narrative included an episode in which Lackobreath is crushed in a crowded highway coach. He reports, "All of my limbs were dislocated and my head twisted on one side" (66). His grotesque appearance and absence of breath convince his fellow travelers that he is a corpse, a theory one passenger tests by giving him "a thump on the right eye." Not wishing to ride with "any such carcasses," the travelers heave Lackobreath out of the coach and thereby fracture his skull "in a manner at once interesting and extraordinary." This fear of traveling with a dead body (a motif Poe would later use in "The Oblong Box") suggests the primitive idea of death as contagion—the fear that contact with the dead somehow contaminated the living and marked them for death. Lackobreath's "corpse" figures as an object of disgust upon which gratuitous violence is inflicted, presumably to counter any supernatural influence.

In all versions of the tale Poe likewise included an episode in which Lackobreath undergoes dissection at the hands of medical experimenters. In the story's original version, the hero is first hanged and then delivered to a "practising physician" who pays twenty-five dollars for an anatomical specimen, only to discover signs of life after cutting off both ears. Unwilling to forfeit his investment, the surgeon makes an incision in Lackobreath's stomach and removes several viscera "for private examination." To determine whether the corpse can be revived, he then summons an apothecary, who applies galvanic charges to the body "with the most unremitting assiduity." In later versions, the apothecary is also said to carry out "several curious experiments" with his battery. Poe's slapstick version of dissection reminds us that medical schools and private anatomists were then actively involved in the procurement of cadavers; in Baltimore (where Poe composed the first version of the story) "great prejudice" against dissection forced teachers at the University of Maryland School of Medicine to use an anatomical theater with concealed dissecting areas and hidden exits to guard against "surprise attacks by irate citizens."[20] Poe's dissection scene plays upon popular scorn for the anatomist, who is seen buying a body (interestingly, the price drops from twenty-five to ten dollars in later versions) and dismembering it with no regard for the humanity of the subject.

Beyond such topical satire, Poe's tale also enacts a verbal predicament that returns us to the paradox of language inherent in the burial narrative. For Lackobreath's misfortunes—the indignities of hanging, mutilation, dissection, and finally premature interment—derive not from his loss of breath but from the loss of words: he is taken for dead because he cannot speak. During the anatomy scene, for example, the victim attempts to refute the assumption of his death by "kicking and plunging with all [his] might," but the experimenters persist, and Lackobreath remarks: "It was a source of mortification to me nevertheless, that although I made several attempts at conversation, my powers of speech were so entirely in abeyance, that I could not even open my mouth" (67). Loss of speech is a mortification both in the ordinary sense of humiliation and in the literal, etymological sense of inflicting death. In a later chapter, the connection between death and the loss of language will figure in the elaboration of Poe's theory of revenge. But for now we should note that in "Loss of Breath" Poe transposed the dialectic between death and writing (inscribed in "MS. Found in a Bottle") into the dialectic of death and speech. Mr. Lackobreath is buried because he cannot verbally affirm his existence; life and language become coterminous, and the loss of one implies the surrender of the other.

But a second figuring of the relationship between language and death arises from the first. Lackobreath's loss of breath and speech does not deprive him of thought or animation, but without the capacity to speak his mind—to translate thought into discourse—he finds himself simultaneously living and dead. In the later versions of "Loss of Breath," when the hero undergoes premature burial his situation provides both a metaphor for the loss of language (to be buried alive is to be held incommunicado) and an implicit gloss on its restoration. Just as Lackobreath has been consigned to the tomb because he has lost breath and speech, so he recovers them in a public vault. Shortly after his interment he begins to explore his environs: "I knocked off . . . the lid of my coffin, and stepped out. The place was dreadfully dreary and damp, and I became troubled with *ennui.* By way of amusement, I felt my way among the numerous coffins ranged in order around. I lifted them down, one by one, and breaking open their lids, busied myself in speculations about the mortality within" (70). Immediately Lackobreath begins to "soliloquize," a parodic Hamlet whose powers of speech have been restored, it would seem, by the spectacle of a "carcass, puffy, bloated, and rotund." This return of language through the contemplation of death marks a significant moment, for here Poe suggests that while mortality deprives the individual of the word (*parole*), it likewise calls forth language (*langue*) as a transhistorical source of continuity in human culture. In Poe's comic scene, the sight of the bloated carcass evokes a verbal response even though Lackobreath has no listener; the image of death lifts the repression of speech as though he had uncovered the primordial origin of language itself. This moment seems to dramatize the idea that consciousness of mortality both creates the need for language and determines its symbolic nature. For just as the intrusion of death into human experience manifested for the first time (one imagines) the concept of permanent loss, so it created the need to designate that which was no longer present. If we trace this myth of language to its origins in Judeo-Christian culture, we might say that although Adam and Eve first used language to name elements in their worldly paradise, they did not understand the word as the sign of an absence until their expulsion from Eden and their entry into a world of pain and death. Indeed, death alone created the radical awareness of a thing-which-is-not-present, which marked the point at which the verbal signifier could enter the field of human consciousness.

Lackobreath's paradoxical recuperation through contact with

death (the reverse of the primitive death-as-contagion) becomes complete when he chances to disturb the body of Mr. Windenough, his counterpart and sexual rival. Windenough has been buried alive, it seems, not because he has "lost his breath" but because he has "caught his breath"—or rather, the misplaced breath of Poe's narrator, who remarks: "The breath so fortuitously caught by the gentleman . . . was, in fact, the identical expiration mislaid by myself in the conversation with my wife" (73). We recall that Lackobreath's loss occurred in the midst of a harangue about his wife's "iniquity," delivered on the morning after their wedding; and so we might conclude that what Lackobreath has lost in intercourse, Windenough has gained. But Lackobreath means to get back his breath (whatever it signifies) and so retains a firm hold on "Mr. W.'s proboscis" until the missing essence is returned. Apart from the intriguing sexual innuendo, which doubles the notion of breath/language as a vital force, this recovery of "mislaid" aspiration makes possible the narrator's escape from the tomb. The resuscitated voices of Lackobreath and Windenough possess enough united strength to summon help, and so the two are rescued from "the dungeons of the sepulchre."

But despite the technical resolution of "Loss of Breath," the point of this breathlessness remains—as it were—cryptic: in what economy of symbolic exchange are we to place the transaction narrated here? In opposing Lackobreath and Windenough, lack and excess, losing and finding, Poe traces the circulation of a breath both as a physiological event and as a play on words. Indeed, the physical transaction can be imagined only as a literalizing of the figurative expressions "losing one's breath" and "catching one's breath." The story's action may thus be said to occur at the threshold of figurality, at that place where the verbal sign begins to constitute a new order of relations, a new logic of reference. Insofar as "breath" is a conventional metonym for "life," we see Poe representing a fantasy world in which loss of life becomes a reversible process; death no longer marks an absolute boundary. If one can accidentally lose his life, he can as easily regain it. Because events in this fantasy are determined by the logic of wordplay rather than probability or causality, such recovery is inscribed from the outset in the punning names of the characters: Mr. Lackobreath will surely recover his lost breath from Mr. Windenough (who will simultaneously be relieved of a superfluity). In the parodic unfolding of "Loss of Breath," language governs metaphysics; the figurative imposes itself upon the literal to redefine the phenomenology of death. The power of words—the aeolist fantasy par excellence—supersedes the fatality of nature and momentarily satisfies the writer's desire to escape the inevitability of death or horror of premature burial.

That which the comic tale suppressed or converted to farce—the psychic impressions of living interment—found expression, however, in another kind of narrative, usually presented as the authentic testimony of a survivor. Relying upon first-person narration, such stories sought to achieve verisimilitude through circumstantial detail, directness, and sincerity of tone. The tale to which Poe's Mr. Blackwood alludes—"The Buried Alive"—popularized what might be called the underground memoir: reprinted freely in American periodicals, it provided a model of self-narrated "death" and burial. While it is tempting to dismiss such narratives as facile hoaxes, the continuing fascination of "The Buried Alive" and its kind requires us to consider symbolic content as well as surface detail. Recent medical and psychological research on the nature of the "near-death experience" lends a curious plausibility, for example, to the supposed death described by the author of "The Buried Alive":

> One day toward the evening, the crisis took place.—I was seized
> with a strange and indescribable quivering—a rushing sound was
> in my ears—I saw around my couch, innumerable strange faces;
> they were bright and visionary, and without bodies. There was
> light and solemnity, and I tried to move, but could not.—For a
> short time a terrible confusion overwhelmed me, and when it
> passed off, all my recollection returned with the most perfect distinctness; but the power of motion had departed. I heard the sound
> of weeping at my pillow—and the voice of the nurse say, "He is
> dead."[21]

The rushing sound, the sense of light, and the presence of disembodied others—all of these impressions match the documented pattern of near-death experience.[22] This congruence helps to explain the effect of authenticity in "The Buried Alive," though it cannot clarify the more intriguing problem of how the writer came to describe these phenomena with such accuracy.

As if to provide a textbook example of the way in which a "minute attention to the sensations" might generate narrative, the writer of this *Blackwood's* tale recounts his own premature burial, relying upon sounds and a rudimentary sense of movement to establish the sequence of events:

> The day of interment arrived—I felt the coffin lifted and borne away—I heard and felt it placed in the hearse. There was a crowd of people around; some of them spoke sorrowfully of me. The hearse began to move—I knew that it carried me to the grave. It halted, and the coffin was taken out—I felt myself carried on the shoulders of men, by the inequality of the motion—a pause ensued—I heard the cords of the coffin moved—I felt it swing as dependent by them—It was lowered, and rested on the bottom of the grave—the cords were dropped upon the lid—I heard them fall. Dreadful was the effort I then made to exert the power of action, but my whole frame was immoveable.
>
> Soon after, a few handfuls of earth were thrown upon the coffin, then there was another pause; after which the shovels were employed, and the sound of the rattling mould, as it covered me, was far more tremendous than thunder. But I could make no effort.—The sound gradually became less and less, and by a surging reverberation in the coffin, I knew that the grave was filled up, and that the sexton was treading the earth, and slapping the grave with the flat of his spade.—This, too, ceased; and then all was silent.

Despite the plain diction and banal details, the passage holds a compelling interest that is bound up not with the specific content nor with the point of view, but with the paradoxical relationship between them. In its unfolding of the "death" and sepulture of a subject, "The Buried Alive" violates the logic of writing, for the account is inscribed by the very subject whose absence the burial certifies. If death marks the forfeiture of language, a memoir of one's interment is always an unwritable record, already an impossible text. Yet here, against the conventions of discourse, writing traces the conditions of its own negation. When the narrator writes, "This is death, thought

I, and I am doomed to remain in the earth, until the resurrection," he anticipates the impossible claim of Monsieur Valdemar: "I *have been* sleeping—and now—now—*I am dead.*"

In recognizing the hopelessness of his situation, the writer of "The Buried Alive" experiences a definitive form of death anxiety—one which recapitulates the imagery of dread that the victim has carried to the tomb. He anticipates that his body will "fall into corruption," and a low sound excites more explicit terrors: "I fancied that the worms and reptiles of death were coming, and the mole and the rat of the grave would soon be upon me." In this nightmarish moment we recognize the primal psychic material exploited in the underground memoir—namely, the fear of one's creaturely condition. Becker writes of man's estrangement from his own form: "His body is a material fleshy casing that is alien to him in many ways—the strangest and most repugnant way being that it aches and bleeds and will decay and die."23 The tale of premature burial articulates a fantasy of ultimate physical entrapment, in which one is beyond rescue (it would seem) and doubly doomed, being both condemned to death and already in the place of death, subject to the horrors of the Conqueror Worm (to borrow Poe's already borrowed phrase24). Yet the narrator of "The Buried Alive" survives his ordeal through the intervention of two grave robbers; he is exhumed, delivered to an anatomy room, and revived when a surgeon makes an incision. His deliverance thus cancels the threat of corruption and converts his experience into a fable of resurrection. Becker notes that such a pattern informs the great monomyth of ancient cultures: "The hero was the man who could go into the spirit world, the world of the dead, and return alive. He had his descendants in the mystery cults of the Eastern Mediterranean, which were cults of death and resurrection. The divine hero of each of these cults was one who had come back from the dead."25 While one cannot claim mythic status for the protagonists of underground memoirs, such narratives implicitly re-enacted the agon of survival, the archetypal triumph of life over death.

The same motif of rescue by grave robbers—known appositely as "resurrection men"—occurs in "Living Inhumation," an account purportedly "from the unpublished diary of C. Hodgson, Esq., lately deceased, formerly of Bristol, (Eng.)." Hodgson's tale, which appeared in the *Saturday Evening Post* of May 24, 1828, emphasizes the sensations of enclosure, tracing the emotional changes and levels of awareness experienced by the victim. Like the narrator of "The Buried Alive," Hodgson falls prey to a paralyzing illness and is presumed dead; his recovery of consciousness within the coffin brings terror, then despair:

> When the real truth flashed upon me in all its fearful energy, I never can forget the thrill of horror that struck through me! It was as if a bullet had perforated my heart, and all the blood in my body gushed through the wound! Never, never, can hell be more terrible than the sensations of that moment! I lay motionless for a time, petrified with terror. Then a clammy dampness burst forth from every pore of my body. My horrible doom seemed inevitable; and so strong at length became this impression—so bereft of hope became my situation—that I ultimately recovered from it only to plunge into the depths of a calm, resolute despair.

What sets Hodgson's narrative apart from others is his attentiveness to the psychology of premature burial. He describes an alternating cycle of hope and dread, and his representation of physical suffering underscores the enormity of the experience: "I shrieked with horror: I plunged my nails into my thighs, and wounded them; the coffin was soaked in my blood; and by tearing the wooden sides of my prison with the same maniacal feeling, I lacerated my fingers, and wore the nails to the quick, soon becoming motionless from exhaustion." Of his confinement he later notes, "Stretched in a position where my changes consisted only of a turn on my side upon hard boards, the soreness of my limbs was excruciatingly painful."

Compared to "The Buried Alive," Hodgson's narrative seems more detailed and more "literary" in its rhetorical effects. In the extremity of his hysteria, Hodgson too has a visionary episode, but here we note the intrusion of conventional Gothic figures:

> Images of men and women, often numberless, in a sort of shadowy outline, came before and round me. They seemed as if limbless from decay. Their featureless heads moved upon trunks hideously

vital; in figure-like bodies, which I have seen drawn from burned dwellings, each being rather a hideous misshapen mass than a human semblance. Thick darkness and silence succeeded; the darkness and silence of a too horrible reality.

Here the author seems to disclose (in the recollection of burned bodies) the unconscious source of his vision, which may owe something as well to the imagery of Blair's *The Grave.* Whether "Living Inhumation" is by virtue of its literariness less "authentic" than "The Buried Alive" is beside the point, however. In Hodgson's narrative, premature interment has become an occasion of writing, a self-conscious project of language directed against the silence and oblivion ordinarily associated with burial. Writing becomes an act of self-preservation in a double sense: by recounting the means through which he attracted the attention of grave robbers, Hodgson produces both the history of his physical survival and a text which insures his survival as a writing subject. Yet this self-preservation is enfolded in an irony: the writer who speaks of his deliverance from the tomb is identified as "lately deceased"; the death he claims to have escaped has claimed him. This irony defines the scene of writing as a moment between two burials, in which the one who writes of escaping death is always already dead.

Though Poe grasped the potential for satire and farce inherent in premature burial, he seems to have been obsessed by claustrophobic memoirs of the sort represented by "The Buried Alive" and "Living Inhumation." After the 1840 publication of *Tales of the Grotesque and Arabesque,* Poe removed passages on the phenomenology of death and burial from his earliest interment piece, "Loss of Breath." Inconsistent with the tale's bantering tone, these excised paragraphs reveal the uncertainty of Poe's response to the interment theme: amid foolery, the sensations specific to a "corpse" evoke an irrepressible dread. One can imagine the young Emily Dickinson—she who would later write "Because I could not stop for death"—absorbing these funereal details:

> During the brief passage to the cemetery my sensations, which for some time had been lethargic and dull, assumed, all at once, a degree of intense and unnatural vivacity for which I can in no manner

account. I could distinctly hear the rustling of the plumes—the whispers of the attendants—the solemn breathings of the horses of death. Confined as I was in that narrow and strict embrace, I could feel the quicker or slower movement of the procession—the restlessness of the driver—the windings of the road as it led us to the right or to the left. I could distinguish the peculiar odor of the coffin—the sharp acrid smell of the steel screws. I could see the texture of the shroud as it lay close against my face; and was even conscious of the rapid variations in light and shade which the flapping to and fro of the sable hangings occasioned within the body of the vehicle. [81]

Here the reader senses—as Poe doubtless did—the intrusion of anxiety, the onset of a panic otherwise denied, textually cancelled, by parodic exaggeration. But while Poe expunged from "Loss of Breath" those passages evoking "the actual terrors of the yawning tomb," he could not exorcise the thought of living interment.

That fear surfaces in his fiction with periodic insistence, sometimes masking itself as situation comedy of the sort observed in "King Pest," where one of the members of the King's junta is "habited, somewhat uniquely, in a new and handsome mahogany coffin" (*CW*, 2:248). More often, however, it occurs as an explicit dread of what Poe would later call "the one sepulchral Idea." In "Berenice" his narrator comes to consciousness only to hear a servant's tremulous account "of a violated grave—of a disfigured body enshrouded, yet still breathing—still palpitating—*still alive!*" (*CW*, 2:218). It appears that Egaeus has buried his cousin hastily so that he can gratify his desire to possess her teeth; that is, interment has created the possibility of a "violation" previously denied. In this psychosexual context, the deathlike trance of the beloved carries the meaning of availability, and premature burial signifies the displacement or concealment of an erotic project. The fate of Berenice anticipates the problematic "deaths" of the Lady Rowena and Madeline Usher, who are both "prepared . . . for the tomb" without an explicit confirmation of their decease; and the pattern of hasty interment at least raises the possibility that Ligeia too has been consigned to the grave mistakenly, perhaps from the narrator's unconscious desire to relieve his own anxieties. Chapter 3 considers Ligeia's return as an act of revenge for premature interment.

The fear of burial alive recurs in *The Narrative of Arthur Gordon Pym* (1838) when the narrator finds that he is trapped in the hold of the *Grampus*: "In vain I attempted to reason on the probable cause of my being thus entombed . . . and, sinking on the floor, gave way, unresistingly, to the most gloomy imaginings, in which the dreadful deaths of thirst, famine, suffocation, and premature interment, crowded upon me as the prominent disasters to be encountered."[26] Later, when the natives on Tsalal trigger an avalanche to kill the crew of the *Jane Guy*, Pym and Dirk Peters find themselves sealed in a cave. The two conclude that they are "lost forever, being thus entombed alive," and Pym takes the occasion to rehearse the terrors of the experience:

> I firmly believe that no incident ever occurring in the course of human events is more adapted to inspire the supremeness of mental and bodily distress than a case like our own, of living inhumation. The blackness of darkness which envelops the victim, the terrific oppression of lungs, the stifling fumes from the damp earth, unite with the ghastly considerations that we are beyond the remotest confines of hope, and that such is the allotted portion of *the dead*, to carry into the human heart a degree of appalling awe and horror not to be tolerated—never to be conceived. [182]

In *Pym* the dread of premature burial signifies the narrator's powerlessness over phenomenal reality; unable to comprehend events—much less to control them—Pym feels buried alive by the irrationality and violence inscribed in the natural order. Indeed, his two scrapes with living interment anticipate his fate as a textual entity: Poe buries his narrator alive, causing him to disappear into a milky vortex, his project of writing interrupted forever by the gesture which enshrouds him, gathering him into an image of death, a "shrouded human figure . . . of the perfect whiteness of the snow."

Pym's remark that inhumation possesses an "appalling awe and horror" because it is "the allotted portion of *the dead*" helps to explain the singular fascination of "The Colloquy of Monos and Una" (1841), a story which—strictly speaking—does not represent premature burial at all. Rather, it purports to depict through a dialogue of spirits the phenomenology of authentic death and permanent burial. On one level Poe here continues to work out a theory of transcendence: Monos and Una have been reunited as disembodied beings after a century of insentient moldering in the grave. But the narrative interest resides in the account offered by Monos of his corporeal death and residual sensations during the laying-out and entombment. In these passages Poe projects a concept of gradual rather than sudden extinction: Monos records first visual and auditory postmortem impressions, then (in the grave) an "abiding sentiment of duration," and finally the replacement of a "consciousness of *being*" with the mere sense of "*place.*" Behind this projection, one recognizes the familiar rhetoric of the premature-burial narrative; in a lengthy paragraph Monos tells Una what he perceived at the hour of death:

> I breathed no longer. The pulses were still. The heart had ceased to beat. Volition had not departed, but was powerless. The senses were unusually active, although eccentrically so—assuming often each other's functions at random. . . . *All* my perceptions were purely sensual. The materials furnished the passive brain by the senses were not in the least degree wrought into shape by the deceased understanding. Of pain there was some little; of pleasure there was much; but of moral pain or pleasure none at all. Thus your wild sobs floated into my ear with all their mournful cadences, and were appreciated in their every variation of sad tone; but they were soft musical sounds and no more; they conveyed to the extinct reason no intimation of the sorrows which gave them birth; while the large and constant tears which fell upon my face, telling the bystanders of a heart which broke, thrilled every fibre of my frame with ecstasy alone. And this was in truth the *Death* of which these bystanders spoke reverently, in low whispers—you, sweet Una, gaspingly, with loud cries. [*CW*, 2:612–14]

Likewise, Monos recalls his being "attired for the coffin," his conveyance to the cemetery, and his burial, which leaves him "in blackness and corruption." In all of this, we note the pattern observed in magazine tales like "The Buried Alive" and "Living Inhumation." The point is not that Poe tried in "Monos and Una" to disguise a familiar formula. Rather, he eliminated the framework of catalepsy, premature burial, and rescue to expose the essential question evoked by such tales: how does it feel to die? This is the point of Pym's reference to "the allotted portion of *the dead*," and this is doubtless the covert fascination of every narrative of living interment.

Poe perceived premature burial as an equivalent to death itself not simply because of its inherent lethality, but also because he believed all burials to be "living" insofar as consciousness extended beyond physical death. In "The Pit and the Pendulum" he declared, "Even in the grave all *is not* lost. Else there is no immortality for man. Arousing from the most profound of slumbers, we break the gossamer web of *some* dream" (CW, 2:682). Much of the power of this celebrated tale derives from the uncertain relationship between consciousness and death. With his opening words—"I was sick—sick unto death with that long agony"—the narrator evokes the psychic environment of death anxiety and upon receiving the death sentence loses consciousness—only to recover it in a manner characteristic of the premature-burial narrative:

> Very suddenly there came back to my soul motion and sound—the tumultuous motion of the heart, and, in my ears, the sound of its beating. Then a pause in which all is blank. Then again sound, and motion, and touch—a tingling sensation pervading my frame. Then the mere consciousness of existence, without thought—a condition which lasted long. Then, very suddenly, *thought*, and shuddering terror, and earnest endeavor to comprehend my true state. [683]

Not for a moment does he suppose himself actually dead, yet through his own anticipations of death he intuits the desperation of his situation, and a "fearful idea" enters his mind: that he will find himself "impeded by the walls of a *tomb*." The fear that he has been entombed alive brings to mind all of the associations by which death is imaged. Though he subsequently determines his receptacle to be a dungeon, the narrator continues to experience his confinement as a premature burial. He is simultaneously a "dead man" (condemned to death) and a living victim, and his elemental struggle seems to unfold at the threshold of consciousness itself, for survival depends upon coherence of thought in the face of horrors dredged up from the unconscious. Like the victim of premature interment, he feels the hopelessness of his predicament; he is oppressed by "the intensity of the darkness"; amid the gloom he descries the imagery of the burial vault, "hideous and repulsive devices" of a "charnel superstition . . . the figures of fiends in aspects of menace, with skeleton forms" (689). The convergence of the walls evokes once again the panic of fatal enclosure, and only the arrival of a deus ex machina (a resurrection man, as it were) saves him from death-in-life. Indeed, for all its historical trappings as a tale of the Inquisition, "The Pit and the Pendulum" amounts to an elaborate fantasy of burial alive, drawing its claustrophobic intensity from the sense of impending annihilation.

Poe's most problematic response to the threat of living interment came, however, in his 1844 tour de force, "The Premature Burial." Here the author combined in a single tale the disparate modes of anecdotal history, burlesque, and underground memoir. The juxtaposition is not entirely successful; in moving from journalistic case studies to a putative recollection of burial to a ludicrous scene of mistaken assumptions, Poe sacrifices unity of effect for parody. In one respect he effectively hoaxes the reader with the formula worked out in *Pym*—eliciting belief and then discrediting his own narrative. When the "victim" in "The Premature Burial" vows to read no more "'Night Thoughts'—no fustian about church-yards—no bugaboo tales—*such as this,*" he implicitly deconstructs his account, dismisses the genre which it represents, trivializes the idea of living inhumation, and leaves the reader holding the shroud. But Poe cannot entirely laugh off what the rest of the narrative affirms: that premature burial indeed occurred and that the very thought obsessed the writer. Noting the complex satiric irony of "The Premature Burial," Thompson calls attention to Poe's oddly ambiguous evocation of "sepulchral terrors" in the last paragraph, just after the "jarring, comic, illusion-breaking reference" to "bugaboo tales." This final reversion to Gothic fear—which according to Thompson leaves us "entertaining the serious possibilities of the absurd situation"— breaks the illusion of comedy to create a twice-cancelled version of living interment.[27]

The cancellation effected in the last paragraph is less a "mistake" or formal lapse than an almost perversely confessional postscript on the relationship between obsession and writing. The story told by Poe's narrator—the account of his fears, his susceptibility to trance-like states, and his embarrassing "rescue" from the berth of a ship—closes with a renunciation of graveyard poetry and other funereal texts. The avoidance of such writing is said to have a salutary effect: "From that memorable night, I dismissed forever my charnel apprehensions, and with them vanished the cataleptic disorder, of which, perhaps, they had been less the consequence than the cause." The story's last sentence returns to the idea of repression, underscoring the need to deny those imaginings capable of consuming us: "Alas! the grim legion of sepulchral terrors cannot be regarded as altogether fanciful—but, like the Demons in whose company Afrasiab made his voyage down the Oxus, they must sleep, or they will devour us—they must be suffered to slumber, or we perish" (CW, 3:969). Yet the existence of the tale itself bears witness to the devouring force of these same sepulchral terrors. The narrator who has renounced the literature of death has subsequently steeped himself in magazine writing on premature burial, so that he can summarize four sensational cases. The writer who perceives the danger of awakening subliminal fears has rehearsed the details of his "burial" and exposed the features of his own dread. Despite the claim that he has dismissed his charnel apprehensions, his writing of a text called "The Premature Burial" manifests a repetition mechanism, through which (like the Ancient Mariner) the reenactment of his fate presumably enables him for a time to relieve its psychic weight.

But while the writing appears to spring from an unconscious need to reconstruct his traumatic experience, the narrator's awareness of his own obsessive tendencies establishes an ironic perspective on obsession itself. Poe complicates the text with ambiguous gestures of self-analysis, as when the narrator remarks: "My fancy grew charnel. I talked 'of worms, of tombs and epitaphs.' I was lost in reveries of death, and the idea of premature burial held continual possession of my brain" (963). Here we observe both self-mockery—inherent in the misquotation from *Richard II*—and what seems to be authentic psychic disclosure. Is the narrator guilty of frightening himself with charnel fancies, or does his predilection for reveries of death reveal an uncontrollable monomania? Both perspectives seem correct: that is, the reading of Young's *Night Thoughts* and the talk of worms, tombs, and epitaphs constitute a perverse, willed response to the problem of burial anxieties. Yet unbidden horrors pervade the narrator's dreams, described as "a world of phantasms, above which, with vast, sable, overshadowing wings, hovered, predominant, the one sepulchral Idea." His preoccupation with interment is at once a parody of the graveyard sensibility and a reflex of dread.

Among other signs that the idea of premature burial holds "continual possession" of his brain, the narrator at one point sketches a "solitary vision," a hallucinatory glimpse of death which seems to crystallize the relationship between historical evidence of living interments (cited in contemporary treatises) and the subliminal force of that threat:

> I looked; and the unseen figure, which still grasped me by the wrist, had caused to be thrown open the graves of all mankind; and from each issued the faint phosphoric radiance of decay; so that I could see into the innermost recesses, and there view the shrouded bodies in their sad and solemn slumbers with the worm. But, alas! the real sleepers were fewer, by many millions, than those who slumbered not at all; and there was a feeble struggling; and there was a general sad unrest; and from out the depths of the countless pits there came a melancholy rustling from the garments of the buried. And, of those who seemed tranquilly to repose, I saw that a vast number had changed, in a greater or less degree, the rigid and uneasy position in which they had originally been entombed. [964]

This vision of writhing corpses recalls Fontenelle's claim that churchyards concealed legions of bodies prematurely entombed, and it marks a subliminal reformulation of the narrator's earlier "factual" observation that "scarcely, in truth, is a graveyard ever encroached upon, for any purpose, to any great extent, that skeletons are not found in postures which suggest the most fearful of suspicions" (961). The difference between this documentary comment and the dream sequence above marks the surface-depth relationship in Poe's treatment of "the one sepulchral Idea" and indicates his awareness of the way in which the material of rational discourse can evoke figures of essential anxiety from the unconscious. In this oneiric panorama of "sad unrest" we discern elemental features of Poe's view of death: lurid decay, residual sentience, melancholy struggles to escape the tomb.

Although the narrator of "The Premature Burial" must not be confused with Poe himself, we note an inherent doubling: the putative writer who speaks of his obsession with living interment is the fictive counterpart of an author who was drawn back to that subject persistently. The narrator is both a victim of compulsion and an observer of compulsiveness; he can laugh at his fondness for "bugaboo tales," but he cannot quite escape the need to write one. He speaks sternly of the importance of "truth," yet he proceeds to tell a story in which living interment does not occur. His tale is nevertheless "true" in the sense that it describes a state of mind rather than an event. These contradictions spring from the simultaneous effort to reveal a fixation while concealing the filiation between author and narrator. Yet insofar as the narrator repeats earlier references by Poe to premature burial, we observe traces of authorial identity. For example, his summary of the case of "Mr. Edward Stapleton" returns to the same story ("The Buried Alive") cited playfully in "How to Write a Blackwood Article." At another juncture, when the narrator discovers himself enveloped in darkness, his description of the "utter raylessness of the Night that endureth forevermore" echoes similar passages in early versions of "Loss of Breath," in *Pym*, and in "The Pit and the Pendulum."[28] When the narrator analyzes the psychic effect of accidental interment, he borrows Arthur Gordon Pym's declaration about burial—that "no incident ever occurring in the course of human events is more adapted to inspire the supremeness of mental and bodily distress"—to observe: "*No* event is so terribly well adapted to inspire the supremeness of bodily and of mental distress, as is burial before death" (961). He revises more of Pym's account in enumerating the elements of this distress:

The unendurable oppression of the lungs—the stifling fumes of the damp earth—the clinging to the death garments— the rigid embrace of the narrow house—the blackness of the absolute Night—

the silence like a sea that overwhelms—the unseen but palpable presence of the Conqueror Worm—these things, with thoughts of the air and grass above, with memory of dear friends who would fly to save us if but informed of our fate, and with consciousness that of this fate they can *never* be informed—that our hopeless portion is that of the really dead—these considerations, I say, carry into the heart, which still palpitates, a degree of appalling and intolerable horror from which the most daring imagination must recoil. [961]

Here Poe specifies the psychic impressions associated with living interment: enclosure, isolation, and helplessness. This projection of the interior, subjective experience balances the subsequent dream sequence in which the narrator sees in a vista of opened graves external signs of the same dilemma. In this doubling of inside and outside perspectives as well as the rhetorical duplication of prior texts, Poe points to the more important doubling of the fictive writer—who claims he now thinks "upon other subjects than Death"—and the author who extracted from death the very life of writing.

By the time he composed "The Premature Burial," Poe had nearly exhausted his own fascination with the "one sepulchral Idea." Only two later stories, "Some Words with a Mummy" and "The Cask of Amontillado," partake of the motif of living burial: the former plays on the notion of galvanic reanimation to stage a whimsical escape from the coffin; the latter evokes the atmosphere of the burial vault to intensify the horror of Fortunato's entombment. But Poe's diverse and protracted use of the subject carries its own irrefutable significance. For him, premature burial was a rehearsal of death, a foretaste of the silence and darkness of which the corpse would be dimly aware. The idea of living interment provided a focus for more generalized anxieties about dying, enabling the writer to explore and particularize his own ideation of death. Yet the writing of such narratives should not be viewed as a morbid exercise, for inscription implicitly confirms the endurance of the victim. In this sense the underground memoir constitutes a literature of survival; the gesture of writing signifies if not an absolute immunity from death at least a provisional victory over the tomb.

That Poe in his scenes of premature burial articulated a culturally shared disquietude may be seen in a last example of periodical writing, an item called "Burying Alive," which appeared in the *Rover* of August 17, 1844. This commentary on Poe's "The Premature Burial" betrays no awareness of the fictitiousness of his case histories. "This is a fearful subject," the unidentified writer opined, "but the well-known fact, that cases do sometimes occur where people are buried alive, renders it proper and important that public attention should occasionally be called to it." This misfortune admittedly did not happen "very often," but the "abundant evidence" of sporadic occurrences prompted the magazinist to reproduce extracts from Poe's "well-authenticated" reports. The ironical, "bugaboo" aspect of the tale seems not to have troubled the writer, whose respectful tone indicates the success of the hoax. Yet from an informed perspective, we see what the *Rover*'s columnist could not: that living interment recurs in Poe's writing not simply as a "predicament," a thematic source of terror, but more importantly as a foretaste of death and as a figure of the writer's essential dilemma. To inscribe his narrative, he draws upon the isolation, dread, and silence which are the terms of his human confinement; and the underground memoir bears witness to the way in which writing is inherently a sign of survival, a heroic resistance to the "one sepulchral Idea."

3

The Horrors of Translation
The Death of a Beautiful Woman

Poe's 1842 tale "The Oval Portrait" tells of a "desperately wounded" traveler who chances to pass a night in a Gothic chateau. Suffering from "incipient delirium," the narrator decides to peruse a volume of art criticism found lying on his pillow; he gives himself over to the book "devoutly" until the approach of "deep midnight," when he adjusts the candelabrum at his bedside and perceives in a dark niche the hitherto unnoticed portrait of a beautiful young woman. The picture possesses an "absolute *lifelikeliness* of expression" that startles the narrator, rivets his gaze for half an hour, and then leads him back to the book (which happens to describe the paintings in the bedroom). The volume provides a brief account—reminiscent of Hawthorne's "The Birthmark"—of a "wild and moody" painter who worked so obsessively to idealize his young bride through portraiture that he did not notice her failing health and so completed his masterpiece only to discover that he had killed the beloved subject.

The tale is exemplary in several respects and provides a condensed allegory of death, life, and art which implies an antagonism between living beauty and its artistic representation. In this sense the story is not so different in implication from Keats's "Ode on a Grecian Urn," which opposes human warmth to the "cold pastoral" of the urn. But the interest of "The Oval Portrait" does not lie in its metaphorizing of aesthetic theory; rather, it resides in the tortured relationships limned by the tale: between the painter and his young bride, between the woman and her painted likeness, between the haunting portrait and the wounded narrator, and between the "quaint" anecdote in the art book and the narrator's truncated story. Each pairing figures an opposition between life and art, between one who gazes and one who is gazed at; more revealingly, each implies a relationship between translator and text or between text and translation. The painter translates his wife in a double sense—into a visual icon and into a lifeless model. Like all translation, this process entails duplication and effacement, a retracing which both mirrors the original and abolishes it in the sense that every translation sacrifices the letter of the original text to reconstitute its spirit in another language.[1] The young bride and the portrait manifest the fatality of translation, inasmuch as the picture lives by virtue of the wife's death; yet the wife paradoxically "lives on" in the painting and her essence in effect sustains the life of the translation.

The narrator, for his part, translates the painting into writing, into a text which is twice removed from the original:

> The portrait, I have already said, was that of a young girl. It was a mere head and shoulders, done in what is technically termed a *vignette* manner; much in the style of the favorite heads of Sully. The arms, the bosom and even the ends of the radiant hair, melted imperceptibly into the vague yet deep shadow which formed the back ground of the whole. The frame was oval, richly gilded and filagreed in *Moresque*. [CW, 2:664]

This rendering of the portrait again involves the slippage of translation; the narrator can tell us about "the true secret" of the painting's effect, its astonishing "lifelikeliness," but the verbal account does not leave us "confounded, subdued, and appalled" as it does the narrator. What has been lost is precisely the life of the twice-translated text; what has been gained is access to the idea of the painting. Yet as if to compensate for the loss incurred by his own translation, the narrator provides yet another version, a historical gloss, culled from the volume of art criticism. This passage explains the initial translation (from bride to portrait) and mediates a recovery of the original subject:

> She was a maiden of rarest beauty, and not more lovely than full of glee. And evil was the hour when she saw, and loved, and wedded the painter. He, passionate, studious, austere, and having already a bride in his Art; she a maiden of rarest beauty, and not more lovely than full of glee: all light and smiles, and frolicsome as the young fawn: loving and cherishing all things: hating only the Art which was her rival: dreading only the pallet and brushes and other untoward instruments which deprived her of the countenance of her lover. [664–65]

But of course this version of the young bride is itself the translation of an irrecoverable text.

The economy of translation always entails gain and loss, but in the final sentence of "The Oval Portrait," Poe's metaphor carries us to the brink of metaphysics and compels us to reflect upon the sense in which the human subject is invariably a text marked for translation. "*She was dead!*" the volume reports, in a phrase which simultaneously closes the woman's life, the critical note, and the narrative itself. Although Poe makes no further mention of his narrator's grievous wound, the catafalquelike bed, "enveloped" by "fringed curtains of black velvet," may indeed be the implied site of his own mortal translation, a supposition given force by the abrupt termination of his story. If we imagine the narrator to be upon his deathbed, his adoration of "the immortal beauty of the countenance" becomes intelligible as a manifestation of his own desire for immortality. Significantly, in the brief account of his gazing at the picture, we see him first startled, then agitated, then subdued, and finally "appalled"—the last term obliquely suggesting the onset of horror and death ("pall"). In the story of the artist and his young bride, he discovers a mirroring of his own decline before the beauty of the portrait.

Like the painter, he produces a translation without realizing its personal cost; the narrator's "gaze" at the appalling image reenacts the artist's final horror: "For one moment, the painter stood entranced before the work which he had wrought; but in the next, while he yet *gazed*, he grew tremulous and very pallid, and aghast" (665–66, my emphasis). What causes the painter to grow "very pallid" (and what later casts a pall over the narrator) is not the discovery that the bride is dead but the more unexpected realization that the portrait possesses a "life itself," a hideous autonomy of being. Here the painter confronts (as will the narrator after him) the scandal of translation, the awareness that his text has taken on an independent life more real to him than that of its original; indeed, the metaphrase has parasitically drained the original of its vitality. In its preternatural vividness, the portrait has become a frightening double of the young bride. Its "lifelikeliness" simultaneously signifies an immortality and a fatality: while the beauty of the portrait will endure, its living counterpart will not; the woman will resemble the sign of herself less and less until she is at last translated into a corpse. In this sense the portrait conveys the same inevitable message of time and mortality which (as Roland Barthes has remarked) every photograph of a human subject bears.[2] This is the shocking truth which appalls the painter and the narrator; this is the discovery which the final sentence of "The Oval Portrait" serves to confirm.

Poe's implication that the fate of the narrator is somehow linked to that of a beautiful young woman places this tale among an important group of "portraits"—writings about doomed beauty and untimely translation. In an early, quasi-autobiographical poem Poe wrote, "I could not love except where Death / Was mingling his with Beauty's breath" (CW, 1:157). In one sense this declaration expresses an entirely conventional Romantic attitude; Mario Praz notes: "To such an extent were Beauty and Death looked upon as sisters by the Romantics that they became fused into a sort of two-faced herm, filled with corruption and melancholy and fatal in its beauty—a beauty of which the more bitter the taste, the more abundant the enjoyment."[3] But as with premature burial, Poe's insistent figuring of the death of beauty—and the beauty of death—obliges us to look more closely at implicit metaphorical attributes. The poet endeavored in "The Philosophy of Composition" to rationalize his obsession with dying young women, calling the theme "the most poetical topic in the world," as if that assertion explained the brooding evocation of the "lost Lenore" and all of the other doomed ladies in his writing. Poe's biography yields plentiful sources for his preoccupation with cadaverous women and mournful men, and in chapter 4 I discuss the pattern of loss which informs his correspondence. Here I want to situate the death-of-a-beautiful-woman motif in relation to conventions of popular literature and to the anthropology of death in the nineteenth century. As noted earlier, Ariès typifies Poe's epoch as "the Age of the Beautiful Death," a period in which dying became a fetishized spectacle, an elaborately prepared departure; in which the deathbed became a site of beatific intimacy; and in which the corpse became an object of idolatry and commemoration. Barton Levi St. Armand comments on the extensions of this practice: "The loved dead themselves became keepsakes, as advances in embalming and the invention of waterproof tombs and airtight burial cases actually allowed sentimentalists to treat the corpse as a metaphorical gem, treasure, or idol it so often is in the lofty lamentations of mortuary verse."[4] As the dead body became an icon, the proliferation of mourning art in nineteenth-century America—with its iconography of urns, plinths, mourners, and weeping willows—helped to feed a melancholy preoccupation with death. This impulse found its consummation in the death of young women, especially unmarried women, whose departures from this life seemed to epitomize the beauty of innocent faith.

In the marketplace of popular literature, death and mourning generated an impressive variety of sentimentalized writing. Washington Irving's lugubrious "biography" of Margaret Miller Davidson typifies the sort of work which sponsored the concept of the Beautiful Death. Irving had first met Miss Davidson in 1833 (before her consumption had been diagnosed), and when he saw her again in 1836, two years before the girl's death, he noted that she seemed—pathetically—more beautiful in her diseased condition:

> The interval that had elapsed had rapidly developed the powers of her mind, and heightened the loveliness of her person, but my apprehensions had been verified. The soul was wearing out the

body. Preparations were making to take her on a tour for her health, and her mother appeared to flatter herself that it might prove efficacious; but when I noticed the fragile delicacy of her form, the hectic bloom of her cheek, and the almost unearthly lustre of her eye, I felt convinced that she was not long for this world; in truth, she already appeared more spiritual than mortal.[5]

Preceded in death by her sister (also a poetess of sorts), Miss Davidson passed away in 1838 at the age of fifteen, attended in her final hour by her mother, who reported in a letter: "She gave me one more look, two or three short fluttering breaths, and all was over—her spirit was with its God—not a struggle or groan preceded her departure."[6] Margaret Davidson's parting was exemplary of a kind of death that seemed devoid of pain, deformity, filth, or horror.

Another work in this genre, Rev. Moses Waddel's *Memoirs of Miss Caroline E. Smelt* devotes fully half of its one hundred fifty pages to the "last sickness and death" of its subject, a girl from Augusta, Georgia, who succumbed at the age of seventeen. During a visit to the bedside of a dying orphan, the girl witnesses for the first time the awful transformation: "I never had such feelings in all my life—I viewed with horror the change in her countenance—I saw her struggles—the sight was more than I could bear." A few days later, Miss Smelt contracts a fever and takes to her own bed, where for more than three weeks she hovers between life and death, dispensing admonitions, blessings, and pious utterances to sundry visitors. But her own transformation is kept tactfully out of sight. Waddel's narrative (based on information supplied by her family) gives a day-by-day account of the girl's rallies and relapses that emphasizes her virtuous suffering, but about her physical symptoms, the account notes only the progress of the fever and the application of "blisters" (poultices). Throughout the ordeal, Miss Smelt is said to have exhibited a countenance of "heavenly serenity" and "celestial beauty," though Waddel does permit himself to reveal that "the necessity of blistering her head" required the removal of her hair. Apposite to such representations, St. Armand observes that the "doctrine of justification by death and suffering allows us to understand the great paradox of the popular gospel of consolation: the mingled emphasis on both the corporeal and the marmoreal—the fascination with a clinical report of excruciating pain and an equal obsession with the calm, marble-like features of the corpse itself, petrified by rigor mortis."[7] Consistent with this pattern, Miss Smelt's parents contemplate her remains a few moments after her decease, and her father declares: "She is gone.—It is death! but oh! I never saw it in so heavenly a form before. It is death! but he has made no ravages upon that face. She is changed a little; but more beautiful than ever. What serene majesty of countenance! and what heavenly calmness! her sufferings are over."[8] The insistence upon the beauty of the dead seems a mandatory reflex of belief, for the perceived loveliness of the girl's corpse operates as a sign of redemption. The father allows that Miss Smelt is "changed a little," but this alteration is an apotheosis of the flesh, a confirmation of her supposed victory over death.

Contemporary gift books and guides to mourning and consolation invariably emphasized the beauty of the last hour and the spiritual uses of grief while ignoring the physiology of dissolution. *The Mourner's Gift* (1837), edited by Mrs. M. A. Patrick, offered a gilt-edged anthology of funereal verses by such purveyors of sentiment as Lydia Huntley Sigourney, Felicia Hemans, and Mrs. H. F. Gould. In 1844, Rev. Rufus W. Griswold (later to blacken Poe's reputation) brought forth a gilt-edged collection entitled *The Cypress Wreath*, with a preface announcing its purpose:

> Our literature embraces many admirable discourses and "poesies with a spiritual harmony," addressed to the heartbroken and desponding, who linger among the tombs. This little volume, the fruit of the editor's desultory reading while he was himself a mourner, it is hoped will leave upon the minds of others in like circumstances, some portion of that happy influence which its preparation had upon his own; leading them to view the FATHER'S dispensations with resignation, and to look more and more to the future life as the scene and source of blessedness.[9]

The emphasis of this "little volume" on a heavenly reunion in "the future life" was calculated to assuage grief and render "the FATHER'S dispensations" palatable if not comprehensible. Griswold's belief in the "happy influence" of such verses as "The Hour of

Death," "On the Death of a Young Girl," and "The Slumber of Death" suggests the importance of mourning as a spiritual exercise. As Karen Halttunen demonstrates, mourning in nineteenth-century America was in fact a complicated performance, both a private, meditative act and a public display of class status; as the etiquette of grief defined itself, mourning became increasingly dissociated from the actualities of death, evolving into a hypocritical system of conventions and proprieties.[10]

Poe's response to the cult of mourning and the Beautiful Death defies easy summary. His poetic treatment of dying women indicates that, to a certain extent, he shared the pervasive sentimental view that death intensified female beauty and even brought about a purification of loveliness. Thus for example in "Lenore" he idealized the departed one:

> The sweet Lenore hath gone before, with Hope that flew beside,
> Leaving thee wild for the dear child that should have been thy
> bride—
> For her, the fair and debonair, that now so lowly lies,
> The life upon her yellow hair, but not within her eyes—
> The life still there upon her hair, the death upon her eyes.
> [CW, 1:337]

This lyric captures the subtle eroticism of a beauty heightened by the implication that Lenore takes to the grave the charms which she had not yet yielded to her "wild" lover, Guy de Vere. But Poe's emphasis (in l. 12) on the death of "innocence" is also consistent with gift-book evocations of the saintly departure. More frequently in his verses, the beauty of the beloved is an obsessive memory; his speakers recall "the rare and radiant maiden whom the angels name Lenore" (in "The Raven") or "the bright eyes / Of the beautiful Annabel Lee." Poe could argue (in "The Philosophy of Composition") that the death of a beautiful woman offered the most poetical subject imaginable because that motif conjoined the essential elements of desire: irresistible loveliness and the impossibility of its preservation or recovery. The ephemerality of such beauty accounted for its force: unlike the timeless beauty of the work of art (the oval portrait), the loveliness of Poe's women is doubly evanescent, being both an aspect of youth (which is lost daily) and a symptom of illness (which must end in death). This aesthetic no doubt developed in part from the much-noted irony that consumption—the all-too-common destroyer in the nineteenth century—actually did enhance physical beauty at an intermediate stage by inducing a feverish glow. In Poe's tales, which deal more directly with the *process* of dying, fated women seem invariably to grow more beautiful as they approach their last hour. Poe implies that through this insidious transformation, temporal loveliness approaches the perfection of eternal beauty, and theoretically at least the corpse of the dead woman briefly incarnates an ideality. But because death also entails physiological decay, the beauty of the just-departed contains an element of terror, since the passage of time implies a subsequent and inevitable mutation to loathsomeness. Death discloses its cruel paradoxicality, being both the source of ideal beauty and its destroyer. Poe could accept the perverse fact that death intensified beauty—he had seen it often enough—but he also saw through the illusion fostered by sentimentalism.

If Poe persistently wrote poems about dead young women, he dwelt less upon the physical attributes of the Other than upon the condition of desolation which her death brought about for his persona. In "The Raven," for instance, the setting mirrors the melancholy speaker's own despair and emptiness: the "midnight dreary," the "bleak December," and the "dying ember" all reflect his sorrowful exhaustion. The outer world seems, on the one hand, a simple projection of his inward condition; yet the poem also enacts the struggle to escape solipsism through a recovered connection with the Other. The contradiction of mourning is that the narrator wishes both to forget and to remember: he has been pondering a "volume of forgotten lore" (repressed material) in order to find "surcease of sorrow" (to deny or repress grief). Paradoxically, he seeks forgetfulness through an act of remembrance, the recovery of lore which has been "forgotten." This conflict between memory and its denial underlies the narrator's response to the raven. While he vows in the second stanza that Lenore will remain "nameless *here* forevermore," he cannot resist naming her: "Lenore" signifies the absence which afflicts him. Thus in stanza five, he opens the door to "darkness," "silence," and "stillness"—images of death's fixity—and perversely whispers the name which he had hoped to repress. A similar ambivalence lodges itself in the famous refrain "Nevermore," which seems on the one hand to manifest the desire to forget (the narrator will nevermore brood upon the lost Lenore) and on the other to serve (as it does for the speaker) as a nagging reminder of the irrevocability of death. Many readers have noted that the mourner poses just those questions to the bird for which the answer "nevermore" seems to portend endless grief, the absence of heavenly redemption (no "balm in Gilead") and the impossibility of spiritual reunion with Lenore.

What seems particularly curious about "The Raven"—in view of the nineteenth-century model of death sketched by Ariès—is the narrator's unconscious and apparently compulsive need to disconfirm the key ideas associated with the Beautiful Death. To read the poem as a self-contained lyric of bereavement is to overlook the historical and cultural dilemma inscribed in the speaker's anxiety. The problem of a spiritual afterlife had become a matter of public dispute, and we see this uncertainty about a heavenly rendezvous creep into stanza sixteen of "The Raven" when the narrator demands: "Tell this soul with sorrow laden if, within the distant Aidenn, / It shall clasp a sainted maiden whom the angels name Lenore" (CW, 1:368). This fantasy of reunion is the only bearable conception of future existence; it alone holds out the hope that the myth of the Beautiful Death is not as empty as the dark world beyond the chamber door. But the narrator poses the question in a way that must elicit a denial from the raven. Already the bird's presence has become the sign of an irrevocable absence; it embodies the idea of despair, and its perching on the bust of Pallas transparently allegorizes the obsessive nature of dejection, in which loss itself becomes a fetish.

Not all of Poe's poems about dying women evoke quite so bleak an imagined future. The possibility of a meeting in paradise seems the implied hope of "Lenore." Here, despite the belief that the "saintly soul" of the woman has "flown forever," and though she seems "doubly dead in that she died so young," Lenore is said to have "gone before" her betrothed, Guy de Vere, to "a high estate within the utmost Heaven . . . to a golden throne, beside the King of Heaven" (CW, 1:336–37). This more sanguine and conventional vision of futurity allows the speaker to replace the dirge with "a Paean of old days," a celebration of the soul floating up to friends above, thus fulfilling the expectation—nurtured by consolation literature—of a "re-creation in heaven of the friendships of earth and communication with spirits."[11] Lenore has gone ahead of Guy de Vere to discover the social opportunities of paradise.

At first glance, physical separation also seems bearable in "Annabel Lee," because the speaker claims an indissoluble spiritual bond:

> And neither the angels in Heaven above,
> Nor the demons down under the sea,
> Can ever dissever my soul from the soul
> Of the beautiful Annabel Lee . . .

Unlike the desolate atmosphere of "The Raven," even the forms of nature seem in "Annabel Lee" to be endowed with the spirit of the dead woman:

> For the moon never beams, without bringing me dreams
> Of the beautiful Annabel Lee;
> And the stars never rise, but I feel the bright eyes
> Of the beautiful Annabel Lee . . .

However, the poem also briefly acknowledges the estrangement imposed by the tomb. The speaker's beloved has been carried off and sealed away:

> . . . her high-born kinsmen came
> And bore her away from me,
> To shut her up in a sepulchre,
> In this kingdom by the sea.   [CW, 1:478]

In the final lines, the mourner speaks of lying down beside his "bride" through "all the night-tide"; that she happens to be "in her sepulchre there by the sea— / In her tomb by the sounding sea" seems a minor inconvenience, perhaps no obstacle at all to the sort of love Poe has in mind, and the poem thus superficially conforms to the idea of a love that finds its romantic completion in death. Indeed, Poe's lyric calls to mind the case, reported by Ariès, of Alexandrine de la Ferronays, who in 1836 climbed down into the open grave of her husband "so that she could touch and kiss, one last time, the coffin that contains everything she has ever loved." The tomb, Ariès reports, became "the object of a daily pilgrimage" for the widow. [12] Poe's poem evokes a similar kind of sentimental devotion, but there is an underlying implication of despair: the speaker accepts the fact of death in referring to "the wind [that] came out of the cloud by night, / Chilling and killing my Annabel Lee." And the "sounding sea" of the final line contrasts ominously with the silence of the sepulchre. The narrator's compulsive return to the tomb thus raises a curious question: why does he try to achieve physical proximity to the corpse if his love is indeed spiritual and lasting? His action seems an unconscious betrayal of anxiety, a reflexive acknowledgment of the very separation which the poem itself seeks to deny.

This pattern becomes more intelligible when we consider "Annabel Lee" in relation to the tomb imagery of "Ulalume." This much-abused poem dramatizes a dialogue between the speaker and his soul, Psyche, which unfolds in the course of a nocturnal encounter in "the ghoul-haunted woodland of Weir." A fatalism compels the excursion, for the speaker has chosen, all unaware, to retrace the way to the burial site of Ulalume on the anniversary of her entombment. Astrological details help to explicate the inner debate: the narrator finds himself attracted to "Astarte's bediamonded crescent" and the physical love she patently represents, being "warmer than Dian," the goddess of chastity. But her allure is deceptive; whereas the speaker imagines that Astarte (the body or flesh) leads toward forgetfulness, the "Lethean peace of the skies," Psyche (the mind) mistrusts Astarte and tries to warn the speaker of danger. Convinced that the star's light "cannot but guide [them] aright," he follows the glow to the end of a vista closed off by the tomb of Ulalume. The sight of the burial vault reveals to the narrator his own perverse obedience to a repetition mechanism:

> And I cried—"It was surely October,
> On *this* very night of last year,
> That I journeyed—I journeyed down here!—
> That I brought a dread burden down here—
> On this night, of all nights in the year,
> Ah, what demon hath tempted me here?"   [CW, 1:418]

The temptress is Astarte, whose association with fleshly charms now reveals the delusion of immortality inspired by female beauty; for the loveliness of Ulalume has not insured the eternality of her soul, much less the incorruptibility of her body. She is the lost Ulalume, recollected by the speaker only as a dread burden, a source of fear and loathing. Now on this night of nights, her tomb has become a cursed site that marks the end of hope and beauty, the withering of human desire: "Then my heart it grew ashen and sober / As the leaves that were crispéd and sere."

Poe's representation of the tomb as an object of both repression and fixation curiously anticipates the theory of "cryptonymy" elaborated by Nicolas Abraham and Maria Torok in their much-discussed study of Freud's Wolf Man.[13] This account merits attention here because it opens up the metaphoricity of the burial vault in Poe as a figuring of the contradictions of bereavement. Abraham and Torok perceived in the case of the Wolf Man evidence of an "artificial unconscious," a forgotten niche in which the subject had deposited the contents of an early traumatic loss. They located this sealed-off space of psychic incorporation, or "crypt," between the "dynamic unconscious" and the "self of introjection"; yet the crypt remained inaccessible to conscious remembrance and unrecognizable in dreams and fantasies. Only through a painstaking decoding or cryptanalysis of the fragmented symbols by which the unnamable had disguised its presence were Abraham and Torok able to postulate the existence of the crypt and identify its contents: the repressed traces of a primal scene of incest involving Wolf Man's father and sister. As Derrida explains in his commentary "Fors," the "seductress sister" was thereafter symbolically buried or cryptically incorporated:

Sealing the loss of the object, but also marking the refusal to mourn, such a manoeuvre . . . is a kind of theft to reappropriate the pleasure-object. But that reappropriation is simultaneously rejected: which leads to the paradox of a foreign body preserved as foreign but by the same token excluded from a self which thenceforth deals not with the other, but only with itself. The more the self keeps the foreign element as a foreigner inside itself, the more it excludes it.[14]

Wolf Man's desire for the sister, together with his horror at her violation, compels the encrypting which is always "an effect of impossible or refused mourning." Thus she remains preserved yet forgotten in this interior which is always "partitioned off from the interior."

Derrida's remark that "the crypt is the vault of desire" provides a gloss not only on Wolf Man's predicament but also on Poe's poetic enactments of loss. For as we see in "Ulalume," the tomb is hidden in a place which the narrator cannot avoid, for the crypt designates a site that is always already within. Ulalume has been incorporated within the narrator's "artificial unconscious" through an act of repression, a refusal to mourn, here indicated (in his ramble with Psyche) by a series of denials: "We noted not the dim lake of Auber, / (Though once we had journeyed down here) / We remembered not the dank tarn of Auber, / Nor the ghoul-haunted woodland of Weir" (416). As in "The Raven," this suppression of memory in "Ulalume" is symptomatic of the encryptment of the beloved, who remains nevertheless undead: "The inhabitant of a crypt is always a living-dead, a dead entity we are perfectly willing to keep alive, but *as* dead, one we are willing to keep, as long as we keep it, within us, intact in any way save as living." Paradoxically, the erection of a tomb in Poe marks a refusal to let go of the beloved, a refusal signified by acts of revisitation; yet the tomb also constitutes an impassable barrier, an effacement of the Other. An irresistible site that cannot be entered; a beloved that cannot be brought to life or allowed to die: such is the dilemma of the subject who constructs a crypt—as Derrida says of the Wolf Man—"to save the living death he has walled up inside him."15

That which the tomb encloses is always "a foreign body," a thing that cannot be named. Death produces its own cryptonomy or secret language, which cannot be deciphered or translated. At "the door of a legended tomb," the speaker in "Ulalume" confronts the horrors of translation; death has converted the object of desire into a foreign, unspeakable "thing that lies hidden in these wolds." The etymology of *translate*, meaning to carry or bear across, lends itself readily to the idea of burial; that which is carried or borne across the pale is encrypted into a language which is always unknown.

The element of defamiliarization, the strangeness of this mortal translation, is elsewhere suggested in Poe's "The Sleeper." Here the conventional poetic notion of death as a sleep (used, for example, in Donne's "Death Be Not Proud") is horribly subverted: rather than providing its traditional comfort—that death, like sleep, is peaceful and refreshing—Poe's lyric evokes the illusion of a sleeping woman in order to induce, through a succession of incongruous details, the gradual perception of her death and the recognition of a hideous *difference*. The poem opens with a speaker standing "at midnight, in the month of June" beneath the window of his beloved: "All Beauty sleeps!—and lo! where lies / Irene, with her destinies." Though there are hints in the first seventeen lines of the grim actuality ("The rosemary nods upon the grave"), Poe otherwise creates the innocent impression of a romantic vigil near his darling. In the second section, however, the suggestion of natural sleep is eroded by questions and allusions. The speaker asks, "Oh, lady bright! can it be right— / This window open to the night?" His query, apparently addressed to the sleeper, offers no direct evidence of her death, but the open window becomes the first sign of the anomalous. Through the casement, the speaker then imagines the "wanton airs" (night breezes) invading the sleeper's room:

> The bodiless airs, a wizard rout,
> Flit through thy chamber in and out,
> And wave the curtain canopy
> So fitfully—so fearfully—
> Above the closed and fringéd lid
> 'Neath which thy slumb'ring soul lies hid.   [CW, 1:187]

By this point, the secret is out. The "closed and fringéd" lid of the coffin tells us all we need to know about the sleeper's condition and about the metaphor of the title; but the speaker continues to play (now perversely) with the notion that his love is *only* asleep. He asks rhetorically, "Oh, lady dear, hast thou no fear? / Why and what art thou dreaming here?" These are not true interrogatives—for the sleeper cannot answer—but rather components of a fiction he tries to sustain. The illusion of natural sleep collapses, however, before the disconcerting otherness of death:

> Strange is thy pallor! strange thy dress!
> Strange, above all, thy length of tress,
> And all this solemn silentness!

Her "sleep" is a cheat, a deception; the metaphor of slumber gives no solace to the speaker, who observes on the one hand that her rest is lurid, unnatural, and who fears on the other that it will be all too much like ordinary sleep and that his beloved may awaken (from a cataleptic state?) in the tomb: "I pray to God that she may lie / Forever with unopened eye, / While the dim sheeted ghosts go by." In what is very nearly the worst line in Poe's poetry, the speaker then implores, "Soft may the worms about her creep!" Here the poet looks ahead to the last, ghastly fate of the beautiful woman: definitive translation by the Conqueror Worm.

In calling poetry the "rhythmical creation of beauty," and then designating the death of a beautiful woman as the most poetical of topics, Poe established an implicit metaphorical relationship between the death of beauty and poetic texts. The poems discussed above may be understood as figurations of the problem of beauty, its earthly fate, and its translation through death—first into an ideal form and then into an object of disgust. As such, these poems appear to allegorize for Poe the fate of poetry: the poetic text stands over and against mundane reality and subjects itself to the "death" of publication (separation) and public judgment (corruption). The recurrent tension between heaven and hell and the occasional suggestion that the woman has been destroyed by calumny (as in "Lenore") or victimized by jealous rivals (implied in the final version of "To One in Paradise" and in "Annabel Lee") strengthen one's sense of a relationship between the poem itself and the fated woman who is its subject. Seemingly cursed by her beauty, the dying woman is typically too fine or pure for earthly survival, too ethereal to be appreciated by vulgar contemporaries. The crucial relationship exists between the woman and the speaker—between the work and its author. Poe seems in this way to dramatize the writer's problematic relationship to his own texts. An unwritten poem exists only as a phantasm of the poet's imagination, but once reified as verse, once translated into the language of the tribe, the writing assumes a life of its own, conditioned by the vagaries of reception. For the poet, the essential beauty of the original idea always remains in some sense untranslatable; yet its "body" (which becomes part of the larger corpus) suffers the indignities of scorn, neglect, envy, misunderstanding, and misquotation.

To place Poe's preoccupation with the death of a beautiful woman in a somewhat broader perspective, we must note its figural relation to the dilemma of all inscription. Insofar as Poe associates the woman with beauty and the poetic sentiment in general, she may be said to incarnate the desire of writing. In an important sense, her power over the writer lies in her otherness or her remoteness; that is, her personal beauty, characterized as a "strangeness," is the physical sign of a difference which is irreducible and inexplicable. Poe says of the poetic sentiment that it is "the desire of the moth for the star," the insatiable longing for the unreachable; likewise the beautiful woman embodies that which compels the writer yet remains unattainable. Writing is a form of nympholepsy.

In the tales and poems about dying women, Poe places this nympholeptic project in the context of a sickening transformation. While the metaphoricity of "translation" refers on one level to the action of death, on another it describes a revolting change in the desire of writing, a reversal of one's relationship to inscription. The vision of beauty, strangeness, and indefiniteness which once impelled composition becomes either lost (no longer present to the writer) or else disgusting and all too present. Caught between these alternative versions of defeat, both consequences of the catastrophe of death, the writer indites his narrative as a therapeutic activity, an exorcising of grief. But writing always proves inadequate to the demands placed upon it by the experience of loss, for the attempt to resurrect the beloved by an act of inscription invariably ends by revealing the impotence of language. That ethereal presence which has been lost or transformed can never be textually recovered, for writing as a play of signs merely substitutes one absence for another. Unlike the reassuring verses promulgated as consolation literature, Poe's variations upon the death-of-a-beautiful-woman paradigm enact the failure of language and the inconsolability of the writer. Indeed, as the desire of inscription becomes sealed off or corrupted, he seems to stage in the dead woman's translation the impossibility of writing.

In their attention to the predicament of the mourner, the writing persona who must contend with the absence of the beloved, Poe's texts reflect a tendency in popular culture itself. Michael Davitt Bell speaks of the "climate of uncertain spiritualism" which helped to produce "the curious combination of spirituality and ghoulishness" in Poe's writing: "Spirituality may have arisen, in its various forms, as a protest against the soul's annihilation in death. Yet, lacking a sense of what 'spirit' was, Poe and his contemporaries could find it, finally, only in this annihilation—in its ultimate 'effect.'" Illuminating the dilemma of Poe's spirituality, Bell observes that

> his pursuit of the "celestial soul" led back, again and again, to the "earthly corpse." Once he had accepted the terms of the spiritualist debate . . . he was trapped, whichever side he chose to take: if spiritual belief led only to the "truly spiritual affection" of the tomb, materialist skepticism hardly offered better. The physical detritus of the soul's triumphant departure was hardly, in a phenomenal sense, to be distinguished from the physical evidence of its absence. If the mind of man could imagine nothing that had not "really"—i.e., materially—existed, then the body was all one could know. Dead flesh was dead flesh.[16]

In his poetry, Poe generally sustained the notion that the dying woman incarnated a "supernal Loveliness"; his grieving narrators long for the lost beloved and seek either proximity to her corpse or communion with her soul, plagued by the uncertainty of spiritual survival. The text seems a last, ambiguous effort to sustain belief in the recoverability of the woman as the "soul" of poetry, if not as a spiritual presence.

Quite a different relationship to the beautiful woman, however, informs the sequence of works including "Berenice," "Morella," "Ligeia," and "The Fall of the House of Usher." In these stories, the woman's death excites horror, even perverse impatience in the narrator, whose fixation upon disgusting physical changes drives him beyond the brink of madness. In place of the beatific reunion of spirits imagined in consolation literature, Poe's fiction dramatizes an implicit antagonism, culminating in a frenzied, sometimes violent encounter with the buried woman. These narratives portray death not as annihilation or separation but as an ambiguous, temporary parting. In a revolting parody of the death of the Other, Poe depicts the return of the beloved not in spiritual terms but as a ghastly reanimation tinged with vampirism. In these tales, the spirit of the beautiful woman does not go floating up to heaven; rather, it remains bound to the undead corpse, condemned to a fitful existence in which the revenant acts out the desires and hostilities of an earlier life. Only in the later, uncharacteristic tale "Eleonora" did Poe permit himself to represent a death with a reassuring, sentimental outcome.

"Berenice" offers a particularly suggestive enactment of the relationship between attraction and repulsion, dread and longing. The narrator, Egaeus, characterizes himself as a visionary: realities have become illusions and "the wild ideas of the land of dreams" constitute the stuff of daily life. This principle of "inversion" (Poe's term) accounts for his tendency to regard physical realities as abstractions and ideas as things having a material substance. Thus it happens that when his cousin Berenice falls ill ("a fatal disease fell like the simoon upon her frame"), he takes an acute interest in her decline, not as a physiological process but as a theoretical instance of mortality. He treats Berenice "not as a being of the earth, earthy, but as the abstraction of such a being; not as a thing to admire, but to analyze; not as an object of love, but as the theme of the most abstruse although desultory speculation" (*CW*, 2:214). Yet although he regards his response to Berenice as wholly conceptual, he admits that he "shuddered in her presence, and grew pale at her approach." Her "desolate condition" afflicts him with both terror and fascination: "an icy chill ran through my frame; a sense of insufferable anxiety oppressed me; a consuming curiosity pervaded my soul" (214). Gradually, the woman's disease transforms her into a living cadaver; she becomes the personification of dissolution, the signs of her illness creating an "appalling distortion of her personal identity." That is, contagion discloses the absolute otherness of death:

The forehead was high, and very pale, and singularly placid; and the once jetty hair fell partially over it, and overshadowed the hollow temples with innumerable ringlets, now of a vivid yellow, and jarring discordantly, in their fantastic character, with the reigning melancholy of the countenance. The eyes were lifeless, and lustreless, and seemingly pupilless, and I shrank involuntarily from their glassy stare to the contemplation of the thin and shrunken lips. [215]

Here there is little beauty in dying; once a brunette, now a blonde, Berenice has become a grotesque version of herself.

The crux of the passage, however, is a subsequent reference to the woman's teeth, which Egaeus somehow associates with ideas. "Tous ses dents étaient des idées," he repeats wildly, as if the insight holds esoteric significance. Recurrently in Poe teeth signify mortality: in "Metzengerstein" the demon horse is said to reveal his "sepulchral and disgusting teeth"; in "The Facts in the Case of M. Valdemar" the narrator reports that the dying man's "upper lip . . . writhed itself away from the teeth"; in "Hop-Frog" the "dead silence" before the murder of the king and his counselors is broken by the "low, harsh, *grating* sound" produced by "the fang-like teeth of the dwarf." Egaeus sees the teeth of Berenice as "long, narrow, and excessively white, with the pale lips writhing about them"; they are both "ghastly" and "irresistible," becoming the paradoxical sign of her disintegration. Because the narrator regards the material world as pure abstraction, he falls prey to the delusion that his peace of mind depends upon physical possession of the teeth. "For these I longed with a frenzied desire," he confesses, preparing us for the final, shocking revelation that he has unconsciously violated the tomb of Berenice and ravaged her "still palpitating" body to extract the "ideas" that were her teeth. What does this bizarre act signify? For Egaeus, the death of the beautiful woman cannot be understood or psychically absorbed; it can only be repressed, translated into a theoretical instance of itself. Yet his unconscious incites an act of aggression against the teeth, the displaced focus of his anxiety. Becker speaks of the transference object, which for the child (as for the childlike Egaeus) represents all that is frightening and uncontrollable in the world:

The transference object always looms larger than life size because it represents all of life and hence all of one's fate. The transference object becomes the focus of the problem of one's freedom because one is compulsively dependent on it; it sums up all other natural dependencies and emotions. This quality is true of either positive or negative transference objects. In the negative transference, the object becomes the focalization of terror, but now experienced as evil and constraint.[17]

Becker concisely remarks: "This is how we can understand the essence of transference: as a *taming of terror*." Egaeus can do nothing about the disease of Berenice, and her hideous transformation confronts him with a reminder of his own impotence and vulnerability. In particular the woman's teeth signify the problem of death; the narrator wants to possess them to control the reality which they represent.

The problem of identity, which arises in "Berenice" as a function of physiological change, also emerges in "Morella," where Poe's narrator ponders the fate of individual essence—the "*principium individuationis*, the notion of that identity *which at death is or is not lost forever*" (CW, 2:231). The tale seems to demonstrate the survival of personal entity when the dying wife ostensibly returns in the form of the daughter whom she has delivered upon her deathbed; the empty tomb, discovered at the story's end, appears to signal the transmigration of the mother's soul. But the matter remains ambiguous, for the death of the second Morella evidently brings to a close the cycle of death and reincarnation. More clearly the story dramatizes Poe's characteristic attraction-repulsion pattern: the narrator's "singular affection" for Morella and the abandon with which he enters into a mystical novitiate give way at length to "horror" and "alienation." As in "Berenice," the signs of the woman's disease obsess the narrator: "In time, the crimson spot settled steadily upon the cheek, and the blue veins upon the pale forehead became prominent; and, one instant, my nature melted into pity, but, in the next, I met the glance of her meaning eyes, and then my soul sickened and became giddy with the giddiness of one who gazes downward into some dreary and unfathomable abyss" (231–32). The "abyss" metaphor is revealing: the narrator observes indications of his wife's impending death and feels himself pulled helplessly toward self-destruction, as if her extinction somehow entailed his own.

Here Poe touches again upon the mechanism we now know as transference. As a maternal, protective figure, Morella stands between the narrator and all that threatens him in the external world; the symptoms of her mortality bring home the fact of his own jeopardy. Becker notes that the idealizing of the Other often occurs in marriage, where the wife (for example) is expected to assure the happiness of the husband and by maintaining her own youthfulness and vitality to affirm his youth—that is, to save him from aging and death. The discovery of her vulnerability seems to deprive him of the illusion of his own immortality: "If a woman loses her beauty, or shows that she doesn't have the strength and dependability that we once thought she did . . . then all the investment we have made in her is undermined. The shadow of imperfection falls over our lives, and with it—death and the defeat of cosmic heroism. 'She lessens' = 'I die.'"[18] The revulsion of Poe's narrator is not a response to Morella herself but to her mortality; we can trace his disgust back to her "cold hand," to the voice whose melody is "tainted with terror," to her "melancholy eyes"—all signs of the fate which she anticipates and symbolizes. His abhorrence of the process of dissolution and his eagerness for the moment of release (through her death) foreshadow the twentieth-century concept of unmentionable, invisible death— the concealed obscenity about which Geoffrey Gorer has written.[19]

In effect, "Morella" presents a grotesque inversion of the sweet parting idealized as the Beautiful Death. Rather than a celestial reunion, Morella speaks on her deathbed of avenging the narrator's loathing: "Thy days shall be days of sorrow . . . the hours of thy happiness are over . . . thou shalt bear about with thee thy shroud on earth" (233). The instrument of his anguish will be the second Morella, whose similarity to the mother becomes "more hideously terrible" with each passing day. The daughter is such a perfect translation of the mother that the narrator, in "an unnerved and agitated condition," gives her the same name—and thus induces her instantaneous death. Underlying the occult action is a recognizable psychological pattern: repression and the subsequent eruption of unconscious material. The narrator's "consuming desire" for Morella's death and his impatience at her slow decline are symptomatic of his "alienation"— his aversion to her touch, her voice, and her eyes, all of which bespeak her fate. By avoiding Morella, the narrator endeavors to protect himself from the contagion of dying. But he cannot escape "the hemlock and the cypress": the child whom he imagined to embody the principle of life and the proof of his own immortality becomes herself the emblem of inescapable death.

Fear and loathing enter the scheme of "Ligeia" in a somewhat different way. Ligeia personifies for the narrator a will to live and a loveliness which verges on the "supernal Beauty" of poetry itself. Poe has evoked the woman from his own poetic text, the youthful "Al Aaraaf":

> Ligeia! Ligeia!
> My beautiful one!
> Whose harshest idea
> Will to melody run . . .   [CW, 1:109]

The fictional text delineates her exquisite strangeness: a "lofty and pale" forehead, skin of "purest ivory," "raven-black hair," teeth of "a brilliancy almost startling," and eyes of "the most brilliant of black." Like Berenice and Morella, Ligeia grows ill and takes on the characteristics of mortal decline: "The wild eyes blazed with a too—too glorious effulgence; the pale fingers became of the transparent waxen hue of the grave, and the blue veins upon the lofty forehead swelled and sank impetuously with the tides of the most gentle emotion. I saw that she must die" (CW, 2:316). Before she dies, however, Ligeia delivers herself of a poem, "The Conqueror Worm," which (as noted in chapter 1) comprises a radical response to consolation literature, positing a grim, naturalistic image of "human gore." Unlike Margaret Davidson, who is said to have died without a struggle or groan, Ligeia listens to the recitation of her poem and then shrieks: "O God! O Divine Father!—shall these things be undeviatingly so?—shall this conqueror be not once conquered?" What Ligeia expresses at this moment is Kierkegaardian "fear and trembling," the characteristic dilemma of the modern age. At the core of this uncertainty is the awareness that despite increasing information and knowledge, the denizen of a secular, technological culture can never entirely surmount what Becker calls the "horror of his own basic animal condition."20

Poe's narrator tells us that he is "crushed into the very dust with sorrow" by Ligeia's death. He voices no expectation of heavenly reunion, but he seizes upon the suggestion of his dying wife that she will return to him through force of will. On the surface, he seems to have participated in her dying moments as the narrator of "Morella" was unable to do, but the second half of the story hints that he too has, in some way, avoided the dying woman, repressed the terror of the transformation, and doomed himself to an inevitable reenactment. In the months after Ligeia's death, he gives himself up to "aimless wandering" and then begins to refurbish an abbey "with a faint hope of alleviating [his] sorrows." But his selection of funereal artifacts (such as the "gigantic sarcophagus of black granite") reveals that, as with the speaker in "The Raven," his effort to forget conceals a stronger urge to remember, to resurrect the departed. He tells us that "in a moment of mental alienation" he has married Rowena, the Anglo-Saxon antithesis of Ligeia, upon whom he projects an irrational hatred rooted presumably in guilt over remarriage (a theme in "Eleonora" as well). As Roy Basler pointed out, the narrator thus cunningly engineers the collapse of Rowena, and the image of his second wife's "pallid and rigid figure upon the bed" brings to mind Ligeia's demise and "the whole of that unutterable wo with which [he] had regarded *her* thus enshrouded" (326).21 A deep psychic necessity impels him to reconstruct in this way the final agonies of Ligeia, perhaps as a symptomatic expression of survivor guilt. During this night of the living dead, Rowena's morbid relapses cause two associated effects: the narrator's shudder of horror at "the ghastly expression of death" and his "waking visions of Ligeia." The mingling of past and present pushes him toward the edge of madness; the woman before him is both living and dead, Lady Rowena and Ligeia, an impossible image of desire and loathing.

While the narrator's treatment of Rowena may be explained as a symptom of his guilt at taking a second wife, a more disturbing possibility surfaces in his fascination with the woman's "corpse." In this preoccupation he reveals himself to be a connoisseur of decay, attentive to the signs of death, the awful work of translation. The narrator's own questioning of the act of inscription illuminates his compulsion:

> But why shall I minutely detail the unspeakable horrors of that night? Why shall I pause to relate how, time after time, until near the period of the gray dawn, this hideous drama of revivification was repeated; how each terrific relapse was only into a sterner and apparently more irredeemable death; how each agony wore the aspect of a struggle with some invisible foe; and how each struggle was succeeded by I know not what wild change in the personal appearance of the corpse? [328–29]

Why indeed does he devote such close attention to the physical condition of Rowena? Such detail of course prepares the reader for the final scene in which the two women merge. But the narrator's scrutiny of the "hideous drama of revivification" reveals a peculiar interest in physiological change, here encountered as the dreamlike repetition of a surreal back-and-forth movement between health and corruption. The narrator experiences a compressed version of all of the declines witnessed by his counterparts in other tales. He describes himself (on the night of his vigil) as paralyzed by "unutterable horror and awe, for which the language of mortality has no sufficiently energetic expression" (327), and yet the text itself betrays an obstinate curiosity about the object of this "horror and awe" and a determination to represent its nature through a system of signs already declared to be inadequate.

What impels him to write is the tacit sense that Rowena's ambiguous condition, her wavering between resurrection and decomposition, expresses both the paradoxical mockery of death and the uncertainty of his own response to its transformation. Though he acknowledges a disgust for his "fair-haired and blue-eyed" second wife, arranges the "bridal chamber" to exacerbate the "nervous irritation of her temperament," and expresses no grief at her apparent demise, he twice makes an unlikely effort to revive her. In the first instance he speaks of his "endeavors to call back the spirit still hovering" (327) and at her second recovery he affirms: "The lady *lived*; and with redoubled ardor I betook myself to the task of restoration. I chafed and bathed the temples and the hands, and used every exertion which experience, and no little medical reading, could suggest" (328). We should probably attribute these efforts not to solicitude but to voyeuristic interest in the cycle of corruption. Each time the woman stirs, she relapses into a more frightful condition; after a first flush of life, "the color disappeared from both eyelid and cheek, leaving a wanness even more than that of marble; the lips became doubly shrivelled and pinched up in the ghastly expression of death; a repulsive clamminess and coldness overspread rapidly the surface of the body; and all the usual rigorous stiffness immediately supervened" (327). At her second relapse, "the color fled, the pulsation ceased, the lips resumed the expression of the dead, and, in an instant afterward, the whole body took upon itself the icy chilliness, the livid hue, the intense rigidity, the sunken outline, and all the loathsome peculiarities of that which has been, for many days, a tenant of the tomb" (328). "Time after time" the same experience repeats itself, as the spellbound narrator finds himself the "helpless prey to a whirl of violent emotions."

The meaning of the scene is complex, for on one level it exposes a cultural and historical anxiety: divested of sentimental illusion, the dead body has become a potentially revolting sight. Yet the memory of a beautiful woman's death superimposes itself upon the narrator's perception of the body's metamorphosis. The "drama of revivification" is "hideous" yet utterly absorbing; and its interest seems to lie in its radical indeterminacy. Rowena is neither living nor dead; she incarnates the indefinable, the anomalous. The seeming reversibility of her condition enables the narrator to contemplate that which can ordinarily be glimpsed only as a transitional moment, as a liminal state—the marginality upon which Poe bases the poetics of translation. If the death of a beautiful woman is "the most poetical topic in the world," its aesthetic value derives neither from female beauty as such nor from death as an ontological event, but from the unstable relation between the two, from the shifting intermediacy of a phenomenon which has no proper place or form or intelligibility. The narrator has witnessed this process before, when its unfolding deprived him of Ligeia; now he examines the back-and-forth movement intently, for in his own contradictory response of horror and fascination he confronts the dilemma of translation. The "language of mortality" has no equivalent word for a transformation of this kind, no means of articulating the in-between nature of dying.

The return of the primordial repressed—that which the apparition of Ligeia represents—seems also to be the (re)animating principle of "The Fall of the House of Usher." Without much difficulty we see Madeline's resemblance to Usher as the locus of his own terror: she mirrors his fate and provides an image of his own eventual disintegration. Like Madeline, Usher is already marked for death by a "cadaverousness of complexion . . . [a] ghastly pallor of the skin." Like Berenice and Rowena, his sister suffers from a "cataleptical" disorder (which conveniently leaves open the possibility that these women only *seem* to die). Madeline's disease has led to "a gradual wasting away of the person," transforming her into a ghostlike presence; even the commonsensical narrator admits that he "regarded her with an utter astonishment not unmingled with dread." Ultimately the illness transforms Madeline into that "grim phantasm, FEAR," with which Usher knows that he must one day struggle. Her apparent death creates a dilemma: Usher cannot believe that she is wholly dead and so refuses to have her interred in the remote family burial ground; yet he cannot persuade himself that she still lives and so has her "encoffined" and entombed in an underground vault. The indefinability of her condition is epitomized by her ambiguous appearance in the coffin: the disease has left "the mockery of a faint blush upon the bosom and the face, and that suspiciously lingering smile upon the lip which is so terrible in death" (CW, 2:410). Usher's decision to place the body in an underground vault provides an obvious trope of repression which is congruent with the house/head metaphor elaborated in the embedded poem "The Haunted Palace" and throughout the story. When Madeline bursts through the door to claim her brother, we witness the figurative eruption of repressed death anxiety into conscious experience, the apparition of that phantasm which will indeed deprive Usher of "life and reason together."

Like the awful return of Ligeia, the appearance of Madeline resembles, in its odd imagery, the surreal quality of a nightmare:

There *did* stand the lofty and enshrouded figure of the lady Madeline of Usher. There was blood upon her white robes, and the

evidence of some bitter struggle upon every portion of her emaci-
ated frame. For a moment she remained trembling and reeling to
and fro upon the threshold—then, with a low moaning cry, fell
heavily inward upon the person of her brother, and in her violent
and now final death-agonies, bore him to the floor a corpse, and a
victim to the terrors he had anticipated. [416–17]

The reference to "now final death-agonies" virtually collapses the
supernaturalistic reading of "Usher" and confirms that Madeline has
been a victim of premature burial. She stands briefly upon the threshold of consciousness before falling "inwardly," touching the psychic
depths of her brother's being. Like Berenice, Morella, and even
Ligeia, she has been transformed by disease into a personification of
death; Usher's own morbid fear of death has caused him to bury her
too hastily, for her illness is the contagion of mortality.

Madeline's resurrection seems, in fact, to partake of revenge; after
a "bitter struggle" to escape the burial vault, she seizes her brother as
if to repay him for the horrors which she has suffered. This action
parallels the reincarnation-as-curse which informs "Morella," and it
resembles as well the ambiguous return of Ligeia. Although the latter
event seems to victimize Rowena rather than the narrator, we must
remember that (unlike Eleonora) Ligeia never sanctions or encour-
ages her husband's remarriage. She signals her reappearance, in fact,
with a gesture of aversion; the narrator writes: "*Shrinking from my
touch,* she let fall from her head the ghastly cerements which had
confined it" (*CW*, 2:330, my emphasis). It is as if the reanimated
woman returns the avoidance she felt in dying. The point is subtle
but important, for we see that in the tales of doomed women, the
parting marks an irreversible alienation to which the horrific reunion
bears witness. In this version of the return as revenge, the ultimate
implication of the translation metaphor becomes clear: death makes
us utter strangers to those who survive us.

For Poe, the death of a beautiful woman posed in absolute terms
the paradox of our creaturely condition. The beauty of woman
seemed a sign of the eternal, an apparent proof of paradise and
immortality. Yet disease transformed beauty into a ghastly parody of
itself, turning desire to loathing and love to disgust. The dying woman became a sign of her own fate, and her dissolution presented a

spectacle at once irresistible and unbearable. In the relation of the narrator to the beloved, Poe staged the inevitable conflict between mind and flesh, between the longing for "Supernal Beauty" and the threat of cessation. Female loveliness manifested for Poe the essence of poetry:

> He feels it in the beauty of woman—in the grace of her step—in the lustre of her eye—in the melody of her voice—in her soft laughter—in her sigh—in the harmony of the rustling of her robes. He deeply feels it in her winning endearments—in her burning enthusiasms—in her gentle charities—in her meek and devotional endurances—but above all—ah, far above all—he kneels to it—he worships it in the faith, in the purity, in the strength, in the altogether divine majesty—of her *love*. 22

Yet the eternality of female beauty could not withstand contamination by reality. Only in poetry, in a work of art—an oval portrait, perhaps—could loveliness escape the "vermin fangs" of the Conqueror Worm. For the beautiful woman was (like Ulalume) destined to become a "dread burden"; she was (like Lenore) always "doubly dead" in that her death marked the end of a particular life and the collapse of that myth of immortality which her beauty seemed to guarantee. Her apparent return from the grave in "Morella," "Ligeia," and "Usher" dramatizes the contradictory desires of memory and forgetfulness experienced by the narrator of "The Raven": the beautiful woman cannot be buried, for the monstrous irony which she incarnates cannot be assimilated by the human psyche. For Poe, her story could never be written; it could only be rewritten, over and over, obsessively, like the repetition of some hideous drama of revivification.

4

The Rhetoric of Dread
Poe's Letters

In both poetry and fiction, as we have seen, Poe's dominant metaphors lead back to the problem of death and its effect upon the one who writes. The death of a beautiful woman is before all else a dilemma of writing, both an experiential ordeal and a test of narratability. Within the space of the poem or tale, Poe devises a trope for this crisis of being and language. But these textual figurations also invite curiosity about the life of writing which produced them. What was the experience of the subject who signed himself "Poe" and how did the catastrophe of death insinuate itself into the particularity of his existence and writerly travail? In an intriguing essay, Eugenio Donato traces the transformations of Flaubert's signature and contends that the works associated with Flaubert's name were in fact generated by the writer's attachment to the dead: "It is these dead who, by being associated with the literary act, put into play a series of texts which produce, in their turn, the space in which a form of writing which engenders the series of texts signed Flaubert becomes possible." Donato shows that during vigils over the bodies of Caroline Flaubert and Alfred Le Poittevin, respectively, the author passed the night by reading, an activity which in each case prefigures Flaubert's "metaphorization of the corpse into a text"—his transposition of the beloved into a "written representation."[1] Le Poittevin, according to Donato, became the guiding spirit of *La Tentation de Saint Antoine,* while Caroline by a complex displacement became Loulou, the dead parrot cherished by Félicité in *Un Coeur simple.* Reconstructing the "fantasmatic scenario of the origin of Flaubertian writing," Donato entertains the possibility that "in the last analysis, the signature of Flaubert belongs to one or several corpses." His hypothesis appears to have broader applicability: might we not speculate that such filiations are symptomatic of writing itself in its modernist phase? In an epoch of doubt is there not for every writer a corpse whose image compels inscription? Through evidence supplied by published correspondence, we shall here consider the idea that Poe, like Flaubert, understood his compositions as a kind of thanatography.

Situated midway in our reflections upon death and writing, this chapter seeks to connect Poe's public, literary expression with the obsessions of his private life—not to generate specific critical readings but to bridge cultural and psychic responses to the new idea of death. The letters indicate that as Poe constructed his literary corpus, he struggled to check a recurrent sense of fatality; attention to this personal reflex reveals the way in which dread impinges upon the activity of writing. This is not to say that the letters give access to privileged autobiographical data masked in the narratives; my concern here is not to correct interpretation but to extend its parameters by regarding the correspondence as a parallel text. Through this complementary script one glimpses the interplay of anxiety and ambition, death and writing, in diverse predicaments registered by different personae. Clearly, letters are products of contingency in ways that most literary effusions are not; however, if letters cannot be read as a concerted and sustained narrative, they nevertheless disclose verbal tendencies and imaginative preoccupations. As we shall see in the following pages, Poe persistently warded off destruction with schemes of literary ascendancy. His correspondence thus supplements our understanding of the life of writing by providing a human grounding for the theoretical issues lodged in the poetry and fiction.

Like Flaubert, Poe discovered the desire of writing in the contemplation of a corpse. In an important sense (analyzed years ago by Marie Bonaparte), he remained fixated upon his dead mother, Elizabeth Poe, reenacting her loss endlessly in later compositions. And amid the biographical evidence, we find many subsequent episodes of separation and bereavement which activated the need to write; recurrently the correspondence confirms the effect of the dead upon the living writer. Yet in another respect these influences seem secondary, for the corpse whose image most often haunts the letters is Poe's own. From the outset, he experienced premonitions of a catastrophe which he tried to escape through textual strategies. In practical terms, literary work provided intermittent income and sustenance for Poe the magazinist, but in a more complicated, symbolic sense, writing also became a defiance of mortality, a resistance to oblivion. In letters, as in fiction and poetry, he elaborated fantasies of retribution and triumph which carry a metaphysical import, and he inscribed visions of a pastoral paradise where he would be insulated from failure, pain, and death. His correspondence cannot, however, be reduced to an organized view of the writer's ordeal; it remains a sequence of disparate texts—outbursts and apologies, introductions and valedictions, reports and requests, confessions and deceptions. But these communications enable us to observe in different personal contexts the nexus of writing and death and the problem of Western culture to which it finally refers.

To open another perspective on these larger issues, I want to examine here what might be called Poe's urgent messages, letters in which writing functions as a call for help. In these texts we observe the writer figuring himself as the inevitable victim—of poverty, illness, treachery, or bad luck—and appealing for deliverance from his fate. In the letters of crisis, Poe taxed his resources as a writer to project images of his own destruction; well before publishing his first tale, he had mastered the rhetoric of dread. By this phrase, I mean to imply a strategy of writing rooted in despair. Poe was surely capable of deviousness—of overstating his distress to elicit help—but the crises in question were more often real than invented. It is moreover pointless to calculate the justifiability of a particular usage; what concerns us is the *way* in which language produces specific impressions and effects. For Poe, the rhetoric of dread involved both a characteristic diction and a conventional formulation of his situation. These letters repeatedly include terms of suffering (such as "wretchedness" and "misery"); mourning ("melancholy," "sorrow," and "depression"); and apology or supplication ("forgiveness" and "succour"). Poe typically describes his plight as a hopeless impasse, a dilemma which the addressee alone can resolve; often he implies that his deliverance from pain, his very survival, depends upon the reader's intervention. As such, his letters display manipulative ingenuity, an intriguing deployment of language to evoke a particular response. While it is unlikely that Poe worked out these strategies solely to coerce friends and relatives, his epistolary efforts nevertheless taught him the value of "effect," which became the cornerstone of his theory of unity of impression in the tale.

In this context, Poe's letter to John Allan on February 21, 1831, acquires considerable interest. Shortly after his dismissal from West Point, an ailing Poe wrote (in "an unsteady hand") to his foster father—as he had often done since their estrangement in 1827—begging for help while prefiguring his own destruction:

> In spite of all my resolution to the contrary I am obliged once more to recur to you for assistance—It will however be the last time that I ever trouble any human being—I feel that I am on [a] sick bed from *which* I never shall get up. . . . My *ear* has been too shocking for any description. . . . I have caught a most violent cold and am confined to my bed—I have no money—no friends—I have written to my brother—but he cannot help me—I shall never rise from my bed—besides a most violent cold on my lungs my *ear* discharges blood and matter continually and my headache is distracting—I hardly know what I am writing—I will write no more—Please send me a little money—quickly—and forget what I said about you— [L, 1:43–44]

Quite apart from the irrelevant question of how sick Poe *really* was, we discover here a rhetorical method not unlike that which informs the final paragraph of "MS. Found in a Bottle" (presumably composed about the same time). After first assuring Allan that his ear is "too shocking for any description," Poe then speaks of its loathsome excrescence, if not to shock Allan at least to suggest through tangible detail the nature of his misery. Using the dash, Poe implies that his words are inscribed with great pain; the short phrases indicate a faltering mind unable to sustain coherence ("I hardly know what I am writing"), so that the markings on paper carry significance both as writing and as physical traces of a struggle for life. Moreover, Poe depicts himself as utterly alone in New York, without resources or hope for survival. Allan is, by implication, both a last resort and the source of Poe's suffering, since he (Allan) has refused to authorize Poe's resignation from West Point and so has deprived him of the travel allowance that would have enabled him to reach New York without hardship. The letter thus lays a double guilt upon Allan: he has created Poe's distress and now must act or be responsible for his demise. The ultimate force of the rhetorical appeal lies in the threat of death; writing derives its ultimate power from the perishability of the writer, as Poe tries to turn his anticipated doom into epistolary advantage. But the reader resisted: John Allan apparently never replied to his foster son's plea.

Collectively regarded, the twenty-seven extant letters from Poe to Allan provide a useful focus for problems of voice and strategy that weave through later correspondence. Poe's habit of projecting his own annihilation to elicit aid can be traced to the 1827 note in which he apprised Allan of his decision to leave home and of his need for cash: "Send me I entreat you some money immediately—as I am in the greatest necessity—If you fail to comply with my request—I tremble for the consequence" (L, 1:8). The same motif informs the last known communication from Poe to Allan: "For God's sake pity me, and save me from destruction" (L, 1:50). We know that Poe suffered a series of reverses from 1827 to 1833—setbacks too involved to summarize here—while continuing to petition his erstwhile protector even after Allan had disowned him. In tone, the letters range from apologetic wheedling to contemptuous sarcasm, as Poe alternately begged forgiveness for his "wayward disposition" and rebuked Allan for parental neglect. Both modes, however, suggest the psychic importance of the break with his foster father, and in this sense the letters represent a desperate project to recover paternal love and care. At the close of his letter of October 30, 1829, Poe confessed, "I am sorry that your letters to me have still with them a tone of anger as if my former errors were not forgiven—if I knew how to regain your affection God knows I would do anything I could" (L, 1:31). A phrase in another letter comes closer to the writer's fundamental fears when he speaks of Allan's silence: "All communication seems to be at an end." Then Poe exposes the crux of the situation: "When I think of the long twenty one years that I have called you father, and you have called me son, I could cry like a child to think that it should all end in this" (L, 1:46). What we see here and elsewhere in Poe's letters to Allan is a primal anxiety which implicitly reenacts—and draws intensity from—Poe's loss of his natural parents in 1811. Though he was not quite three years old when Elizabeth Poe died (on December 8, 1811), Poe had already reached an age at which fear of separation from the mother had become conscious. Her death, accompanied by the mysterious disappearance of the father, David Poe, must have ingrained a terror of permanent separation in the child's psyche. Robert Jay Lifton's discussion of the emergence of a death concept in early childhood helps to illuminate the biographical circumstances in question:

> Separation is the paramount threat from the beginning of life and can give rise, very early, to the rudiments of anxiety and mourning. . . . From the age of six months, connection and separation become more specifically associated with a particular person, usually the mother, as do manifestations of separation anxiety and infantile mourning. Actual death imagery, the beginning awareness that living creatures die, occurs during the last half of the second year of life. . . . The child shapes an increasingly formed notion of being or becoming dead.[2]

Elsewhere, Lifton draws the important conclusion that "imagery of separation, present from the beginning of life, is the basic precursor for the idea of death."[3]

My purpose here is not to launch another psychoanalytic study of Poe. Rather, I want to establish the effect of separation anxiety on Poe's conception of death. As we see, the threat of parental loss triggered imagery of personal destruction, which in turn compelled the urge to write. Poe portrayed himself recurrently as an unloved, abandoned child; his deepest need was to reestablish his connection with a parent who had not only ceased to give him affection but who had also stopped communicating. Allan's remoteness, his silence, and his suspension of care amounted to a symbolic death that repeated Poe's infantile separation from his parents. It was a loss that Poe sought to forestall or prevent through correspondence, as writing became an unconscious protest against death, a struggle to avoid an absolute sundering of the parental bond. On another level, this fixation on separation seems to manifest the insecurity of the existential self in the modern world. That is, Poe's fear of orphanhood made him peculiarly responsive to the radical homelessness and dread which characterize the crisis of death. H. P. Lovecraft has remarked that a "cosmic panic" suffuses Poe's writing; the letters to Allan describe a local encounter with that global anxiety.

After the rift of 1826, Poe returned to the Allan home only once—to mark another separation, the death of his foster mother, Frances Valentine Allan, on February 28, 1829. That event (which led to Allan's remarriage and Poe's formal disinheritance) remained a source of bitterness; in a letter of January 3, 1830, Poe recalled the experience in terms calculated to wound the surviving parent: "I came home, you will remember, the night after the burial—If she had not have died while I was away there would have been nothing for me to regret—*Your* love I never valued—but she I believed loved me as her own child" (*L*, 1:41). Poe's reference to loss and leavetaking had been occasioned by another, more recent separation: his brief meeting with Allan in late 1830, perhaps at West Point, which culminated in a scene bearing the stamp of finality. Poe wrote to his foster father: "When I parted from you—at the steam-boat, I knew that I should never see you again" (*L*, 1:41). But despite the asperity of the January 3 letter, Poe continued to beg Allan's assistance, and his letters of late autumn, 1831, betray eagerness to recover the status of son. When he says of Allan's long silence that he could "cry like a child to think that it should all end in this," he gives voice to a fear so elemental that it carries him back to infancy and the trauma of birth. "I am ready to curse the day when I was born," Poe vows to Allan, lamenting his "flagrant ingratitude" (*L*, 1:46) as if it were a congenital defect.

But the penitent found Allan unmoved by gestures of atonement; after the parting in late 1830 Poe must have recognized the hopelessness of his epistolary project. Lifton points out that the ultimate implication of separation anxiety is the child's fear of his own annihilation in a world where all protection has been lost. In Poe's case, Allan's complete abandonment seems to have activated a terror of destruction rooted in childhood memory. Poe's last letters to Allan are thus infused with a sense of dread and with images of deprivation; he saw himself, on December 15, 1831, as "suffering every extremity of want and misery without even a chance of escape," and two weeks later he wrote of his "extreme misery and distress," while assuring Allan: "If you knew how wretched I am I am sure that you would relieve me" (*L*, 1:49). Apposite to Poe's self-representation is Lifton's observation that "the inner sense of 'disintegrating'—of falling apart—is often associated with separation and isolation."[4] Poe's final plea to his foster father to be saved "from destruction" apparently had no effect, and John Allan's break with Poe became irrevocable on March 27, 1834, when the Richmond merchant passed beyond the reach of earthly correspondence. Poe's numerous letters had elicited occasional financial aid, but they could not evoke parental care nor could they resolve the problem of estrangement. His letters served as a resistance to the epistolary silence which became, increasingly, a figure of death's silence. Writing made possible a postponement, a gradualizing of loss, but it could not reformulate Poe's relationship to Allan. On those occasions when Poe secured a response, he won a symbolic deferral of absolute abandonment; but his (presumably) never-answered letter of April 12, 1833, marked the end of writing to Allan and the surrender of that desire which the writing had sustained.

The letters to Allan constituted the first crucial challenge of inscription for Poe, insofar as he attempted to produce a text that would save him from dissolution. The stakes were high: Allan's patrimony could have ensured Poe of that aristocratic modus vivendi to which he aspired throughout his career. It would surely have enabled Poe to complete his studies at the University of Virginia and to vie for that "eminence in public life" which Allan had taught him to prize. But the rupture compelled Poe in 1827 to pursue the life of writing. Whether he would have published *Tamerlane and Other Poems* had the rift not occurred is a moot question; nevertheless his search for literary fame seems crucially motivated by his broken relationship to Allan and the symbolic threat of annihilation which it entailed. In a key letter of December 22, 1828, Poe (by then a published poet) wrote from his military post at Fort Moultrie:

> If it is your wish to forget that I have been your son I am too proud to remind you of it again—I only beg you to remember that you yourself cherished the cause of my leaving your family—Ambition. If it has not taken the channel you wished it, it is not the less certain of its object. Richmond & the U. States were too narrow a sphere & the world shall be my theatre—. . . . If you determine to abandon me—here take [I my] farewell—Neglected—I will be doubly ambitious, & the world shall hear of the son whom you have thought unworthy of your notice. [*L*, 1:12]

The last lines imply that Poe conceived of his belletristic pursuits as a kind of revenge; public notice would compensate for paternal neglect. The quest for fame thus spurred by Allan's silence offered a symbolic solution to the problem of orphanhood, the trauma of abandonment, and the menace of death. Such a formulation seems implicit in Poe's forthright declaration: "Neglected—I will be doubly ambitious, & the world shall hear of the son whom you have thought unworthy of your notice."

Poe's craving for recognition propelled him—significantly, about the time of Allan's death—into the burgeoning American magazine world, where he hoped to establish his identity as a writer while confirming his worth as a son. His correspondence to various acquaintances reveals the process by which he sought to create a self, to invent a public image as a man of letters. This project was bound up, from the beginning, with his notion that periodicals represented the wave of the literary future and that his own fate depended upon an association with some prominent journal. After frustrating editorial stints with the *Southern Literary Messenger* and *Burton's Gentleman's Magazine*, however, he fixed on the scheme of publishing his own monthly magazine. Shortly after his break with Burton, Poe assured a friend: "As soon as Fate allows I will have a magazine of my own—and will endeavor to kick up a dust" (L, 1:119). Here the dream of proprietorship reveals itself for the first time; as the publisher of a periodical, Poe imagined that he could secure his own immortality. That he conceived of the longed-for journal in such extravagant terms can be surmised from his letter to William Poe on August 14, 1840, in which he vowed: "If I fully succeed in my purposes I will not fail to produce some lasting effect upon the growing literature of the country, while I establish for myself individually a name which that country 'will not willingly let die' " (L, 1:141). Speaking of the same magazine project five months later, he assured Joseph Evans Snodgrass, "I must now do or die—I mean in a literary sense" (L, 1:152). As these comments make plain, the projected magazine had both pragmatic and psychosymbolic objectives. While Poe's remarks may be read as conventional expressions of ambition, we see behind them the unresolved problems of identity and survival. Poe's determination not to "die," not to allow his name to be forgotten, seems less a response to death as a figurative, literary oblivion than a struggle against the literal obliteration of the writer, a fate one escaped through writing itself, through the symbolic immortality guaranteed (or so Poe imagined) by the creation of a great magazine. At the risk of oversimplifying, it appears that ownership of a literary periodical became the dominant compensatory fantasy of Poe's adult life, a dream engendered by separation anxiety and dread of death, which saw Poe winning public admiration, asserting his self-worth, establishing a "name" (that is, supplanting the father by becoming his own creator), and, in the face of his personal mortality, insuring the survival of his writerly identity.

Such a pattern of symbolization was possible for Poe because he believed intensely in the future of periodicals and in their inevitable centrality to literary culture. In a series of nearly identical letters to noted authors of the day, Poe sought in the summer of 1841 to enlist their support for the *Stylus* (the never-to-be-realized successor of the never-published *Penn*) by extolling the periodical as an embodiment of what he liked to call "the *rush* of the age":

I need not call your attention to the signs of the times in respect to Magazine literature. You will admit the tendency of the age in this direction. The brief, the terse, and the readily-circulated *will* take [the] place of the diffuse, the ponderous, and the inaccessible. Even our Reviews (lucus a non lucendo) are found too massive for the taste of the day—I do not mean merely for the taste of the tasteless, the uneducated, but for that also, of the few. The finest minds of Europe are beginning to deal with Magazines. In this country, unhappily, we have no journal of the class, which can either afford to compensate the highest talent, or which is, in all respects, a fitting vehicle for its thoughts. In the supply of this deficiency there would be a point gained, and the project of which I speak has originated in the hope of supplying it. [L, 1:164]

This passage, from a letter to John Pendleton Kennedy, was repeated almost verbatim in correspondence with Irving, Longfellow, and Halleck; Poe thought so much of these views that he recast them later as "Marginalia" items.[5] Poe indeed hoped to feature the "finest minds" of America in his *Stylus*, for he believed that the accelerated pace of an urban, industrialized culture entailed a transformation of both reading and writing, toward "the brief, the terse and the readily-circulated"—in a word, toward the magazine as the principal vehicle of literary expression.

Lewis P. Simpson is surely correct in describing Poe's dream of a quality periodical as a "quest for an authoritative literary community in America."[6] My own reading of the project differs from his only in its emphasis on the personal motives which he places in the background. My insistence on the magazine as a compensatory fantasy, a symbolic overcoming of human finitude, locates Poe's obsession in a nexus of half-conscious motives. Clearly, Poe had exalted notions of what might be achieved for "the Republic of Letters" by enlisting "the most distinguished pens" of America. But he also envisioned the journal as a life-or-death project through which he might overcome his ingrained sense of exclusion, achieve meaningful connection with "the elite of our men of letters," and insure the remembrance of his name by later generations. In a March 30, 1844, letter to James

Russell Lowell—in which he urged a "coalition" of writers to avoid being "devoured, without mercy, by the Godeys, the Snowdens, et id genus omne"—Poe adverted to the problem of his literary survival: "My Life is not yet written, and I am at a sad loss for a Biographer" (*L,* 1:246). The need to perpetuate his name was not satisfied by the biographical sketch Lowell subsequently produced, and by late 1846, a month before the pathetic demise of his wife and cousin, Virginia Clemm Poe, the author had begun to regard his magazine as a project conditioned by the reality of death—his own death: "Touching 'The Stylus':—this is the one great purpose of my literary life. Undoubtedly (unless I die) I will accomplish it—but I can afford to lose nothing by precipitancy. . . . I have *magnificent* objects in view—may I but live to accomplish them!" (*L,* 2:330). Poe's brief ownership of the *Broadway Journal* (from October 24, 1845, until its collapse on January 3, 1846) seems to have counted for nothing in this quest; in his mind only a quality monthly would suffice.

The author's last, improbable bid to realize his fantasy informs Poe's late correspondence with Edward H. N. Patterson of Oquawka, Illinois, which developed about five months before his fatal seizure. "All my prospects, pecuniary as well as literary, are involved in the project," Poe wrote to Patterson on May 23, 1849, noting (with some urgency), "if we attempt it we *must* succeed" (*L,* 2:443). The disasters of the previous three years—the death of Virginia, the failure of the *Broadway Journal,* and the refusal of marriage by Sarah Helen Whitman—had (as we shall see) awakened in Poe a sense of dread, an explicit premonition of his own annihilation. He wrote to Patterson with the urgency of one who realizes that he has little time to live—and less time to create the powerful journal which would save him from death's obscurity. Simpson wryly observes of the Patterson episode: "Here the story becomes ludicrous, for Patterson, it seems, wanted to publish the *Stylus* in Oquawka, an impractical, not to say ironic, location from which to consider 'the general interests of the Republic of Letters,' not to mention those of Pure Art."[7] But despite his hesitation about Oquawka, Poe agreed to the venture and even planned an autumn journey to Illinois to negotiate the arrangements. Refusing to compromise his notion of a quality journal, however, Poe dismissed Patterson's suggestion of a "$3 Magazine," which smacked of "namby-pambyism and frivolity," and insisted on a five-dollar subscription. Declining health may have intensified Poe's determination; having suffered during the summer of 1849 from the effects of cholera—"debility and congestion of the brain"—he was in no mood to scale down his immortality project. He apologized to Patterson for the delay in answering his letters, opposed the idea of a cheaper publication, and then admitted ruefully: "I fear that *now* it is too late" (*L*, 2:457). As if he intuited the fate which would overtake him two months later, Poe seemed forced to abandon the hope which he had sustained for so long. But he found it difficult to write off the *Stylus:* "It is not impossible, indeed, that, with energy, the first number might yet be issued in January," he advised Patterson in closing. Poe had, however, run out of energy, and the "one great purpose" of his "literary life" remained a figment of his failing mind.

Alongside his correspondence with John Allan and his letters associated with the magazine project, Poe's epistles to a handful of women—most of them mothers or sisters in a symbolic if not literal sense—constitute a third distinct sequence of messages. They are filled, once again, with the fear of abandonment and sense of vulnerability, but in his letters to women we also see Poe gripped by a fatalistic attraction to death. If the correspondence with his father embodies an agon of defiance and an intensified desire for fame, his missives to women are marked by a passive melancholy amounting at times to an explicit death wish. In the earliest extant letter to a female addressee, Poe wrote on August 29, 1835, to Maria Clemm: "My dearest Aunty, I am blinded with tears while writing this letter—I have no wish to live another hour" (*L*, 1:69). In view of the biographical facts, this distress is understandable; having left his impoverished aunt and cousin in Baltimore while he sought work in Richmond, Poe had just learned that a prosperous kinsman, Neilson Poe, had offered to take Virginia into his care. The author regarded the proposal as a dire threat: "It is useless to disguise the truth that when Virginia goes with N. P. that I shall never behold her again—that is absolutely sure" (70). Already engaged to edit the *Messenger*, Poe wanted to bring Maria and Virginia Clemm to live with him in Richmond, but his hopes of domestic felicity were temporarily crushed.

Poe's response to the arrangement is curious, both in its theatricality and in its revelation of a complex relationship with the Clemms. He agonized: "But the dream is over. Oh God have mercy on me. What have I *to live for*? Among strangers with *not one soul to love me.*" Here we encounter again a vestige of infantile separation anxiety in this pairing of emotional abandonment and physical annihilation. The letter projects itself as a textual defiance of death, a last bid for survival. Having procured a "sweet little house" in which to make Virginia and her mother comfortable, Poe reacts to Neilson Poe's offer as a thwarted provider and neglected child. The possibility of losing his child-love drives him to the verge of suicidal despair:

> My last my last my only hold on life is cruelly torn away—I have no desire to live and *will not.* . . . I love, *you know* I love Virginia passionately devotedly. I cannot express in words the fervent devotion I feel toward my dear little cousin—my own darling. . . . You both have tender hearts—and you will always have the reflection that my agony is more than I can bear—that you have driven me to the grave—for love like mine can never be gotten over. [69–70]

Here Poe resorts to a form of manipulation practiced in his letters to Allan: he alludes to his impending death in a way which assigns blame to the reader of the letter ("you have driven me to the grave"). Poe's closing line was calculated to reinforce the sense of fatality: "Let me have [from Virginia] a letter, bidding me *good bye*—forever—and I may die—my heart will break—but I will say no more."

Within the conventions of the billet-doux, the notion that one will die without the other is the most hackneyed of declarations. But Poe's connection to Virginia is more complicated than that of rejected suitor. In the postscript note attached to his letter to Mrs. Clemm, he addresses a few words to the girl: "My love, my own sweetest Sissy, my darling little wifey, think well before you break the heart of your cousin" (71). Virginia is here not only his sweetheart and fiancée but also sister ("Sissy") and wife ("wifey") as well as blood relative ("cousin"). Their lives are implicated by more than love; in this incestuous, exact figuring of their relationship, she is both spouse and sibling, a fragile child whose implicit vulnerability seems the key to Poe's intense identification. Beyond familial and affectional ties, the two are linked by common insecurities; here Poe wishes to protect Virginia from a father surrogate of uncertain devotion, to spare her the fate he has known himself. The prospective loss of his "dear little cousin" thus entails a double catastrophe, separating him forever from his intended and consigning the girl to a possible reenactment of his own abandonment. He has "no wish to live another hour" because the proposed arrangement threatens the symbolic project of saving himself from poverty and orphanhood by rescuing his double, the diminutive "Sissy." To create a haven for her in the "sweet little house" in Richmond would amount to a rewriting of his own past, a compensatory effacement of his own homelessness and rejection. The house would be a virtual paradise, a shelter from death. That Maria Clemm seemed to welcome Neilson Poe's proposal struck Poe as a betrayal, a perversion of mother love: "Oh Aunty, Aunty you loved me once—how can you be so cruel now?"

Poe's letter to Mrs. Clemm implies more than verbal posturing; as a subsequent letter indicates, he was evidently experiencing a suicidal crisis. On September 11, 1835, he wrote to his sometime benefactor, John Pendleton Kennedy: "I am suffering under a depression of spirits such as I have never felt before. I have struggled in vain against the influence of this melancholy. . . . Write me immediately. Convince me that it is worth one's while—that it is at all necessary to live" (*L*, 1:73). Though he professed not to know the cause of his despair, Poe was apparently (as Ostrom speculates[8]) uncertain about his position with the *Messenger;* but that anxiety was in turn linked to his need to provide a Richmond home for Maria and Virginia Clemm. Without the maternal affection of the one and the wifely (or sisterly) companionship of the other, Poe had fallen into a state of doubt and "incoherency." He appealed to Kennedy not for any explicit intervention with Thomas White but simply—more poignantly—for a raison d'être: "Console me—for you can. But let it be quickly—or it will be too late." Visualizing his own death, Poe sought from his literary sponsor a motive for both life and writing.

The nature of Poe's psychic reliance on Virginia defies interpretation. But we can trace its effect in certain letters, most tellingly in a missive to George Evelith, written nearly a year after Virginia's death. Here Poe writes as the desolate husband, recounting the history of his wife's decline and its effect upon his own being. This is an extraordinary passage—not only as a revealing instance of epistolary self-presentation but also as a disclosure which throws into question the relation between lived experience and literary practice:

> Six years ago, a wife, whom I loved as no man ever loved before, ruptured a blood-vessel in singing. Her life was despaired of. I took leave of her forever & underwent all the agonies of her death. She recovered partially and I again hoped. At the end of a year the vessel broke again—I went through precisely the same scene. Again in about a year afterward. Then again—again—again & even once again at varying intervals. Each time I felt all the agonies of her death—and at each accession of the disorder I loved her more dearly & clung to her life with more desperate pertinacity. But I am constitutionally sensitive—nervous in a very unusual degree. I became insane, with long intervals of horrible sanity. During these fits of absolute unconsciousness I drank, God only knows how often or how much. As a matter of course, my enemies referred the insanity to the drink rather than the drink to the insanity. I had indeed, nearly abandoned all hope of a permanent cure when I found one in the *death* of my wife. This I can & do endure as becomes a man—it was the horrible never-ending oscillation between hope & despair which I could *not* longer have endured without the total loss of reason. In the death of what was my life, then, I receive a new but—oh God! how melancholy an existence. [*L*, 2:356]

This passage merits full citation because it demonstrates a bizarre intermingling of life and writing: Poe's private, epistolary record of Virginia's illness and death echoes the rhetorical patterns in "Berenice," "Morella," and "Ligeia." Reversing the assumed relationship between the author's vicissitudes and his texts, Poe here recalls the lustrum of Virginia's decline (1842–1847) in language that doubles the tales of the 1830s, as if those stories anticipated the pathetic actuality of the writer's loss.

In the letter to Evelith, Poe presents himself (unconsciously?) as the counterpart of his own fictional protagonists, "constitutionally sensitive—nervous in a very unusual degree." His mental torment is said to derive from the "horrible never-ending oscillation between hope and despair." Like the narrator of "Morella," he comes to see his wife's death as the only release from a cycle of collapse and recovery which threatens his sanity. Virginia's successive crises, each of which causes Poe to feel "all the agonies of her death," remind one of the "hideous drama of revivification" in "Ligeia," in which "each terrible relapse" by Rowena "was only into a sterner and apparently more irredeemable death." These parallels suggest that in some basic sense, the life of writing had overtaken the reality of Poe's experience, so that imaginative episodes began to blur with actual events, creating a metafiction of personal suffering. Indeed, the distinction between literature and experience has been superseded by the sense that Poe has become his own Gothic victim and that his life is a text already inscribed in the horror of his earlier tales. Like so many of his fictional characters, Poe seems to perceive that the loss of the beautiful, dying woman entails his own doom: "In the death of what was my life, then, I receive a new but—oh God! how melancholy an existence." Five months later he confessed to Marie Louise Shew: "Unless some true and tender and pure womanly love saves me, I shall hardly last a year longer, alone" (L, 2:373). About his prospects for survival, Poe was uncannily correct: fifteen months after the letter to Mrs. Shew, he was dead.

Poe did not, of course, expire from want of female affection. But he evoked that notion of fatality repeatedly in letters to various women, appealing for protection from imminent disaster. The two principal recipients of such correspondence, Sarah Helen Whitman and Annie Richmond, both served for a time as soulmates to the bereaved author, and Poe's letters to them seem almost a rewriting of those narratives in which an agitated, helpless protagonist falls under the thrall of a beautiful woman. Poe's singular romance with Mrs. Whitman requires no further biographical elaboration, but the letters of late 1848 enable us to see the courtship as a play of fantasy situated within the margins of writing. This is not to deny the significance of their several encounters but simply to suggest that the relationship was inherently "literary" insofar as both saw their romance through poetic metaphor, indulged in incessant quotation, wrote verse to each other, and imagined their correspondence as an elaboration of poetic sentiments and motifs. Moreover, Poe seems consciously to have regarded his pursuit of Mrs. Whitman as an enactment of his quest for a beautiful, ideal woman. Underlying the real romance—and etched in its epistolary traces—is the notion of fatality, the implicit sense of doom that was never far from Poe's consciousness.

In his long letter to Mrs. Whitman on October 1, 1848, Poe lamented the impotency of language, the lack of those words (he told her) "that might enable me to lay bare to you my whole heart." Voicing a commonplace frustration, Poe felt the inadequacy of the letter as an expression of passion and imagined a mystical solution to the impasse: "My soul, this night, shall come to you in dreams and speak to you those fervid thanks which my pen is all powerless to utter" (L, 2:390). One can hardly resist the Freudian suggestion of sublimation, a union achieved in fantasy rather than through the phallic instrument of self-expression, the pen. Poe became enamored of Mrs. Whitman because he felt that her "poet-nature" enabled her to share his deepest sentiments. He confessed to her: "A profound sympathy took immediate possession of my soul. I cannot better explain to you what I felt than by saying that your unknown heart seemed to pass into my bosom—there to dwell forever—while mine, I thought, was translated into your own" (L, 2:384). This process of "translation" took another, more literal and literary form. His early poem, "To Helen," a tribute to the beloved mother-figure, Helen Stith Stannard, became in the context of his late romance an uncanny anticipation by Poe of his devotion to Sarah Helen Whitman. He said of the youthful lines: "They expressed all—*all* that I would have said to you—so fully—so accurately and so exclusively, that a thrill of intense superstition ran at once throughout my frame" (385). Poe saw the later affair figured in the earlier verse, whose "absolute appositeness" convinced him that he was fated to find the poetess from Providence, and that having made that discovery, his "Destiny, for good or for evil, either here or hereafter" was "in some measure interwoven" with that of Mrs. Whitman.

Here again art seems to have eclipsed life; past writing has provided the script for present experience. Poe drew upon the coincidental title and content of the early poem as part of an elaborate strategy to win the woman's consent to marriage; he sent her a copy of the printed text, without inscription or explanation, thus in effect translating "To Helen" into a prophetic tribute to Mrs. Whitman. He then composed a second poem, "To Helen," which surpassed the original in length and ardor if not in beauty. Poe imagined that the second "Helen" poem would have a miraculous effect on his beloved; situating their relationship within the field of writing, Poe declared himself (in the poem) to be "enchanted / By thee, and by the poetry of thy presence" (CW, 1:445). When he sent the verses to Mrs. Whitman, he entertained the fantasy that the writing itself would transmit to him the sensation of the reader's warmth and tenderness: "The mere thought that *your* dear fingers would press—*your* sweet eyes dwell upon characters which *I* had penned—characters which had welled out upon the paper from the depths of so devout a love— filled my soul with a rapture which seemed *then* all sufficient for my human nature" (L, 2:386). Here the words on the page not only communicate desire but become themselves a site of pleasure—for the writer as well (presumably) as the reader. Yet for all of the figurative intimacy afforded by writing, Poe was unable to shake the awareness of distance and the fear of being misunderstood. He wrote to Mrs. Whitman subsequently:

> In pressing my last letter between your dear hands, there passed into your spirit a sense of the *Love* that glowed within those pages:—you say this, and I feel that indeed it *must* have been so:— but, in receiving the paper upon which your eyes now rest, did no shadow steal over you from the *Sorrow* within?—Oh God! how I now curse the impotence of the pen—the inexorable *distance* between us! [L, 2:391]

In referring to "the paper upon which your eyes now rest," Poe seems intent on projecting a presence, evoking a putative intimacy which cancels the inexorable distance of correspondence. The sorrow to which he alludes may have its origin in the assumed impotence of the pen: despite its capacity to encode desire, the pen can never "connect" the lovers and (as a phallic sign) can only testify to the absence of the Other. Poe finally questions the vicarious pleasure his words have given to Mrs. Whitman and worries about the inadequacy of his epistolary gesture.

If Poe's courtship with Mrs. Whitman tested the power of words, its philosophical crux was the problem of metaphysics. Specifically, the two pondered together and in correspondence the nature of the soul and the relationship between souls in the realm of death. Poe imagined Mrs. Whitman as the incarnation of his own recurrent fantasy, the idealized, dying woman:

> As your eyes rested appealingly, for one brief moment, upon mine, I felt, for the first time in my life, and tremblingly acknowledged, the existence of spiritual influences altogether out of the reach of the reason. I saw that you were *Helen*—*my* Helen—the Helen of a thousand dreams—she whose visionary lips had so often lingered upon my own in the divine trance of passion—she whom the great Giver of all Good had preördained to be mine—mine only—if not now, alas! then at least hereafter and *forever,* in the Heavens. [*L,* 2:387]

The idea of a romance consummated "hereafter and *forever,* in the Heavens" was a familiar contemporary myth which converted the tomb into a place of ardent commemoration and the cemetery into a romantic site for living lovers. Interestingly, in Poe's letters to Mrs. Whitman, we learn that one of their passionate encounters occurred in the Providence burying ground: "During our walk in the cemetery I said to you, while the bitter, bitter tears sprang into my eyes— 'Helen, I love now—now—for the first and only time' " (383).

Poe drew a mournful pleasure from the notion that Mrs. Whitman would be his in death, and in apparent reference to her precarious health he asked rhetorically at one point: "May not this terrible [disease] be conquered?" (389). This echo of Ligeia's plaintive demand, "shall this Conqueror be not once conquered," exhibits once again the peculiar relationship between Poe's past writing and his current romance. In speaking of the disease, he seems unconsciously to connect the woman to the dying fictional character with whom his narrator is apparently reunited in the final moments of the tale. Voicing the quintessential nineteenth-century concept of union in death, Poe remarked in the same letter that, should Mrs. Whitman's illness prove to be fatal, he would happily join her in death: "If you *died*—then at least would I clasp your dear hand in death, and willingly—*oh, joyfully—joyfully—joyfully*—go down *with* you into the night of the Grave" (390). This generous proposal seems not to have evoked the desired response, and in a subsequent letter, Poe confessed to a "sad foreboding at heart" as he told the widow of a second, solitary visit to the cemetery to find "the very spot where my arm first tremblingly encircled your waist" (*L*, 2:397). This return to the churchyard seems a revealing gesture, signifying Poe's attraction to the idea of communion in death, and, it may be, his desire to pass beyond the grave.

Indeed, Poe's letters to Mrs. Whitman following his unsuccessful courtship and the subsequent suicide attempt disclose a mounting sense of approaching dissolution. "I am calm & tranquil," he wrote to her on November 14, 1848, "& but for a strange shadow of coming evil which haunts me I should be happy" (*L*, 2:400). A week later he confided: "*Still* the Shadow of Evil *haunts* me, and, although tranquil, I am unhappy. I dread the Future" (*L*, 2:405). Unconsciously his comment echoes Roderick Usher's premonition of terror: "I dread the events of the future, not in themselves, but in their results." Poe likened himself intuitively to the protagonist of his great tale, that despairing victim bound fatally to a dying woman whom he could not marry. He seems to have become increasingly unable to separate life and writing, to distinguish the experiences of his last years from those texts concerned obsessively with pallid women and doomed men. To Mrs. Whitman he finally suggested that his very survival depended upon her devotion: "My sole hope, now, is *in you*, Helen. As you are true to me or fail me, so do I live or die" (*L*, 2:410). Poe's desperate entreaties to the poetess finally betray a desire to rewrite the ur-narrative of the ethereal, cadaverous bride, to construct an outcome in which the melancholy protagonist achieves earthly bliss with his mystical lady while securing at the same time literary celebrity. In one of his last letters to Mrs. Whitman, Poe fantasized: "Would it *not* be 'glorious,' *darling*, to establish, in America, the sole unquestionable aristocracy—that of intellect—to secure its supremacy—to lead & to control it? All this I *can* do, Helen, & will—if you bid me—and aid me" (410). Here we see a remarkable convergence of Poe's quest for dominance in the republic of letters and his desire for the ideal woman, the "Helen of a thousand dreams." But he could not escape the insidious pattern of abandonment and loss. In January 1849, he penned his last known letter to Mrs. Whitman, begging her collaboration in a face-saving explanation of the postponed marriage. Poe hoped only that the "unhappy matter" of their broken engagement might "die quietly away" (L, 2:421).

Histrionic as this correspondence may be, when we consider it next to the letters to Annie Richmond, we note parallels, repetitions, and variations which suggest the compulsive nature of Poe's late missives to sympathetic women. The author did not meet Mrs. Richmond until the summer of 1848, and his correspondence with her seems to have begun in October of that year, about the time that Poe was wooing Mrs. Whitman. If he imagined the latter to be his ethereal beloved, he seems to have regarded Annie as a virtual reincarnation of the dead Virginia Poe. "But oh, *my darling*, *my* Annie, my own sweet *sister* Annie, my *pure* beautiful angel—*wife* of my soul—to be mine hereafter & *forever in the Heavens*," Poe rhapsodized, "how shall I explain to you the *bitter, bitter* anguish which has tortured me since I left you?" (L, 2:401). Conflating the roles of "darling," "sister," and "wife," he addressed Mrs. Richmond with extraordinary intimacy and traced a fantasy of domestic contentment:

> It is not *much* that I ask, *sweet sister Annie*—my mother & myself would take a small cottage at Westford—oh *so* small—so *very* humble—I should be far away from the tumults of the world—from the ambition which I loathe—I would labor day & night, and with industry, I could accomplish *so* much—Annie! it would be a Paradise beyond my wildest hopes—I could see some of your beloved family *every* day, & you often—oh VERY often—I would hear from you continually—regularly & *our* dear mother would be with us & love us both—ah *darling*—do not these pictures touch your inmost heart? [402]

Poe's persistent use of the word "sister" and his reference to Mrs. Clemm as "our" mother bespeaks an almost pathological confusion, in which the deceased wife and the unattainable "darling" become one. The same transposition helps to account for parallels between "Annabel Lee" (a lyric patently inspired by Mrs. Richmond) and

"Ulalume," the poetic product of his mourning for Virginia. From the letter cited above, we see that Poe entertained the illusion of a "Paradise" in which he and Annie shared a childlike happiness under the loving protection of Mrs. Clemm, a bliss defined as an escape from "ambition" to a cottage where Poe would paradoxically "labor night & day" to "accomplish so much," presumably as a writer. If this letter recalls the August 29, 1835, letter to Mrs. Clemm (in which he describes the "sweet little house" awaiting the aunt and cousin), it also resembles the letter one month earlier to Sarah Helen Whitman, in which he describes a cottage of "simple beauty" beside "some quiet river" and imagines the idyllic life that the two might share. Out of the same reveries Poe fashioned "The Domain of Arnheim" and "Landor's Cottage," works which chronologically bracket his epistolary visions of rural retirement and suggest once again the interpenetration of life and writing.[9]

The insistence of this fantasy material establishes an important point about Poe's late correspondence: inscription has become dissociated from actuality and increasingly fixed on phantasmic scenes. Earlier tales and poems, previous letters, recurrent hallucinations— all merge as Poe returns to the same images, the same formulations. Both Helen and Annie will be his—if not on earth, then "hereafter and *forever*, in the Heavens." He exalts "the crystal Heaven" of Helen's eyes (*L*, 2:388) and "the clear Heaven" of Annie's (*L*, 2:401). To both he confesses a horrible foreboding of ill and begs for love as a desperate restorative. To Annie Poe confided the details of his suicide attempt and his anticipation of dissolution in words which might have been spoken by one of his own enervated protagonists: "I am so *ill*—so terribly, hopelessly ILL in body and mind, that I feel I CANNOT live, unless I can feel your sweet, gentle, loving hand pressed upon my forehead. . . . Is it not POSSIBLE for you to come—if only for one little week?—until I subdue this fearful agitation, which if continued, will either destroy my life or, drive me hopelessly mad" (*L*, 2:403). Like Roderick Usher, Poe conceived that life and reason were in jeopardy, and he found himself increasingly oppressed by "the grim phantasm, FEAR." Five months before his death, he wrote to Mrs. Richmond: "I am full of dark forbodings. *Nothing cheers or comforts me. My life seems wasted—the future looks a dreary blank:*

but I will struggle on and 'hope against hope'" (*L*, 2:438). The sustaining "hope" of his last summer was the thought of moving to Lowell, Massachusetts, to live near Annie. On his ill-starred last visit to Richmond, Virginia (the city and state ironically uniting the names of his sister-wives), Poe wrote to Mrs. Clemm: "I *must* be somewhere where I can see Annie. . . . I want to live *near* Annie. . . . Do not tell me anything about Annie—I cannot bear to hear it now—unless you can tell me that Mr. R. is dead" (*L*, 2:458–59). With a wedding ring at the ready, Poe entertained the ghoulish illusion that Annie's husband might die, even as he felt the approach of his own end.

The final weeks of Poe's life—at least as reflected in letters—betray the urgency of his search for a bride, as if that tactic alone could forestall his physical and psychic disintegration. At the same time that he wrote Mrs. Clemm of his desire to marry Annie Richmond, Poe was courting his childhood friend, Sarah Elmira Royster. He informed Mrs. Clemm on September 18, 1849, that he was about to return to New York and confided: "If *possible* I will get married before I start" (*L*, 2:461). But Poe did not secure a bride; nor did he return to Fordham and Mrs. Clemm. His distance from Maria Clemm indeed seems to have been one of the principal agonies of his last months. On July 19, he wrote to her of a recent derangement: "Most of my suffering arose from that terrible idea which I could not get rid of—the idea that you were dead" (*L*, 2:455). In a letter of the same week he asked plaintively, "Oh God, my Mother, shall we ever again meet?" (*L*, 2:454). Poe's anxiety readily discloses a reactivated dread of permanent separation from the mother, a panic which intensified premonitions of his own death. Ironically, on a journey to drum up support for the *Stylus*—that abortive scheme for symbolic immortality—Poe sought a bride to solace his dying hour and to ease the torment of separation from "Muddy." Though this recapitulation no doubt oversimplifies the psychic tensions of his final weeks, it does suggest the recurrent themes of his correspondence. Simultaneously preparing for death and seeking to evade or postpone it, Poe poured the contradictions of his situation into letters, as if writing alone could effect a reconciliation with fate. A bout of cholera in Philadelphia led him to suggest to Mrs. Clemm—in a letter penned exactly three months before his death—a version of that simultaneous departure which he had once suggested to Mrs. Whitman:

> The very instant you get this, *come* to me. The joy of seeing you will almost compensate for our sorrows. We can but die together. It is no use to reason with me *now*; I must die. I have no desire to live since I have done "Eureka." I could accomplish nothing more. For your sake it would be sweet to live, but we must die together. You have been all in all to me, darling, ever beloved mother, and dearest, truest friend. [*L*, 2:452]

Here Mrs. Clemm is the composite of possible female roles, his "darling," "beloved mother," "truest friend," and (implicitly) his virtual wife. The idea that they will "die together" makes the prospect of annihilation bearable, for death will thus reunite him with the mother figure from whom death had estranged him so many years before. But Poe's bad luck continued to the end: he did not die with Mrs. Clemm and instead departed from this world, alone, in a Baltimore hospital, calling confusedly for "Reynolds," a name perhaps associated (as A. H. Quinn once suggested[10]) with that great vortex in the polar seas which promised "some exciting knowledge—some never-to-be-imparted secret, whose attainment is destruction."

5

Revenge and Silence
The Foreclosure of Language

If writing creates a space in which one can construct fantasies of beauty and triumph while securing an earthly, literary immortality, it follows that writing must also become a site of conflict, a contested space. Poe's career as a man of letters illustrates this uneasy relationship between the symbolic and the pragmatic. Literary battles occupied his attention more or less continuously after 1835, and contrary to the myth that he worked in melancholy isolation, the facts (adduced by Sidney P. Moss) show how fully he was immersed in a warfare which involved reputations, cliques, and artistic standards.[1] As a cultural phenomenon, critical assault did not begin in the nineteenth century (one thinks, for example, of the Scriblerians and their foes), but the advent of professional authorship and the commercialization of literature changed the terms of such combat. Writing had always entailed the risks of failure, misunderstanding, or neglect; but as it became a livelihood, slashing reviewers wielded a seemingly lethal power. "Keats fell by a criticism," Poe wrote in "The

Duc de L'Omelette" (1832), alluding to the popular belief that the poet had succumbed not to tuberculosis but to critical savagery. In "The Man that Was Used Up" (1839), Poe developed an outrageous conceit of dismemberment from the colloquial notion of "using up" or abusing an author in print. The same phrase recurs in "The Literary Life of Thingum Bob, Esq." (1844), a burlesque depicting (in none too veiled terms) the strategies of an American magazinist who suffers and inflicts verbal wounds. Discovering a hostile review of his poetry, Thingum Bob admits, "As I perused this I felt myself growing gradually smaller and smaller, and when I came to the point at which the editor sneered at the poem as '*verses,*' there was little more than an ounce of me left" (*CW*, 3:1130). However, Thingum Bob perseveres, acquires control of four periodicals, merges them into "one magnificent Magazine," and secures a fame which "extends to the uttermost ends of the earth," thus enacting a fantasy of the life of writing remarkably similar to the one sketched out in letters in the previous chapter.

This seemingly trivial narrative displays two important features of Poe's relationship to inscription. One is the general concept of literary activity as battle, quite literally a contest for survival; the other is the notion of words, writing, as a source of violence. In *Saving the Text*, Geoffrey Hartman speculates on the "tremendous impact words may have on psychic life," and he answers Derrida's essay on Plato's *Phaedrus*—which "shows that writing itself may be viewed as a poisoned gift"—by pointing out the potential of language for both hurt and healing, indeed for a healing which can only come through words that wound.[2] The notion of writing as a wounding seems at first glance a preposterous extension of metaphor: one speaks of brutal facts, cutting remarks, vicious gossip, and so forth, as if to acknowledge by hyperbole the insubstantiality of words, which are said never to hurt us as do sticks and stones. Yet the adage effaces the distinction between bodily and psychic wounds and so ignores the potency of language, which enters the ear or eye unbidden to inflict its suffering. In "The Power of Words" (1845), Poe theorized that words possessed a "physical power," since the creation of the cosmos was itself an effect of speaking. But the substantializing power by which words create something out of nothing also endows them with the capacity to injure. "Words—printed ones especially—are murderous things," he remarked in the "Marginalia" series.[3] Throughout Poe's fiction, language and violence intertwine suggestively, and in tales like "The Literary Life of Thingum Bob, Esq." this convergence seems a transparent projection of the savagery ascribed to the magazine world itself. But in a remarkable series of tales concerned with enemies and adversaries, Poe develops a more complex concept of word-wounds and elaborates a theory of verbal revenge which carries us into the domain of metaphysics toward the radical meaning of silence.

The place of language in the poetics of revenge moreover marks another intersection of writing and death. For Poe imagined the agon with a double or adversary to unfold on the plane of discourse as well as on the level of overt force. While only a few of the texts within this sequence deal directly with what Derrida would call "the violence of the letter," most hinge upon the silencing of an opponent through a foreclosure of language, a tactical expropriation—or should we say purloining?—of the letter. This was a kind of retaliation that Poe the man of letters well understood; in 1839 he wrote to a Baltimore journalist: "It is always desirable to know *who are* our enemies, and what are [sic] the nature of their attacks. I intend to put up with nothing that I can *put down*" (L, 1:114). But the tales of crime and vengeance cannot be reduced to fanciful simulations of literary conflict, for the stakes are much higher. These fables of aggression hinge on reciprocal fear, on an antagonism of identification grounded in mutual resemblance and ineluctable hostility; they are situated between perverseness and ratiocination, between the criminal's audacity and the detective's analysis. They finally articulate a connection between the desire for revenge and ontological dread, projecting violence as displaced anxiety. In this paradigm, the attempt to impose silence reveals itself as a desperate stratagem for avoiding or deferring the silence beyond writing.

Poe's reflections on the psychosymbolic implications of revenge apparently began with a slender narrative titled "Von Jung, the Mystific," later simply called "Mystification" (1837). Composed while Poe was completing *The Narrative of Arthur Gordon Pym*, the tale affords a gloss on the novel (to be discussed in the next chapter), for it deploys writing as a weapon, a means of vanquishing an enemy through interpretive confusion. The plot is simple enough: a prank-ster named Von Jung decides to humiliate Hermann, a self-pro-claimed authority on the code of duelling. The hero contrives to offend Hermann and then answers his demand for satisfaction with a note referring the self-styled expert to an obscure passage in a Latin duelling text—knowing that Hermann will be both unable to under-stand the citation and incapable of admitting confusion. The ploy is a perfect mystification: Von Jung displays his cunning and reduces his foe to silent embarrassment. Insofar as Von Jung's letter demolishes Hermann and obviates the duel, Poe's narrative transcribes the writ-erly myth that the pen is mightier than the sword.

"Mystification" illuminates one other aspect of the defiance of writing. Poe remarks of the cryptic passage on duelling: "The lan-guage was ingeniously framed so as to present to the ear all the outward signs of intelligibility, and even of profundity, while in fact not a shadow of meaning existed" (CW, 2:303). Von Jung seizes upon a passage which parodies the discourse of duelling manuals; but more important, the text parodies the concept of writing as a trans-mission of meaning. Words have become disconnected from any normative or determinate signification. Verbal signs flaunt their own provisionality. The only available "reading" of the nonsense requires a playful reinvention of reading itself: "The key to the whole was found in leaving out every second and third word alternately, when there appeared a series of ludicrous quizzes upon single combat as practised in modern times" (303). Here we encounter the perverse pleasure of cryptography: the use of language to close itself off from common understanding, to defy the uninitiated. The code of the duelling text leads us from the unintelligible to the ludicrous; writing operates as a devious opacity when the outward signs of coherent discourse signify only their own vacuity. What the recondite text finally relates, according to the narrator, is a "most horribly absurd account of a duel between two baboons." Monkey business, in short.

This depiction of writing as a play of signs and a space of rivalry establishes a paradigm of verbal revenge, from which Poe would construct more intricate and deadly formulations. His attention to the "art mystifique," the craft of befuddlement, leads directly to the detective story, which "Mystification" anticipates in the tutelary relationship between a genius and his less discerning narrator-companion; in the emphasis on mystery and disclosure; and in the gamesmanship between the genius and a rival. At issue is the concept of control: the rival advances claims of expertise, but the genius privately lays a trap, calculating the precise gesture by which he will confound the adversary and reduce him to speechless confusion. To see "Mystification" as a precursor of the Dupin stories is to perceive in the latter a struggle for ascendancy rooted in revenge and based ultimately upon the inherent capacity of words to inflict mortal wounds, to impose silence. That is, language holds the key to intellectual rivalry, which is finally a contest for survival.

Initially, Poe seems to have directed the revenge of writing, the rage for control, against the reading public itself through various "quizzes," hoaxes, and parodies. In "The Man of the Crowd," another exercise in mystification, he invited readers to surmise the secret of a mysterious old man—even as he dangled before them the metaphor of a text which "does not permit itself to be read" (CW, 2:506). The whole weight of the story presses upon us the significance of the stranger's mad behavior; the narrator asks us to assume a correspondence between external appearance and intrinsic truth, between surface and depth, so that the particulars of the old man's appearance (the "diamond" and the "dagger" observed beneath his cloak) figure as signs of his sinister nature. Yet the very profundity of the narrator's reading masks its absurd irony, for closer inspection suggests that the stranger's inexplicable actions are symptoms of the narrator's own fanatical pursuit.[4] The old man has good reason to fear the narrator, who stalks him for a night and a day, masked by a handkerchief (512) which resembles the guise of a robber. The narrator thus inadvertently transforms *himself* into "the type and the genius of deep crime." Patrick Quinn rightly observes that the narrator "fails to see and recognize himself" in his double.[5] The would-be detective's headlong effort to read the book that will not permit itself to be read, to construe the "wild history" written within the stranger's bosom, leads him to confuse surface and depth, to ignore the obvious in his pursuit of the hidden. He commits the mistake Poe later associated with the French inspector, Vidocq: "He erred continually by the very intensity of his investigations. He impaired his vision by holding the object too close. . . . Truth is not always in a well" (CW, 2:545). And Poe seduces the reader of "The Man of the Crowd" with the same interpretive delusion, beguiling us with the outward signs of intelligibility, even of profundity, while grounding the narrative in an absurd misreading. The narrator's "man of the crowd" theory obscures the ironic truth that each man prompts the other's perverse behavior; between the two wanderers lies a gulf of silence and mutual dread. Here in a preliminary way Poe approaches one of the crucial insights of the revenge sequence: anxiety projects itself as aggression to create a climate of potential violence.

The impulse to confound the reader through misdirection, concealment, and deferral led Poe to the threshold of a new kind of writing, the tale of ratiocination. By recasting Von Jung the prankster as Dupin the sleuth, he inscribed his defiance of the reading public within the difference between the detective and his less astute foils: the narrator, the Prefect of police, and (in "The Purloined Letter") the criminal rival. Poe strove to bewilder readers so that Dupin's solution might seem the miraculous sign of genius. Yet he was conscious of the inherent gimmickry, for he later wrote to Philip Pendleton Cooke:

> You are right about the hair-splitting of my French friend:—that is all done for effect. These tales of ratiocination owe most of their popularity to being something in a new key. I do not mean to say that they are not ingenious—but people think them more ingenious than they are—on account of their method and *air* of method. In the "Murders in the Rue Morgue," for instance, where is the ingenuity of unravelling a web which you yourself (the author) have woven for the express purpose of unravelling? The reader is made to confound the ingenuity of the suppositious Dupin with that of the writer of the story. [L, 2:328]

The last sentence acknowledges both Poe's mystification of the public and the secret pleasure of the text. But the passage also suggests why he finally abandoned the genre: the game was too easy, the effect of mystification too readily achieved, and credit for ingenuity mistakenly accorded to the detective rather than his creator.

Nevertheless, in "Rue Morgue" and "The Purloined Letter" Poe engaged in games more complicated than his letter to Cooke would suggest. In these tales he incorporates internal strategies and conflicts in which mystification becomes associated more explicitly with silence and death. For example, Dupin reveals his solution of the crime in "Rue Morgue" through a scene carefully contrived to demonstrate his acumen. Just as the detective explains to the narrator how the murders have been committed by an orangutan, the animal's owner appears at the door, his arrival on cue confirming Dupin's godlike control. When the owner, a sailor, offers to pay for the recovery of his pet, the detective stupefies him by demanding information about the crime. The speech act inflicts a mortification: "The sailor's face flushed up as if he were struggling with suffocation. He started to his feet and grasped his cudgel; but the next moment he fell back into his seat, trembling violently, and with the countenance of death itself. He spoke not a word. I pitied him from the bottom of my heart" (*CW*, 2:563). The sailor finally stammers out a confession, a fact less important than his stupefaction and his inability to lift a cudgel. He has been literally disarmed by language through a strategy of ascendancy embellished in later tales. In "Rue Morgue" Dupin traps his prey by a choice made by the victim, whose tongue-tie signifies his powerlessness and asserts the detective's incomprehensible mastery. Thus rendered speechless, the victim exhibits "the countenance of death itself," as the detective achieves a linguistic foreclosure.

The sailor provides the detective genius with only a momentary challenge, and revenge plays no part in Dupin's scheme. At the end of "Rue Morgue," however, Poe alludes to a more important opposition: the sleuth's rivalry with the Prefect of police. The Prefect cannot conceal his "chagrin" at Dupin's solution of the mystery, and Poe's detective observes wryly: "I am satisfied with having defeated him in his own castle" (568). In "The Mystery of Marie Rogêt" (that forgettable experiment in forensic narrative) we learn that Dupin never explains his solution of the "Rue Morgue" case to the Prefect, thus leaving the latter in a condition of attenuated mystification.

Beating someone at his own game is precisely the fascination of "The Purloined Letter," and in the third of the Dupin stories Poe situates the action between ratiocination and revenge. Here the detective's strategies of obfuscation have a more complicated objective, for he is simultaneously playing three games: one with his companion (the narrator), one with the Prefect, and one with the Minister D____. These contests unfold in a tale larded with references to game-playing and broadly conceived as another challenge to the reader's perspicuity. Recent considerations of doubling and repetition, possession and dispossession, have yielded—especially in the commentaries of Lacan, Derrida, and Barbara Johnson—some of the most densely provocative criticism bearing upon Poe. Amid its various controversies, this sequence of readings takes for granted the essentially symbolic, grammatological struggle acted out in "The Purloined Letter." At issue is the control of writing and the appropriation of the power inherent in the signifying letter. This agon culminates in a gesture of revenge which effectually silences the letter's thief in a double deprivation of language.

In the guise of a story about crime and analysis, "The Purloined Letter" presents an oneiric narrative of doubling and subdividing. Barbara Johnson notes that "the narrator and Dupin are doubles of each other, and Dupin himself is first introduced as a Bi-Part Soul, a sort of Dupin Duplex, 'the creative and the resolvent.' The Minister, D____, has a brother for whom it is possible to mistake him, and from whom he is to be distinguished because of *his* doubleness (poet *and* mathematician). Thus the Minister and Dupin become doubles of each other through the fact of their both being already double, in addition to their other points of resemblance, including their names."[6] Johnson leaves out of account here the Prefect, whose personality is said to be divided into "the entertaining" and "the contemptible," and whose quantitative methods associate him with the mathematical side of Dupin and the Minister D____. Within the dramatic configuration, however, he functions as a counterpart of the narrator, remaining ignorant of the letter's whereabouts until the moment of the detective's revelation. Significantly, all three men are literally in the dark as the story opens; the Prefect and the narrator remain figuratively so until the sleuth illuminates them.

This network of oppositions suggests that the action of the tale is traversed by adversarial relations. As Johnson notes, even Dupin and the narrator, ostensibly companions and housemates, were brought together initially (in "Rue Morgue") by a textual rivalry of the sort repeated in "The Purloined Letter"—common desire for exclusive possession of "the same very rare and very remarkable volume" (CW, 2:531–32). At stake in "The Purloined Letter" is another rare screed, upon which depends both the Queen's honor and—implicitly—the stability of the royal government. But the story has less to do with political power than with intellectual ascendancy. Domination is here purely a function of mind; Poe conceives of a fantasy world in which the hierarchy of power coincides with the hierarchy of intelligence. He thus differentiates between the mental ability of the Prefect and the Minister D___ and then dramatizes the more subtle distinction between D___ and Dupin to suggest that differences of intellect are real, consequential, and demonstrable.

The battle of minds lies close to the surface of the tale and leads, perhaps too easily, to a simple analogy with Poe's ambitions for literary authority and control. Although Poe contends that important truths are "invariably superficial," the lesson of "The Purloined Letter" is that the simple and obvious may be more difficult to perceive than the complex and concealed. And so we are obliged to attend more closely to the implications of these surface rivalries and to the instrumentality of the letter. Through their own intellectual contest, Lacan and Derrida have laid bare the psychosexual matrix of the intrigue (the repressed, primal scene implied by the letter) as well as the letter's inherently phallic function in the economy of sexual symbolism.[7] Dupin himself recognizes the letter as a tool whose force lies in its potential: "It is this possession, and not any employment of the letter, which bestows the power. With the employment the power departs" (CW, 3:977–78). To disseminate the letter's meaning is to lose the power it possesses as an instrument of violation (in both the legal and sexual senses). Though this analogy degenerates into farce when we conceive of the story as a search for the severed phallus, the idea of the letter as a floating signifier, the mark of an unspecified referent, returns us to the problem of writing at a deeper level of contemplation. Here we move beyond the vicissitudes of Poe's career as a writer to confront the more radical Derridean sense of writing as violence, as an intrusion which destroys forever the copresence of orality.

Obviously Poe could not have foreseen the deconstruction of language and philosophy carried out by Nietzsche, Heidegger, and Derrida. But in positing the letter as a source of power, he seemingly intuits the provisionality of all language: for what the Queen receives as a sign of desire (the love letter) becomes, in the possession of the Minister D____, a seal of domination; what arrives as a signifier of devotion leaves the Queen's bedroom as a marker of deception and betrayal. Poe dramatizes the potential of language to effect change, to shift the balance of power, to reconstitute reality itself (which as a mental construct is already mediated by words). In the triangular contest between Dupin, the Minister D____, and the Prefect, the urge to possess the letter is rooted in a more fundamental desire to control events by appropriating the signifier: to dictate. The etymology of the verb "dictate" suggests the essential relationship between language and power which discloses the value (both symbolic and pragmatic) of the purloined letter. To possess it is to seize the sign of authority, for all structures of power are inherently rooted in language and its capacity to articulate the fiat by which power justifies itself.

Poe implies that the purloining of the letter always entails a loss which is literally unspeakable: the Queen sees the Minister D____ pick it up in the royal boudoir but cannot object because the King is present; nor can she protest the loss subsequently, since the very acknowledgment of the letter's existence involves scandal. This initial scene of dispossession becomes the model for Dupin's own re-purloining of the letter later in the story. Imagining the Queen's silence and powerlessness at the moment of her loss, the detective discovers his strategy of retribution, for he grasps the inherent principle of language: to lose the letter is to forfeit power, to suffer a symbolic death. Since both Dupin and D____ are poets, they understand the power of the word as an arbitrary function of its deployment. They understand the paradox by which the usefulness of the letter resides in the deferral of use; by which the simplest of stratagems can seem the oddest. D____ entrusts his possession of the letter to two strategies of paradoxical misdirection: he "hides" the correspondence in plain sight and then absents himself from home to permit an exhaustive search by the police. Dupin notes that the Prefect has been "thoroughly mystified" by the Minister D____'s principle of concealment: "And the remote source of his defeat lies in the supposition that the Minister is a fool, because he has acquired renown as a poet" (986). Because the Prefect approaches crime as a matter of arithmetical simplicity, he cannot conceive of an imaginative deployment of the letter; he cannot comprehend the play of language and the game of power to which its concealment belongs.

But this is the special advantage of Dupin, who identifies his thoughts so closely with those of the Minister D____ as to anticipate his designs. Much has been made of the mechanism of repetition which appears to operate in Dupin's repurloining of the letter from D____. For Lacan, the gesture confirms the insistence of the primal scene which occurs at the moment of the theft.[8] Yet can we not assume that Dupin's desire for the scandalous text, like that of the Minister and the Prefect, arises from an unspoken compulsion to observe the scene betokened by the letter but acted out *prior* to its inscription? Can we not conclude that Dupin repeats the method of the theft as an unconscious reenactment of D____'s violation of the Queen's sexual privacy—itself a symbolic version of an earlier penetration? This scenario of unconscious repetition implies a vertiginous historical regression, a movement backward before the letter, before writing, toward an archetypal crime of defiance and appropriation. At the origin of this perspective might we not expect to find a myth of writing figured as sexual transgression?

Intriguing as such a reading may be, it also repeats the mistake of the Prefect, who probes the hidden and unseen while overlooking what is before his eyes. For on a conscious level, Dupin reenacts the method of the theft as a deliberate, private amusement, a strategy infinitely more satisfying than defeating the Prefect "in his own castle." The pleasure of the game lies in the relationship between two scenes: the detective's revelation of the letter's recovery and the implied but unwritten sequel, D____'s discovery of the letter's loss.

The former scene involves another application of the "*art mystifique*," for Dupin has obtained the letter without the knowledge of the Prefect or the narrator. That the sleuth has not confided in his confidant underscores the importance of mystification as a sign of ascendancy. Rather than enlisting the narrator's assistance, he hires a confederate to create the diversion which permits him to steal the document. Thus when the Prefect calls to report his lack of progress in solving the case, Dupin stuns both of his intellectual inferiors by producing the letter. The scene calls to mind both the confusion of the sailor in "Rue Morgue" and the perplexity of Hermann in "Mystification":

> I was astounded. The Prefect appeared absolutely thunderstricken. For some minutes he remained speechless and motionless, looking incredulously at my friend with open mouth, and eyes that seemed starting from their sockets; then, apparently recovering himself in some measure, he seized a pen, and after several pauses and vacant stares, finally filled up and signed a check for fifty thousand francs, and handed it across the table to Dupin. The latter examined it carefully and deposited it in his pocketbook; then, unlocking an *escritoire*, took thence a letter and gave it to the Prefect. This functionary grasped it in a perfect agony of joy, opened it with a trembling hand, cast a rapid glance at its contents, and then, scrambling and struggling to the door, rushed at length unceremoniously from the room and from the house, without having uttered a syllable since Dupin had requested him to fill up the check. [983]

The loquacious Prefect, who in "Marie Rogêt" is said to have discoursed for "seven or eight leaden-footed hours" in the company of Dupin, is here reduced to apoplectic silence. Thus "speechless and motionless" he seems to have been struck dead, a fate prefigured in the story's opening scene when the Prefect responds to the suggestion that the mystery is "a little *too* self-evident" by declaring: " 'Oh, Dupin, you will be the death of me yet!' " (975). Dupin's revelation of the letter deprives both the narrator and the policeman of the system of letters constituted as language. Though the Prefect recovers language to the extent of writing a check (thus acknowledging Dupin's ascendancy), he departs "without having uttered a syllable."

The mystification of the Prefect serves a more important purpose, however, providing Dupin with a simulation of the events that will take place in the privacy of the Minister D——'s apartment. By substituting for the purloined letter a facsimile bearing a cryptic inscription, he has insured the unfolding of a second scene of speechless confusion, which will occur when D_____, flushed with the sense of his own power and sagacity, goes to the card rack to get the letter: "Being unaware that the letter is not in his possession, he will proceed with his exactions as if it was. Thus will he inevitably commit himself, at once, to his political destruction. His downfall, too, will not be more precipitate than awkward" (993). We imagine with Dupin the scene of mortification, the symbolic death inflicted by the loss of the letter (itself a reenactment of the Queen's agony), and the perplexity evoked by the lines from Crébillon. Barbara Johnson observes that the literary reference takes its place in the scheme of doubling by directing D_____ back to a tragedy of violent reversals: "It is a *letter* which informs King Atreus of the extent of his betrayal, and serves as an instrument of his revenge. . . . A Queen betraying a King, a letter representing that betrayal being purloined for purposes of power, an eventual return of that letter to its addressee, accompanied by an act of revenge which duplicates the original crime— 'The Purloined Letter' as a story of repetition is *itself* a repetition of the story from which it purloins its last words."9 And as the handwriting discloses the identity of the robber, Dupin establishes intellectual dominance according to his own previously articulated formula: " 'Here, then . . . you have precisely what you demand to make the ascendancy complete—the robber's knowledge of the loser's knowledge of the robber' " (977). D_____ is left outraged but silent, since he can hardly protest the theft of that which he has stolen. Beyond the objective of defeating his rival, Dupin has the additional satisfaction of turning the game back on D_____ so that the minister by his own act brings about his "political destruction," feels the cruelty of his scheme, and experiences in his mystification the greater intellect of his fellow poet and mathematician.

In the final paragraph, Poe adds one final twist to the torturous plot: he reveals that Dupin has been inspired not only by the desire to aid the Queen, bewilder the Prefect, and assert his mental superiority over D_____, but by the desire to repay D_____ for an "evil turn" done to Dupin in Vienna. That is, the destruction of the Minister marks a repayment, the deferred but inevitable return of evil to its source. Yet the disclosure of the revenge motif (also implicit in the allusion to Crébillon) identifies "The Purloined Letter" as a significant revision of the ratiocinative tale. The difference between criminal and sleuth, between sinister compulsion and analytical genius here collapses in a fusion of personalities and motives. Dupin's elaborate repetition of D____'s strategy betrays a complicated idea of retribution involving identification with an adversary, a strategy of deception, ironic mystification, self-imposed ruin, and symbolic silence. Dupin's deep-seated longing for vengeance marks a new insight by Poe: that even the godlike detective hero is subject to base obsessions and unconscious (or half-conscious) impulses. The conflation of Dupin and D____ illustrates the important principle that Max Bird has located in the classic "detective" stories of the Western tradition, works like *Oedipus Rex* and *Heart of Darkness*:

> We are all criminals in our dark hearts, all capable of Kurtz's savagery. Our natures are in fact double, each of us criminal and each of us cop. The thin line that divides normal human society from the underworld also runs through each of us, dividing our normal selves from our own personal underworld, our own criminality. The detective and the criminal, as Sophocles may be telling us, form one person, not two. And the startling mirror effect, the startling similarity between our best and our worst selves, may be the first (and most important) clue to the mystery of who we are.[10]

Bird's comment, so apposite to the doubling of "The Purloined Letter," enables us to see the last Dupin story as an intersection of two fictional modes. It represents the apotheosis of ratiocination, a line of analytic fantasy that the author exhausted late in 1844 with "The Oblong Box" and "Thou Art the Man." And it marks a convergence with a seemingly antithetical mode characterized by irrationality, murder, and compulsive confession: the tale of perverseness.

This narrative of violence emerged about the time that Poe began to formulate the detective story, and we can trace a parallel fascination through "The Purloined Letter." At this point, however, Poe seems to have reached an impasse, recognizing that the master sleuth, despite his Gothic eccentricities and his "Bi-Part Soul," evinced a rationalism incompatible with madness and finally less interesting. As his 1846 letter to Cooke indicates, he found himself trapped by mechanical repetition; he discovered that in celebrating the exploits of a supremely analytical mind, he was perforce bound to tell the same story over and over. Perhaps because madness has always been more various and intriguing than reason (psychiatry has far less to say about the latter), Poe shelved his detective hero and in subsequent tales of crime confined himself to the perspective of the psychopath. This was not a wholesale rejection of ratiocination, however, for he continued to endow his perverse narrators with a passion for analysis. In five brilliant tales, Poe explored the terrors of a criminal driven to detect and silence himself after silencing an adversary.

For all the variations in Poe's best fiction, Patrick Quinn argues that "the themes are basically two: analysis and obsession." He makes the further distinction that whenever a master analyst dominates the narrative, Poe employs a narrator who stands off and observes; but when the story relates the "twisted fears and agonies" of an obsessive personality, "no intermediary is brought into play."[11] But the dichotomy is not quite so tidy as Quinn suggests: the Dupin of "The Purloined Letter" engages in ratiocination as a form of vengeance, while (as I intend to show) his murderers seem most analytical as they perpetrate violence and most deranged as they solve their own crimes. The penchant for self-detection emerges briefly at the close of "Berenice," where the narrator alludes to the grisly violation of his cousin and speaks of the "ivory-looking" objects scattered about the floor. But the nature and result of the crime are both ambiguous: Berenice is reportedly "still alive" and Egaeus has no conscious recollection of what he has done. Not until Poe composed "William Wilson" did he reify the ironic potential of a story narrated from the perspective of a criminal mind.

One of the chief embarrassments of "William Wilson" is that its meaning is a little *too* obvious—as if Poe had temporarily abandoned his strictures on didacticism to fashion an edifying tale about conscience. Here Quinn provides a representative view: " 'William Wilson' is a first-person account of a man's struggle with, evasions of, and final disastrous victory over, his own conscience, the spectre in his path."[12] One can hardly dispute the notion that in killing his counterpart, the insistent representative of ethical constraint, Wilson does turn himself into an amoral monster, the perpetrator of "unpardonable crime." Leaving aside the problematic nature of the double and his "murder"—Poe situates the action uneasily between nightmare and reality—we are virtually obliged to read the story as an allegorical portrayal of moral conflict. Yet oddly enough, the narrative has little to do with ethics; there is nothing like the dilemma of choice we encounter, for example, in Hawthorne's "Young Goodman Brown." Instead, the narrative sketches a complicated relationship between schoolboy adversaries. Moreover, as we enter the inner world of revenge compulsion, we find a story quite different from the surface allegory of conscience.

That "William Wilson" concerns itself more intensely with a love-hate rivalry than with moral conduct becomes apparent in Poe's elaboration of the antagonism between the narrator and his double. By virtue of the imperiousness of his disposition, as well as his "noble descent," the speaker has gained "an ascendancy" (again the crucial term) over all of his schoolmates except one: "My namesake alone . . . presumed to compete with me in the studies of the class—in the sports and broils of the play-ground—to refuse implicit belief in my assertions, and submission to my will—indeed, to interfere with my arbitrary dictation in any respect whatsoever" (CW, 2:431). Again we find a struggle for the right to dictate, this one curiously reversed from that earlier story of schoolboy conflict, "Mystification," insofar as the narrator finds *himself* perplexed by his opposite: "In his rivalry he might have been supposed actuated solely by a whimsical desire to thwart, astonish, or mortify myself; although there were times when I could not help observing, with a feeling made up of wonder, abasement, and pique, that he mingled with his injuries, his insults, or his contradictions, a certain most inappropriate, and assuredly most unwelcome *affectionateness* of manner" (432). The agon displays a curious ambivalence, as if each recognizes himself in the other and so cannot act out the violent possibilities of the encounter. The narrator detests his counterpart's "intolerable spirit of contradiction" yet admits: "I could not bring myself to hate him altogether" (433). He perceives a "strong congeniality" in their temperaments, and this likeness blunts the resentment which might otherwise have erupted into "a more serious and determined hostility."

Personal resemblance also begins to intensify the narrator's vexation, however. The identity of their names exacerbates Wilson's aversion to his "uncourtly patronymic, and its very common, if not plebian praenomen." He hears in his namesake's whisper "the very echo" of his own voice and senses that his rival has achieved a perfect imitation of himself, a realization all the more galling because the double expresses his triumph through "strangely sarcastic smiles," sneers, and a "disgusting air of patronage." The implicit ascendancy of the second Wilson illustrates a kind of parody: by affecting an ironic semblance of the narrator and mocking him through sneers and chuckles, he absorbs Wilson's identity only to display his mastery over it. The "intolerable arrogance" of this "sarcastic imitation" leads the narrator to contrive a nocturnal prank, presumably an act of retribution. When he attempts to carry out his stratagem, however, he makes a horrifying discovery; in a scene which prefigures the murder of the old man in "The Tell-Tale Heart," the narrator steals into the bedroom of his sleeping enemy:

> Having reached his closet, I noiselessly entered, leaving the lamp, with a shade over it, on the outside. I advanced a step, and listened to the sound of his tranquil breathing. Assured of his being asleep, I returned, took the light, and with it again approached the bed. Close curtains were around it, which, in the prosecution of my plan, I slowly and quietly withdrew, when the bright rays fell vividly upon the sleeper, and my eyes, at the same moment, upon his countenance. I looked;—and a numbness, an iciness of feeling instantly pervaded my frame. [437]

What the narrator sees fills him with "an objectless yet intolerable horror," which holds the key to the revenge compulsion enacted in the latter half of the story. For in the features of the sleeping double he discerns a frightening *difference:* "Were these,—*these* the lineaments of William Wilson?" The otherness of the still, recumbent figure provides an unexpected revelation, a prophetic image of death, which leaves the narrator "awe-stricken." As the light falls "vividly upon the sleeper," he receives a portentous glimpse of his namesake's fate and perhaps recognizes in it his own mortality as well. The event instantly alters the narrator's life and compels him to break off his hostilities with the second Wilson; he leaves the halls of the school "never to enter them again."

The ensuing years trace a pattern of escape and pursuit that reminds us of numerous parallels between "William Wilson" and "The Man of the Crowd." Here the narrator projects *himself* as the victim of a nemesis, and repeated intrusions of the double lead to scenes of humiliation and horror. Recurrently, the namesake frustrates the schemes of the narrator, driving him to ever more outrageous depravity. Whether the double actually intervenes or whether a paranoid Wilson imagines his presence cannot be determined. Clearly the narrator blames his misfortunes upon his "arch-enemy and evil genius," whose "apparent omnipresence and omnipotence" reduce him to "bitterly reluctant submission." His desperate act at the end of the tale manifests a desire to escape his tormentor, to achieve control over his chaotic existence.

Whether a wholly imagined scene or an actual murder experienced as hallucination (as in Basler's interpretation of "Ligeia"), the killing of the Doppelganger fits readily into an allegorical grid as the slaying of conscience. But understood as the outcome of revenge compulsion, the event becomes more problematic and suggestive. In the feud between the two Wilsons, Poe implies that such antagonisms have a life of their own, which absorbs and consumes its participants. Triggered by what René Girard would call a "mimetic rivalry," a mutuality of desire, the opposition enforces a perverse bonding, in which each develops an obsessive awareness of the other and moves toward an intimate identification. The two begin to anticipate each other's strategies and even to assume each other's natures. Poe also suggests that profound rivalries never have a determinate origin; every wound is the reciprocation of a previous injury stretching back across an irrecoverable history of enmity. The economy of revenge insures the recirculation of malice, even as it erases the distinction between self and other. Knowing that his action will prompt retaliation, the rival in effect seeks his own suffering; yet the desire of ascendancy, for the ideal, unanswerable revenge, insures the ceaseless repetition of the exchange. Because the rival uncovers and exploits our vulnerabilities, he becomes associated with those attributes of self which we seek to deny or efface. He comes at last to personify the self that we loathe, so that in seeking the destruction of the rival we strive to rid ourselves of our own most vexing qualities. Within the prison-house of revenge, every fight is a fight to the death, the permanent silencing of one's enemy. But since the rival is also a displaced image of self, the attack upon one's double is always inherently a suicidal gesture. This, I think, is the sense of the spectral Wilson's final remark: "*In me didst thou exist*—and, in my death, see by this image, which is thine own, how utterly thou hast murdered thyself" (448).

The mechanism of self-destruction initiated by dread receives further elaboration in three related tales of crime, "The Tell-Tale Heart," "The Black Cat," and "The Imp of the Perverse." None of these works involves an explicit act of retribution, unless it be the narrator's attempt in "The Black Cat" to avenge his imagined persecution by the feline. Their importance to the unfolding concept of revenge lies rather in the revelation of a mind radically divided against itself. In these tales we find a series of rational confessions by crazed murderers, whose natures are not simply "double" (as in Bird's "criminal/cop" model) but pathologically opposed. Here the narrator's relationship to his victim is almost incidental to the perverse scheme by which each contrives to commit a perfect crime and then to insure his own execution through spontaneous confession. The strategy of murder—premeditated in "The Tell-Tale Heart" and "The Imp of the Perverse," more impromptu in "The Black Cat"— reflects a compulsion to exhibit intellectual superiority by carrying out a scandalous crime with sangfroid and precision in a way which deceives police and public while assuring one's impunity. But each murderer also betrays himself, as if the urge to prove one's sagacity through a private act also contains within itself the contradictory need to have the deed publicly acknowledged, even at the cost of self-destruction.

This mechanism of self-betrayal discloses its psychic origins in "The Tell-Tale Heart." The narrator supposes that his murder of the old man is gratuitous ("Object there was none"), but he nevertheless explains how the man's "vulture" eye, "a pale blue eye, with a film over it," has excited his homicidal ingenuity: "Whenever it fell upon me, my blood ran cold; and so by degrees—very gradually—I made up my mind to take the life of the old man, and thus rid myself of the eye forever" (*CW*, 3:792). His rationale makes a strange kind of sense, for the crime is ultimately rooted in death anxiety: the "vulture" reference indirectly evokes the idea of carrion, while the film over the eye recalls the glassy look of the dead, the "glaze . . . impossible to feign," as Emily Dickinson writes. To rid himself of the eye and the terror which it represents, the narrator contrives a plot of ironic deception: "I was never kinder to the old man than during the whole week before I killed him." Nightly he rehearses the crime, hoping to see the "Evil Eye," and daily he feigns solicitude: "And every morning, when the day broke, I went boldly into the chamber, and spoke courageously to him, calling him by name in a hearty tone, and inquiring how he had passed the night" (793). His stealth gives him a heady sense of his "powers" and "sagacity"; the secret rehearsal creates the illusion of mastery over dread.

The analytical side of the narrator has in effect determined to rid itself of the fearful, mortal side by destroying its projected symbol. Poe implies this unconscious motive through the narrator's deliberate excitation of horror during his last and fatal visit to the old man's room: "Presently I heard a slight groan, and I knew it was the groan of mortal terror. It was not a groan of pain or of grief—oh, no!—it was the low stifled sound that arises from the bottom of the soul when overcharged with awe. I knew the sound well. Many a night, just at midnight, when all the world slept, it has welled up from my own bosom, deepening, with its dreadful echo, the terrors that distracted me" (794). For the narrator, the old man epitomizes that portion of his own being vulnerable to midnight terrors. When he opens a crack in his lantern (repeating the gesture of William Wilson), he sees the vulture eye, "with a hideous veil over it that chilled the very marrow in [his] bones" (795). This emblem of death, coupled with the old man's mortal terror and his groan of pain, stirs the narrator's *own* death anxieties; when he hears the "hellish tattoo" of the victim's heart, he too feels overwhelmed by fear: "And now, at the dead hour of the night, amid the dreadful silence of that old house, so strange a noise as this excited me to uncontrollable terror." Precisely to rid himself of this dread, the narrator kills the old man at "the dead hour of the night" because the hour of midnight corresponds to the onset of his own distracting terrors; he dismembers the corpse—as if to deconstruct the horror of death—and conceals the remains beneath the floor to repress forever the anxiety associated with the victim and his Evil Eye.

The narrator shortly finds himself in the grip of a different compulsion, however. When the three police officers arrive, he welcomes their search "in the wild audacity of [his] perfect triumph." But the triumph is not perfect, for it has missed its real target. The *"low, dull, quick sound,"* presumably the ticking of a death-watch beetle in the wall, becomes confused with the memory of the "hellish tattoo" of the old man's heart and evokes once again the narrator's own fear of annihilation. His frenzy at the imagined sound may represent the outpouring of guilt; but again (as in "William Wilson") Poe's emphasis is less on the problem of conscience than on the nature of psychotic obsession. For the narrator, the killing of the old man was an indirect plot to kill himself, to eradicate the death-haunted alter ego to whom he is bound in a fatal, schizophrenic relation. Robert Jay Lifton's analysis of the schizophrenic's response to death illuminates Poe's characterization: "In schizophrenia, unlike the other conditions [neuroses], the imagery of annihilation is likely to dominate all constellations of the self. The schizophrenic lives in 'a world pervaded by the threat of destruction.' To counter this threat, he may himself destroy. Very often his target of destruction or 'murder' is his own self."[13] The imagined beating of the old man's heart becomes a tormenting sign of failure; unable to destroy his fearful self by killing another, the narrator has only one way to complete his suicidal project—to confess his crime and assure his execution. "I admit the deed," he shrieks, "tear up the planks!—here, here!—it is the beating of his hideous heart!" (797). But of course the irrepressible organ belongs to the narrator, whose willingness to tear up the planks marks a last, desperate attempt to lay bare his "hideous heart" and thus to silence its "dreadful echo."

In a recent theoretical excursus on "The Tell-Tale Heart," Robert Con Davis has reached a similar conclusion about the crime as an instance of repressed death-obsession. Using the model of the Lacanian "Gaze," which explores the unconscious convergence of subject-object relations in the act of seeing, Davis shows how the narrator and the old man are bound together by the voyeuristic fear of being seen—ultimately—by that Death which stalks "with his black shadow before him." Transforming this absence into a "totemic presence, an imaginary object," the narrator aims to protect himself from the deadly gaze: "In the terrified old man's 'vulture eye,' 'his Evil Eye,' Death will emerge as an object visible and present to the narrator—capable of being mastered." His strategy fails because at the moment of expected revelation, the veiled eye discloses only an absence, holding the narrator "in the gaze of that which he sought to grasp." Davis contends that the murder derives from the need to destroy differences within the triadic relationship constituted by the narrator, the old man, and death—to efface the positionality of the Gaze. Through the crime the narrator "expresses what amounts to a desire for death. The killing of the old man simultaneously negates this desire and satisfies it in that the narrator destroys difference by deferring its inscription." Yet this mechanism of self-destruction is set in motion by the narrator's inability to naturalize or accommodate the "irreducible difference" of death; the murder and dismemberment of the Other only creates anew the need to displace the anxiety of difference.[14]

Both "The Black Cat" and "The Imp of the Perverse" recount similar crimes of self-destruction. In the former tale, Poe identifies perverseness as a patently self-directed impulse which motivates the murder of the cat: "It was this unfathomable longing of the soul *to vex itself*—to offer violence to its own nature—to do wrong for the wrong's sake only—that urged me to continue and finally to consummate the injury I had inflicted upon the unoffending brute" (*CW*, 3:852). The action has as its object the ruination of the soul, the repudiation of hope for a heavenly afterlife. Like Hawthorne's Ethan Brand, the narrator seeks to commit "a deadly sin that would so jeopardize [his] immortal soul as to place it—if such a thing were possible—even beyond the reach of the infinite mercy of the Most Merciful and Most Terrible God" (852). This wish to inflict upon the self an everlasting death manifests itself in violent behavior toward others. The immediate focus of the narrator's hostility is his "favorite cat," Pluto, whose eye he gouges out in a fit of rage. Not content with disfiguring the animal, the narrator then admits, "One morning, in cold blood, I slipped a noose about its neck and hung it to the limb of a tree." The gesture is extravagant and revealing: Lifton notes that the schizophrenic, in response to "grandiose (paranoid) images, delusions, and hallucinations," frequently resorts to "caricature" to mock his own imagined death.[15] The motif of hanging holds the key to the narrator's fixations upon destruction; on the day of the animal's death, a fire produces a strange bas-relief image on a plaster wall, the figure of a "gigantic cat" with a rope about its neck—or so the narrator perceives it.

The idea of hanging returns like the material of a recurrent nightmare. When the narrator obtains a second black cat, he notices that a patch of white fur on the animal's breast has assumed a "rigorous distinctness of outline": "It was now the representation of an object that I shudder to name—and for this, above all, I loathed, and dreaded, and would have rid myself of the monster *had I dared*—it was now, I say, the image of a hideous—of a ghastly thing—of the GALLOWS!—oh, mournful and terrible engine of Horror and of Crime—of Agony and of Death!" (855). This instrument of execution now emerges as the ultimate source of the narrator's awe; he both dreads the gallows and longs to inflict "Agony and Death" upon his monstrous other self. His unpremeditated murder of his wife—a crime of blind rage rather than calculation—leads to the self-incriminating Freudian mistake of walling up with her corpse the still living black cat. Like the "hideous heart" that will not stop beating, the cat functions as a sign of irrepressible terror, urging upon the narrator its insistent meaning and driving him to confess his deed to complete his own perverse strategy of self-destruction. "The Black Cat" presents itself as a death row confession, penned on the eve of the narrator's execution; he writes to "unburthen" his soul but still does not comprehend the events which "have terrified—have tortured—have destroyed" him. He fails to see that it is not the "hideous beast" but his craving for self-punishment that has "consigned [him] to the hangman."

The key to his death wish may be contained in his associations with the two cats, both of which are black, have only one eye, and become objects of loathing. Their similarity suggests a repetition mechanism, an insistent phantasmic manifestation of the phenomenon they unconsciously represent. The implicit psychic meaning is self-evident: one cat is named Pluto, reminding us of the underworld of death; the other carries the sign of mortality, the gallows. The narrator's cruelty toward them is a displaced violence, through which (as Becker explains) desire for death translates into aggression: "Human aggressiveness comes about through a fusion of the life instinct and the death instinct. The death instinct represents the organism's desire to die, but the organism can save itself from its own impulsion toward death by redirecting it outward. The desire to die, then, is replaced by the desire to kill, and man defeats his own death instinct by killing others."[16] But this ostensible victory over death is cancelled by the very action which seems to inflict defeat, for the cost of the deed is the criminal's death. Poe implies that the act of murder is always reflexive, always the symptom of an irresistible but deflected urge to die, always a perverse stratagem for resolving the agonizing problem of one's own mortality. The action of "The Black Cat" neatly illustrates Karl Menninger's concept of suicide as "the death penalty self-inflicted."[17]

Similarly, "The Imp of the Perverse" registers the confession of a condemned criminal who has spontaneously betrayed himself. Although less complex than "The Black Cat," the story develops an idea adumbrated elsewhere in Poe—not the principle of "perverseness" (which is merely repeated) but the notion of the perfect crime. The narrator says of the murder he commits: "It is impossible that any deed could have been wrought with a more thorough deliberation. For weeks, for months, I pondered upon the means of the murder. I rejected a thousand schemes, because their accomplishment involved a *chance* of detection" (CW, 3:1224). To escape detection is to defeat the ratiocinative mind and in some sense to escape responsibility for one's actions; it is inherently an exercise in intellectual self-gratification, a defiance of sacred as well as social law. Following DeQuincey, Poe contemplated an aesthetics of murder, in which—as Joseph Moldenhauer has argued—the perfect crime arises from a desire for ideality, the absolute realization of a mental construct.[18] But Poe's criminal-artists are also schizoid, incapable of reconciling their conflicting desires; and so the perfect crime remains unachievable. If the act of murder involves the attempt to destroy that part of the self which suffers mortal anxiety, then the criminal's mistake (the incriminating clue, the perverse disclosure) betrays an unconscious identification with the victim, who is inevitably a symbolic substitute for the true object of the violence, the killer himself. There is always a trace of complicity, a sign of filiation between the murderer and the corpse. To commit the perfect crime is to efface the relational identity, to effect a total dissociation of the self from its double, so that the act of violence does not follow its inevitable circular route back to the perpetrator. It is to destroy the doomed, mortal self with impunity, so that the sagacious, godlike self can be free of its nemesis. But as the narrator of "The Imp of the Perverse" discovers, the perfect crime cannot eliminate the connection between the murderer and his victim, which is inscribed in the memory of the crime and the bond of mortality it recalls.

The concept of the fatal bond brings us at last to "The Cask of Amontillado," that most tightly wound of Poe's narratives of obsession, which consolidates the poetics of revenge and underscores the linguistic nature of violence. Here we have a tale of confession, implicitly the testimony of a man who has for fifty years been unable to forget his cunning crime; here we encounter the murder of a double to even a score; here too emerges an elaborate strategy of mystification and deception, meant to exhibit the genius of the perpetrator; here we witness the imposition of a fatal silence, broken only by the belated telling of the tale. Appropriately, this story brings us back to the correlative of Poe's literary life, for as several scholars have observed, "The Cask of Amontillado" is a product of Poe's war with the New York literati in the 1840s and in some sense embodies the author's desire to avenge the attacks of Hiram Fuller and Thomas Dunn English.[19] To read the story solely as a gloss on Poe's literary battles, however, is to miss much of its intricacy as a critique of revenge. Here the mechanism of rivalry discloses its self-consuming fatality as Poe confronts the implications of those violent motifs ingrained in his writing.

The author grounds the feud between Fortunato and Montresor in an immemorial antagonism: "The thousand injuries of Fortunato I had borne as best I could" (CW, 3:1256). Presumably Montresor has returned many of these injuries to perpetuate the cycle of vengeance, though he implies that he has merely endured them. But now Fortunato has "ventured upon insult," and Montresor takes this literally as a mortal affront, punishable by death. He vows to take revenge in a way that will be definitive and theorizes about the nature of ideal retribution: "I must not only punish, but punish with impunity. A wrong is unredressed when retribution overtakes its redresser. It is equally unredressed when the avenger fails to make himself felt as such to him who has done the wrong." Perfect revenge precludes the possibility of response, and the victim must recognize both the futility of his situation and its retributive nature. In this way the avenger achieves the triple satisfaction of knowing that he has (1) "punished" the wrongdoer; (2) insured himself against subsequent injury; and (3) demonstrated to the adversary his superior intellect. Montresor's idea of revenge casts light on Dupin's triumph over the Minister D____, and it obliges us to examine "The Cask of Amontillado" as a culmination of Poe's thinking about retaliation.

For the narrative presents abundant evidence of a complex strategy, developed at length to eliminate the possibility of risk. Montresor's scheme depends first on ironic doubleness; the avenger adopts a manner precisely the opposite of his real intentions: "It must be understood that neither by word nor deed had I given Fortunato cause to doubt my good will. I continued, as was my wont, to smile in his face, and he did not perceive that my smile *now* was at the thought of his immolation" (1257). This duplicity of demeanor calls to mind the tactics of Von Jung, the visits of Dupin to the Minister D____, and the cheerfulness of the narrator in "The Tell-Tale Heart." Secondly, the strategy depends upon a shrewd analysis of the rival to discover his special vulnerability. Montresor remarks of his nemesis: "He had a weak point—this Fortunato—although in other regards he was a man to be respected and even feared. He prided himself on his connoisseurship in wine." Like Hermann, the self-styled expert in dueling, and the Minister D____, the bold *intriguant* who "dares all things," Fortunato too has his fatal vanity. The avenger's insight comes from a studied identification with his counterpart, an emulation that has (as we shall see) unforeseen consequences.

The strategy of revenge next requires a trap, formulated to exploit the adversary's weakness. But to demonstrate the acuity of the avenger, the snare must be so devised that the victim falls into it by choice, thinking that he is proving his *own* intelligence. And the trap must involve an element of play: the victim must *have* a choice. Coercion has no place in perfect revenge, for the victim must realize belatedly that he has trapped himself. This realization occurs as a moment of *anagnorisis* in the Aristotelian sense, for the victim discovers at the source of his downfall an ineluctable *hubris*. The trap reveals the ascendancy of the avenger with the victim's awareness that he can neither extricate himself from his predicament nor retaliate in kind. Finally, the scheme must silence the enemy, denying even the limited retaliation of the retort. This foreclosure of language may result from the slaying of one's nemesis, but its more satisfying realization occurs through a humiliating predicament that shuts up the victim both literally and figuratively. The dupe discovers that his situation is unspeakable: there is no one to whom he can appeal and no one else to blame for his misfortune.

There is ample evidence of contrivance to achieve the sort of revenge outlined above. When the old rivals reach the underground niche destined to be the site of the inhumation, Fortunato finds himself suddenly fettered by a chain and padlock recently installed for the crime. Montresor then uncovers "a quantity of building stone and mortar" readied for the occasion. And he draws from his cloak the trowel used earlier as an ironic claim of Masonic confraternity with Fortunato. These revelations leave the victim in a condition of mystification: he is said to be "stupidly bewildered" and "astounded" by his abrupt confinement. But these are only the most obvious marks of premeditation. Montresor has already provided a series of subtle clues which in prefiguring his deadly intentions seem to mock Fortunato's dullness, his ineptitude as a reader of signs. Montresor carries out his crime during the carnival season, perhaps to mask his activity or to insinuate through the convention of masking the duplicitous nature of his invitation to Fortunato. Poe notes too that as the two descend into the family vault, the narrator pulls over his face a mask of black silk, as if signaling his role as an executioner. The location of the Amontillado—deep in the catacombs amid the dead—also points toward the fatality of the scheme; Montresor appears to have chosen the site because it epitomizes the decline of his own family, a decline for which he implicitly holds Fortunato and his family accountable. When Fortunato drinks a draught of Médoc "to the buried that repose around us," Montresor ironically toasts his adversary's "long life." Later Montresor offers Fortunato a drink of the wine whose name (in English) portends entombment: "De Grâve."

Drink becomes associated with death in the physical arrangement of the vault: "We had passed through walls of piled bones, with casks and puncheons intermingling" (1260). In a recess of suspicious dimensions, located within a "deep crypt . . . lined with human remains," Montresor claims to have placed the sherry: "Herein is the Amontillado." At this point the Amontillado reveals its metaphoricity; for Montresor the drink has been from the outset a secret, figurative reference to death itself, and in promising a taste of Amontillado, he has of course been speaking of Fortunato's destruction. The very name of the drink may punningly allude to the victim's fate, for as Charles W. Steele has suggested, the repeated references to Amontillado play on the Italian word *ammonticchiato,* meaning "collected in a heap" (*CW,* 3:1265n18). Although Mabbott associated this phrase with the pile of bricks (actually building stones) uncovered by Montresor, the pun operates more daringly as a hint of death in relation to the bones lining the catacombs, especially the heap which marks the site of immurement: "From the fourth [side] the bones had been thrown down, and lay promiscuously upon the earth, forming at one point a mound of some size. Within the wall thus exposed by the displacing of the bones, we perceived a still interior recess, in depth about four feet, in width three, in height six or seven" (1261). Montresor has apparently "collected in a heap" the remains of his ancestors to make room for Fortunato's bones; the pun on Amontillado captures the irony of the latter's fate (to die among one's enemies) and its repetition taunts the victim to discern the veiled signification. Steele notes that at the climactic moment Montresor causes Fortunato to repeat the name of the drink a final time, as if to allow him one more opportunity to grasp the deadly pun. This word play confirms the metaphorical purpose of the sherry and discloses the verbal subtlety of the game by which Montresor means to take revenge.

But despite the flawless execution of his scheme, the narrator in telling his story betrays a lingering anxiety. Though half a century has elapsed since the deed, his precise recollections indicate that Montresor has been haunted by his memory of the crime if not by a theological sense of guilt. Whether or not he is telling his story to a confessor (the "you" of the second sentence), he has clearly become a victim himself, the psychological captive of his own perfect strategy. The anxiety which evokes the story and calls into question the avenger's impunity seems rooted in Fortunato's last words, his desperate effort to laugh off his mortal predicament as a "very good joke." Montresor's repetition of the victim's phrases—"Let us be gone" and "For the love of God"—reveals the essential paradox of revenge, for the echoing suggests the intense mimetic involvement of the murderer with his prey. The strategic need to acquire intimate knowledge of the nemesis, to identify with his mind and sensibility, creates an ironic bond. This reciprocity asserts itself on the level of discourse in the give-and-take between the adversaries, who provide each other with a series of playful replies. Each defines the role of the other, and the opposites begin to merge, a point suggested by their names. Montresor and Fortunato, treasure and fortune, become at last indistinguishable.

This relationship is broken, however, by the silencing of Fortunato, whose last utterance torments the narrator:

> "For the love of God, Montresor!"
> "Yes," I said, "for the love of God!"
> But to these words I hearkened in vain for a reply. I grew impatient. I called aloud—
> "Fortunato!"
> No answer. I called again—
> "Fortunato!"
> No answer still. I thrust a torch through the remaining aperture and let it fall within. There came forth in return only a jingling of the bells. My heart grew sick—on account of the dampness of the catacombs. [1263]

Montresor's sickness of heart is indeed prompted by the dampness of the catacombs, for his identification with Fortunato compels him to share the horror of living inhumation. The victim's silence affects him as no verbal reply could, for it signifies the silence of mortality and foretokens his own death. Like William Wilson, he discovers in the killing of his hated double the price which retribution—even the most flawlessly conceived—exacts from the perpetrator. The victim of revenge is invariably the self; silence always prefigures its own return.

In representing the anxiety of silence, "The Cask of Amontillado" registers Poe's awareness of the destructive circularity of revenge. As we know, the author was at the time of composition in the midst of a vicious literary war with Hiram Fuller and Thomas Dunn English; to see Poe as Montresor and English as Fortunato does not, however, elucidate the tactics of reprisal, much less account for the ironic insistence of the remembered crime.[20] In developing a theory of revenge, a project stretching over a dozen years, Poe was responding less to momentary irritations or particular personalities than to an inveterate sense of persecution and injustice, grounded in his notion that (as he said in the "Literati" papers) "quacks" always had an apparent advantage in profit and public esteem over "men of genius." And in a deeper sense he was probing the metaphoricity of the word-wound and locating the origins of violence in death anxiety.

Yet his last tale of vengeance, "Hop-Frog," dispensed with the verbal subtlety and intellectual play inscribed in earlier tales. Here the avenger occupies the role of freak and outcast; he is the "little man," whose grotesque strategy enables him to triumph over power, wealth, and brutality. There is no sense that in taking revenge Hop-Frog has slain a double, acted out a desire for self-punishment, or imposed a silence of symbolic import. The dwarf realizes a retribution uncomplicated by guilt or memory, as he transforms the king and his privy-councillors into "a fetid, blackened, hideous, and indistinguishable mass" (CW, 3:1354). In "Hop-Frog" Poe effaced the psychic complications of violence to articulate a fantasy of revenge with impunity. But the happily-ever-after ending betrays the fairy tale; only in a purely imaginary world, Poe seems to acknowledge, can one silence an enemy and escape the consequences.

The tales of adversarial relationship conversely suggest that consequences follow because the enemy is always one's self; conflict and aggression metaphorize a fatal schism within the self. If, as Michael Davitt Bell remarks, "the essential Poe fable . . . is a tale of compulsive self-murder," that compulsion appears to spring from the need to destroy the counterpart who incarnates our human frailty.[21] As we see most clearly in "The Tell-Tale Heart," the urge to murder ultimately derives from the midnight terrors, the existential dread afflicting the murderer. Surely the craving for intellectual ascendancy from "Mystification" to "The Cask of Amontillado" arises from a related fear of defeat, silence, or mortification—versions of symbolic death. The effort to resolve the metaphysical problem through verbal revenge manifests the desire to displace anxiety, to escape mortality through an act of angelism. Allen Tate has observed that Poe "thinks of language as a potential source of quasi-divine power" through which he can construct fantasies of transcendence and control.[22] In the tales examined here, the defeat of an adversary hinges on a dispossession of the word; the protagonist claims for himself the prerogatives of language, thus denying the fate of silence which he has imposed on his nemesis. Yet the very effort to secure life through an appropriation of language condemns the criminal to a sentence, an act of writing, a death-house confession (or its equivalent), in which inscription already signifies that absence or fatality which the writer had sought through vengeance to avoid. "Words—printed ones especially—are murderous things," and through the act of writing by which they make known their secret deeds, Poe's narrators assume a textuality which completes the perverse self-destruction of the speaking subject.

6

Unreadable Books, Unspeakable Truths

Longer and more troubling than any other work in the Poe corpus, *The Narrative of Arthur Gordon Pym* has become the pivotal text in current discussions of the author. The notable discontinuities which thwart conventional explication have engendered several recent studies concerned with the novel's self-referential aspects. In important ways, *Pym* calls into question key theoretical relationships: between writer and reader; between text and meaning; between language and truth. We have come to understand the narrator's voyage as a series of interpretive crises which collectively suggest the unreadability of the signs constituted by nature and culture. And when we recall that Von Jung, in "Mystification," referred his adversary to a book "ingeniously framed so as to present to the ear all the outward signs of intelligibility, and even of profundity, while in fact not a shadow of meaning existed," it is hard to resist the notion that Poe was slyly alluding to his strategy in *Pym*. [1] In this chapter I want to explore the implications of illegibility, focusing first on the nature of the hermeneutic dilemma which the reader shares with Pym, and then shifting attention to the metaphysical crux of this impasse. The narrator's abortive quest for meaning seems ultimately related to his progressive immersion in the phenomenology of death; Pym's rehearsals for death and his confrontations with the body of death epitomize the unreadability of lived experience as they disclose the origins of radical uncertainty.

Like "MS. Found in a Bottle," *Pym* stages the progressive disorientation of a narrator who disappears within a fold of the text he is said to inscribe. But far more explicitly than the short story, the novel challenges its own textual status by flaunting its problematic "authenticity"; the narrator successively discovers the unstable or illusory nature of sensory perception, rational thought, social order, and divine providence. He finds the world pervaded by a violence that discloses only the precariousness of life and the imminence of death. Amid horror and despair, only writing seems to provide a source of coherency; Pym sustains identity by registering the ordeal of self-preservation. But finally writing too reveals its provisionality: Pym vanishes in the white vortex, the victim of textual necessity or authorial whim. His fate reminds us (like Borges's "The Circular Ruins") that one never knows whether he is the creator of a dream or the effect of someone else's dream.

If the novel refuses to yield a consistent, unifying meaning, contemporary criticism has nevertheless noted suggestive repetitions within the text. The present effort to deconstruct uncertainty in *Pym* builds upon two principal insights into its recurrent figurality. The first derives from the early work of Patrick Quinn, who has characterized *Pym* as a "profoundly oneiric drama" dominated by "the pattern of recurrent revolt" and by "the theme of deception." Quinn maintains that rebellion and duplicity parallel an ongoing conflict between appearance and reality: "Pym is caught up in a life in which nothing is stable, in which nothing is ever really known."[2] Edward Davidson has subsequently reinforced the idea that deception in Poe's novel is inherent in "the very construction of the world itself," forcing upon Pym the realization that "everything, even the most logically substantial, is an illusion."[3] The perception of Pym's voyage as a metaphor for intellectual or imaginative discovery has clarified the epistemological matrix of the novel and shifted attention to the philosophical crisis figured by the narrator's perplexity. But both Quinn and Davidson assumed that their respective readings bracketed an intelligible thematic consistency. Neither considered the text itself as an extension of the radical confusion represented within its pages. Consequently neither had much to say about internal, narratorial contradictions or about the framing notes which—as we shall discuss later—render the entire narrative problematic.

The second metaphorical implication has been located in the last decade as a result of poststructuralist inquiries into the self-sustaining and self-referential nature of writing, particularly the *écriture* characteristic of modernism. *Pym* has become focal for theoretical critics because it calls attention to its own insufficiency as a written text, raises the question of how writing can—under any circumstances—represent truth, and demonstrates through narrative action the slippery relationship between inscription and meaning, sign and referent. Jean Ricardou initiated this reconsideration of *Pym* with his observation that the narrator's adventure allegorizes a voyage "au bout de la page," which in its black-white oppositions forms "une dramatisation de l'antagonisme encre-feuille." Ricardou concludes that in symbolizing the movement toward the end of the written page, the very gesture by which it has been constituted, *Pym* illustrates the way in which modernist writing evokes a material world only to mirror its own textual strategies. A subsequent essay by John Carlos Rowe has probed the "metaliterary" aspect of the novel: "This text enacts the deconstruction of representation as the illusion of the truth and prefigures the contemporary conception of writing as the endless production of differences." Rowe sees Pym's voyage as the journey toward a "metaphysical" center which is endlessly "displaced, disrupted, deferred" by "the very effort of writing such a story." Likewise, John Irwin projects the narrator's voyage as a search for the origins of language in the mythic emergence of human self-consciousness. But by placing in doubt the credibility of the narrator, the novel—in Irwin's view—forces us to contemplate the inability of language to deliver primary truths: "Since in a narrative the certainty of our knowledge seems to rest upon the credibility of the narrator, putting the latter in question puts the former in question, thereby directing our attention to the coincidence between the limits of knowledge and the limits of the written discourse."[4]

Irwin's remark suggests the point at which earlier discussions of revolt and deception begin to intersect with more recent commentaries on the self-referential nature of *Pym*. It now seems clear that the narrative itself partakes of the metaphysical crisis which it represents; whatever confusions of purpose inhere in its chaotic plot and brutal images, *Pym* in some sense reflects upon the life of writing and the profound indeterminacy of texts. As the narrator struggles to record the "truth" of his adventures by translating remembered scenes into verbal signs, he inadvertently betrays both his own inability to "read" the text of phenomenal experience and the incapacity of language to register its overwhelming nature. And beyond the anxieties of writing consciously noted by Pym, Poe permits us to apprehend problems and inconsistencies of which the narrator is unaware; by casting doubt (in the concluding note) on "the entire truth of the latter portions of the narration," the author forces us to regard the narrator and the narrative as elements of a colossal deception, a plot against the reader.

Poe initiates his covert reflections on the hazards of reading and writing in the introductory note. Here, the putative narrator identifies two obstacles which have supposedly delayed the composition of the text: Pym says he doubted his ability "to write, from mere memory, a statement so minute and connected as to have the *appearance* of that truth it would really possess"; and he feared that the incidents to be related were "of a nature so positively marvellous" that the public would regard his account as "merely an impudent and ingenious fiction." These remarks express a surface concern for the relationship between language and truth and assume the possibility of a verifiable correspondence between words and facts which can be distinguished from the spurious referentiality of fiction. But both comments also undercut the notion of a distinction between truth and fiction. In suggesting the difficulty of affecting the *appearance* of the truth inherent in his statement, Pym acknowledges a potential slippage between remembered experience and its verbal reconstruction. Here Poe subtly insinuates that appearance and reality may not coincide, and that if fact can have the look of fiction, fiction can surely masquerade as fact. The truth of a memory (itself an indeterminate criterion) cannot insure the impression of truthfulness. Ironically, Pym implies that his task is to create through "minute and connected" detail that illusion of truth which the writer of fiction would call verisimilitude. His remark contains a further irony insofar as Poe covertly signals the controlling strategy of the hoax: to contrive the appearance of truth in a statement which possesses no grounding in fact. Pym's ostensible concern that his narrative will be perceived as "an impudent and ingenious fiction" likewise adverts to its actual nature. Through the mask of "A. G. Pym," Poe alludes to an underlying objective—to produce an ingenious deception—while evincing a high-minded concern for its reception as truth.

Poe confuses the issue of truth further when Pym recalls the counsel of "Mr. Poe," formerly of the *Southern Literary Messenger:* "He strongly advised me, among others, to prepare at once a full account of what I had seen and undergone, and trust to the shrewdness and common sense of the public—insisting, with great plausibility, that however roughly, as regards mere authorship, my book should be got up, its very uncouthness, if there were any, would give it all the better chance of being received as truth" (*IV*, 1:55–56). Here the true author fictionalizes himself to enforce the impression that his narrator is an actual, living personage. Behind the pretense of complimenting the public on its collective "shrewdness and common sense," Poe manifests scorn for readers disposed to regard "uncouthness" as a sign of truth. And once again he insinuates his underlying tactic—to produce the sense of authenticity through an affected crudeness—with the impunity of one who knows that his irony will not be discerned by those at whom it is directed. The author's implied mockery bears out the accuracy of Daniel Hoffman's remark that "for Poe, satire serves to display the follies of mankind— and the personal superiority of the Artist-Genius to the generality of fools."[5] In the guise of Pym, who later proves to be a caricature of the American fool, Poe intimates that the reading public cannot possibly distinguish between fact and fable.

As if to give the problem of truth one last twist, the preface refers finally to the two installments of the narrative published earlier in the

Messenger as the work of Poe. Obviously the author had to manufacture some explanation for the prior association of his own name with the story of Pym's adventures. Accordingly, Pym explains how "Mr. Poe" induced him to supply "facts" which were then published "*under the garb of fiction.*" Poe's name was attached to the pretended fiction, he adds, so that it would be received as an invention by readers of the magazine. But the ruse backfired: despite the "air of fable" introduced by Mr. Poe, "the public were still not at all disposed to receive it as fable." Here real fiction is characterized as pretended fiction to bolster the illusion of its factuality; but in retrospect we see that the only pretense is Poe's attempt to pass off the magazine installments as a deceit. Indeed, Pym's explanation of how "fact" was palmed off as fiction by the use of Poe's name merely reverses the strategy of the longer narrative.

In accounting for the decision to compose his statement, Pym reports that many clever readers saw through the *Messenger* ploy because the "facts" of his narrative carried with them "sufficient evidence of their own authenticity." He implies that truth is inherent in the notation of detail and circumstance, an exactness of observation couched in verbal signs and yet somehow independent of style— for the "air of fable" evoked by "Mr. Poe" has not changed "a single fact." With this declaration the author arrives at the philosophical crux of the preface, the relation of the written text to the truth (or truths) which it purports to record. By equating truth with fact, Pym implies that the presence of verifiable data establishes the truth of a text quite apart from stylistic eccentricities or fabricated details. Yet this argument obscures the fact that writing always involves the representation of appearances. Even the simplest declarative sentence ("the sun is shining") refers not to a pure, immanent fact but to what the speaker or writer wishes his audience to construe as a fact. For example, the semblance of precision and objectivity in Pym's later notation, "At noon of this day we were in latitude 78° 30′, longitude 40° 15′ W," hides the reality that these verbal and numerical signs contain no inherent validity and manifest instead only the desire of a writer to represent himself in such a situation. Writing may convey facts—truths confirmable by both writer and reader—but the actual marks upon the page constitute neither truth nor fiction. They merely point to phenomena which might be empirically true. But the truth of which Pym speaks lies forever outside the text, beyond the field of writing. In effect, Poe evokes the concept of the fact to sustain the illusion of legitimacy and authority which facts produce in a culture that prizes rational, scientific discourse—such as travelogues of the kind emulated by *Pym*. As the novel itself demonstrates, however, any textual distinction between truth and fiction must remain intractably problematic.

The interpretive questions raised in the preface rapidly assume concrete form. As the narrative opens, Poe establishes a paradoxical persona: a young man who is simultaneously innocent and devious, a perpetual victim of misleading appearances and a participant in countless deceptions. His ingenuous recitation of family history (a standard feature of the imaginary voyage) leads to a preliminary episode in which Pym fails to perceive the intoxication of his friend Augustus and so nearly loses his life in a nighttime caper aboard the *Ariel*. But Pym is "resuscitated from a state bordering very nearly upon death," and he manages to hide from his family the effects of a ghastly neck wound, blithely remarking that "school-boys . . . can accomplish wonders in the way of deception." This back-and-forth movement between blindness and dissimulation in the *Ariel* sequence typifies the contradictory nature of Pym, who freely admits his predisposition to trickery even as he solicits the confidence of the reader. Alternately deceiving others and being deceived by his own impercipience, the narrator fails to recognize a connection between his duplicity and the treachery inherent in phenomenal experience. Yet this failure of insight makes possible the more comprehensive deception perpetrated by Poe. For Pym's inability to discern analogies between his contrivances and the plots of others (like the natives of Tsalal) or the more incomprehensible scheme of nature itself conceals the analogical relationship between those deceptions which occur as events in the narrative and those "quizzes" encountered by its reader. This theoretical distinction becomes clearer when we examine Pym's relationship to the fraudulent letter by which he covers his departure from home.

Written and possibly delivered by Pym's counterpart, Augustus, the note, supposedly from a Mr. Ross in New Bedford, invites Pym to spend a fortnight with his sons, Robert and Emmet. The stratagem succeeds, and shortly after the letter's arrival, Pym departs to begin his long adventure. Everything about the missive hints at its double nature: the invitation to spend two weeks with two boys actually enables two other boys to go to sea together. Three chapters later— after Pym experiences living burial as a stowaway—we find that the letter is itself the duplicate of an earlier forgery duplicating the hand-writing of Mr. Ross. This fact comes to light when Augustus accounts for the note warning Pym of the mutiny above decks:

> Having concluded to write, the difficulty was now to procure the materials for so doing. An old toothpick was soon made into a pen; and this by means of feeling altogether, for the between-decks were as dark as pitch. Paper enough was obtained from the back of a letter—a duplicate of the forged letter from Mr. Ross. This had been the original draught; but the handwriting not being suffi-ciently well imitated, Augustus had written another, thrusting the first, by good fortune, into his coat-pocket, where it was now most opportunely discovered. Ink alone was thus wanting, and a sub-stitute was immediately found for this by means of a slight incision with the penknife on the back of a finger just above the nail—a copious flow of blood ensuing, as usual from wounds in that vicinity. The note was now written, as well as it could be in the dark and under the circumstances. It briefly explained that a muti-ny had taken place; that Captain Barnard was set adrift; and that I might expect immediate relief as far as provisions were concerned, but must not venture upon making any disturbance. It concluded with these words: *"I have scrawled this with blood—your life depends upon lying close."* [92]

This paragraph recreates a primal scene: writing emerges from darkness and blood, bearing a message of dire importance. Augustus must wound himself to inscribe the words which stand between Pym and death. Inscription entails the sacrifice of life's blood to produce the enduring, written word which sustains life and breaches the gap of silence (always potentially the void of death) between writer and reader.

Ironically, Augustus uses the reverse side of the duplicitous letter to indite his warning of treachery and danger; thus an instrument of betrayal becomes a means of salvation. Such at least is the writer's intent, but meaning is invariably hostage to the vagaries of reading, a problem already illustrated through the tortuous process by which Pym discovers the note and glimpses a portion of its fateful message. The first five paragraphs of chapter 3 in effect create a paradigm of unreadability, staging the crisis of interpretation recurrently encountered in *Pym*. In considerable detail Poe depicts first the finding of the note (which has been attached to Pym's dog, Tiger) and then his effort to discover an inscription by rubbing phosphorus on the paper:

> I placed the slip of paper on the back of a book, and, collecting the fragments of the phosphorus matches which I had brought from the barrel, laid them together upon the paper. I then, with the palm of my hand, rubbed the whole over quickly, yet steadily. A clear light diffused itself immediately throughout the whole surface; and had there been any writing upon it, I should not have experienced the least difficulty, I am sure, in reading it. Not a syllable was there, however—nothing but a dreary and unsatisfactory blank; the illumination died away in a few seconds, and my heart died away within me as it went. [78]

Failing to perceive a message, Pym tears up the note but later recovers the scraps to check the unexamined side. There he sees "several lines of MS. in a large hand," but ironically, in his desire to "read all at once," he can discern only the last seven words: "*blood—your life depends upon lying close.*" Pym observes that the entire message could not have aroused as much "indefinable horror" as this "fragmentary warning," for it is precisely the ambiguity of the communication which evokes panic. The disjointed reference to "mystery, and suffering, and terror" creates a "paroxysm of despair," as the narrator succumbs to interpretive anxiety. Without invoking the name of death, the cryptic message activates Pym's sense of dread; indeed, its uncertainty becomes a figure of the indecipherability of death. In this crucial scene, reading proves itself a risky business, literally an exercise in obscurity. Try as he might, Pym cannot grasp the entire message; writing and reading prove to be ineluctably separate activities, each the function of a subjectivity operating under different pressures at different times, struggling with an arbitrary and imperfect system of signs.

Even as he deconstructs the act of reading, Poe transposes the scene into an interpretive dilemma for the reader of *Pym*. For between the narrator's account of finding "a dreary and unsatisfactory blank" on one side of the paper and Augustus' explanation that he penned his message on the back of the original letter to Mr. Ross, Poe constructs an unresolvable contradiction. Instinctively, one dismisses the problem as an instance of authorial carelessness, for (as the recent edition by Burton Pollin has shown) the narrative is full of inaccuracies. Yet the puzzle bears the mark of intentionality: Poe incorporates a hint of his doubleness by locating a vital message on the reverse side of a duplicate of a forged letter. As I contended in an earlier essay, the letter from Augustus actually bears two messages, one visible and one invisible.[6] The seven words, *"blood—your life depends upon lying close,"* offer a fragmentary warning of revolt and deception, of the cruelty and illusoriness of the world. The blank side carries an equally unsettling message, which reveals to the alert observer (if not to Pym) our inescapable limitations as readers of texts. John Carlos Rowe has more recently commented on this supposed textual error: "The note demonstrates the difficulty of transcending the differential system of language to deliver a unified truth. The note is a palimpsest—*the* palimpsest of language itself, whose messages are always intertexts. Writing appears to defer the presence it desires by constituting a divided present that prefigures its own erasure. Meaning may be situated only within the functions produced by this play of differences."[7] Rowe implies that the unreadability of the invisible message is symptomatic of the "erasure" produced by the delay between writing and reading. But in another sense, the "dreary and unsatisfactory blank" constitutes the only possible representation of that silence which constitutes the obverse of language. What lies on the other side of the fragmentary warning—the reality of death as opposed to its verbal representation—must remain unreadable, for it is precisely the never-to-be-imparted secret, the inscrutable blankness toward which Pym is moving from the beginning of his voyage.

A later scene in *Pym*, overlooked by both Rowe and Irwin, grimly illustrates the way that Poe projects nature and phenomenal experience as an unintelligible text in which death figures as the ultimate cipher. Here Pym's encounter with a complex emblem of fatality brings the writer to the margins of discourse and the limits of intelligibility. The beginning of chapter 10 finds the narrator and Augustus—along with the half-breed Dirk Peters and a man named Parker—shipwrecked and clinging to the hulk of the *Grampus*. Hungry and exhausted by their ordeal, the men have unsuccessfully tried to recover some provisions from a submerged cabin. Suddenly Augustus spies a ship on the horizon; he turns pale, his lips begin to quiver "in the most singular and unaccountable manner," and he loses the power of speech. The appearance of the ship has the same effect on Pym: "I sprung to my feet as if a musket bullet had suddenly struck me to the heart; and, stretching out my arms in the direction of the vessel, stood in this manner, motionless, and unable to articulate a syllable" (122–23). Curiously, this image of apparent deliverance suppresses language and produces the sensation of sudden death.

Such a reversal appropriately introduces an episode defined by paradox and suffused by ironic inversions so overwhelming that language cannot represent their nature. For Pym and his companions encounter a ship littered with corpses—not the benign "ghosts of buried centuries" figured in "MS. Found in a Bottle" but rotting, stinking cadavers. As the vessel approaches, the castaways attribute its erratic movement to a helmsman "in liquor." And they fancy that a tall sailor on the bow is reassuring them: "He seemed by his manner to be encouraging us to have patience, nodding to us in a cheerful although rather odd way, and smiling constantly so as to display a set of the most brilliantly white teeth" (123). Here Poe depicts interpretation as flagrant self-delusion, for the reading posited by Pym turns out to be not only incorrect but also foolish in its assumption that phenomenal reality can be reduced to rational coherence. Significantly, the narrator's recognition of his misperception occurs within the context of a celebration of divine benevolence:

The brig came on slowly, and now more steadily than before, and—I cannot speak calmly of this event—our hearts leaped up wildly within us, and we poured out our whole souls in shouts and thanksgiving to God for the complete, unexpected, and glorious deliverance that was so palpably at hand. Of a sudden, and all at once, there came wafted over the ocean from the strange vessel (which was now close upon us) a smell, a stench, such as the whole world has no name for—no conception of—hellish—utterly suffocating—insufferable, inconceivable. [124]

In this passage as elsewhere in *Pym,* Poe inscribes the idea of providential order only to erase it with an instance of deception, violence, or death. The ship which seems to promise the castaways a "glorious deliverance," thereby furnishing a sign of God's mercy, reveals itself as a ghastly emblem of their corporeal fate. And the stench which turns Pym's attention from providence to putrefaction surpasses verbal expression: its nature is "inconceivable" and therefore unspeakable.

As the black ship sails past, Pym and the others discover the horrific reality signified by the stench. Here again Poe projects the desire of language to break the silence of death, even to establish a dialogue with the dead:

Shall I ever forget the triple horror of that spectacle? Twenty-five or thirty human bodies, among whom were several females, lay scattered about between the counter and the galley, in the last and most loathsome state of putrefaction! We plainly saw that not a soul lived in that fated vessel! Yet we could not help shouting to the dead for help! Yes, long and loudly did we beg, in the agony of the moment, that those silent and disgusting images would stay for us, would not abandon us to become like them, would receive us among their goodly company! [124]

As if unable to surrender their original, mistaken expectation of imminent rescue by the Dutch ship, the survivors of the *Grampus* paradoxically clamor to join the dead crew in order to preserve their own lives. They are simultaneously repulsed by these "silent and disgusting images" and long to enter into their "goodly company." At this moment of extremity, death and life become confused; the living victims confront a vision of what they will become and beg for deliverance as if death alone offers the possibility of life.

And within the economy of symbolic exchange in *Pym*, such proves to be the case. The cry of the castaways finds an answer in the scream of a gull, which is "gorging itself with the horrible flesh" of the tall sailor on the bow. Life feeds upon death in an act of predation which anticipates—and in some sense inspires—the cannibalism episode two chapters later. But the image of the dead sailor also discloses to Pym his own vacuous misreading; this figure which earlier seemed to be "encouraging" the four survivors has been animated only by "the exertions of the carnivorous bird." Indeed, when the body swings round to reveal the face, Pym grasps the sickening irony of his previous assumptions: "The eyes were gone, and the whole flesh around the mouth, leaving the teeth utterly naked. This, then, was the smile which had cheered us on to hope! this the—but I forbear" (125). Unable to contemplate further the difference between death and life, Pym suspends his rereading of the text as if dimly conscious of the pitfalls of interpretation. While the narrator elsewhere seems bereft of memory or intelligence (or both), he nevertheless confronts in this scene the limits of his own knowing. As he gazes at the decomposing back and face of the tall sailor, he senses that the disconfirmation of his initial reading does not amount to the "truth" about the man or the vessel. Rather, it reveals the more profound enigma embodied by the ship, about which he admits: "I have, since this period, vainly endeavored to obtain some clew to the hideous uncertainty which enveloped the fate of the stranger." His ruminations upon its fate are in fact speculations on the origin and meaning of death itself and the "hideous uncertainty" of its phenomenal manifestations. However, the text of death cannot be read, for as Pym finally realizes: "It is utterly useless to form conjectures where all is involved, and will, no doubt, remain for ever involved, in the most appalling and unfathomable mystery" (126).

Between these two sites of hermeneutic perplexity—the note from Augustus and the ship of death—Poe brackets the problem of unreadability in *Pym*, positing an analogy between two texts: the world of signs encountered by Pym and the devious narrative attributed to him. And while both texts have been in the most literal sense inscribed by Poe, the unreadability of the novel simply transcribes an unreadability already implicit in the textuality of being. Freud claimed that all anxiety was rooted in the fear of death, and in *Pym*, Poe alludes to the radical source of uncertainty through the narrator's repeated encounters with and rehearsals for his own annihilation. In virtually every instance, Pym's immersion in the phenomenology of death yields a more disturbing awareness of its unintelligibility and its threat to the myth of personal immortality. More broadly, the resistance of death to interpretation and naturalization finally jeopardizes the illusion that knowledge itself rests upon a bedrock of coherent experience. Death is not simply an isolated, unsolved problem in an essentially intelligible world; it is the defining reality which enables one to see the provisionality, even the unreality of our usual ways of conceptualizing self and existence.

In a sequence of scenes related to those already discussed, Poe illustrates the power of death to disrupt or invalidate the act of interpretation. The first of these occurs when Pym as a stowaway on the *Grampus* submits to temporary burial in an "iron-bound box." With characteristic naïveté, the narrator tells us: "I proceeded immediately to take possession of my little apartment, and this with feelings of higher satisfaction, I am sure, than any monarch ever experienced upon entering a new palace" (69). Perceiving the box as an "apartment" rather than a coffin, Pym fails to recognize that he has entered what Michel Ragon calls "the space of death."[8] In mythic readings of *Pym*, this symbolic burial at the beginning of the voyage is said to portend a rebirth into a more enlightened selfhood. Yet the discernible effect of Pym's misreading is disorientation and terror; he falls into a long sleep, awakens "strangely confused," loses all sense of time, and—prefiguring the dilemma of the Norwegian fisherman in "A Descent into the Maelström"—finds that his watch has stopped altogether. Now out of time literally and symbolically, he discovers that a piece of cold mutton has turned to "a state of absolute putrefaction," imaging the fate which he risks in his little apartment. His consequent fear of sleep transparently displays an anxiety about the sleep which never ends.

During his slumber, Pym also experiences dreams "of the most terrific description" in which he is smothered by "demons," throttled by "immense serpents," and surrounded by leafless trees waving their "skeleton arms." These oneiric projections reveal the psychic itinerary of Pym's voyage. But far from indicating an incipient rebirth, they point toward a dread till now masked by a conscious fantasy of adventure. Before boarding the ship, the innocent youth declares, "My visions were of shipwreck and famine; of death or captivity among barbarian hordes; of a lifetime dragged out in sorrow and tears, upon some gray and desolate rock, in an ocean unapproachable and unknown" (65). This daydream, which forms the ostensible basis of the burial nightmare, derives from the same works of romance which would later inspire Tom Sawyer's scheme to liberate Jim in *Huckleberry Finn*. But Pym's dream of annihilation later in the same chapter marks a transformation of the fantasy and suggests the intrusion of death as a semiconscious fear. In the darkness of the hold, which simulates the black confines of the grave, Pym experiences a recurrence of his "gloomy imaginings," which include "the dreadful deaths of thirst, famine, suffocation, and premature interment." Now these images of extinction bring him close to madness and imply an antithetical relationship between reason and the thought of death.

In a subsequent episode, Poe deconstructs the visual horror of death to reveal its phantasmic, undecidable nature. Significantly, he couches this experience of "reading" death within a double strategy of deception—one aimed at fictional characters within the text and one directed at the reader of the text. The passage in question depicts the process by which Pym becomes a "corpse," impersonating a dead sailor named Hartman Rogers. Until this scene, the narrator has remained hidden beneath the deck of the *Grampus*; when the mutineers divide into two factions, Augustus, who sides with Dirk Peters, decides to enlist Pym's help in defeating the mate's gang. Augustus brings Peters down to Pym's hiding place, where the three plot to overthrow the other faction. Poe frames the ensuing deception of the rival gang with a piece of narrative trompe-l'oeil, for Pym suggests that a surprise attack will have greater success if he disguises himself to resemble Rogers, who was evidently poisoned by the mate. He observes:

Rogers had died about eleven in the forenoon, in violent convulsions; and the corpse presented in a few minutes after death one of the most horrid and loathsome spectacles I ever remember to have seen. The stomach was swollen immensely, like that of a man who has been drowned and lain under water for many weeks. The hands were in the same condition, while the face was shrunken, shrivelled, and of a chalky whiteness, except where relieved by two or three glaring red splotches, like those occasioned by the erysipelas: one of these splotches extended diagonally across the face, completely covering up an eye as if with a band of red velvet. [107]

The gruesome details obscure the fact that Pym could have observed neither the "violent convulsions" of Rogers nor the "horrid and loathsome" appearance of his body a few minutes after death. While it is true that Pym, several hours later, helps to remove Rogers' shirt and to drop the body overboard, his eyewitness report of the man's death throes amounts to a "quiz" of the reader; Pym was hiding below decks when Rogers died.

Yet this misrepresentation conveys a psychic truth. For the visual spectacle of death is irresistible; the sight of the corpse exerts a disquieting hold, in this case prompting the narrator to imagine a scene he could not have observed. We find ourselves engrossed by Pym's depiction of the dead sailor, perhaps for the same reason that the child never forgets his first sight of a corpse. Because we know death only through the signs of its presence, which are themselves signs of an absence, signifiers of mortality have a tantalizing opacity. The strange aspect of the corpse—the "look of distance on the face of death," as Emily Dickinson phrased it—raises the question of the dead body's relationship to the departed being. Resemblance and difference cancel each other; the corpse both is and is not the self that was. Morin remarks that the most violent *perturbations funéraires* arise from the conflict between the idea of personal immortality and the signs of decay: "La terreur de la décomposition n'est autre que la terreur de la perte de l'individualité."[9] At bottom the phenomenon of decomposition evokes the fear that individual essence disappears forever at death. The transformation of Rogers into a repulsive object poses precisely this threat, exciting a gesture of psychic denial. The narrator notes that the mate, getting a glimpse of the "disgusting condition" of the body, orders the remains sewn up in a hammock and accorded the rites of sea burial. "Having given these directions he went below, as if to avoid any further sight of his victim," Pym reports, limning a scene which anticipates the isolation and conceal-ment of death in the twentieth century.

If the mate suffers from guilt, he also fears the physical signs of death. Thus, when Pym disguises himself to imitate the "horrible deformity of the swollen corpse," his masquerade produces a fatal shock. Indeed, the narrator can barely endure his *own* reflected im-age: "As I viewed myself in a fragment of looking-glass which hung up in the cabin, and by the dim light of a kind of battle-lantern, I was so impressed with a sense of vague awe at my appearance, and at the recollection of the terrific reality which I was thus representing, that I was seized with a violent tremour, and could scarcely summon resolu-tion to go on with my part" (109). Pym accounts for his "violent tremour" as an effect of recognition, a sudden "recollection" of the dead man's appearance. Yet the reaction is more complex than that, for the disguise itself—a shirt stuffed with bedclothes, white woollen mittens filled with rags, a face rubbed with chalk and streaked with blood—consists of ludicrous makeshift effects. These contrivances arouse fear not through mimetic efficiency but because their blatantly semiotic function (as signs of the signs of death) points to the dead end of the signifying chain, to signs which themselves have no proper intelligibility. For the signifiers of death refer solely to a lack, to the absence of life, rather than to an immanent signified. If death con-stitutes an actual presence, its signification is forever deferred within the life world of human signs. And so the clinical symptoms of dissolution mark a semiotic disruption, an impasse to meaning which thus insures both their unreadability and their irresistible fascination.

When Pym appears before the sailors in the guise of Rogers, the scene in effect deconstructs the experience of terror. Poe notes that while an apparition of doubtful authenticity can evoke only a partial "anticipative horror," the phantasm simulated by Pym has an abso-lute effect: "The mate sprang up from the mattress on which he was lying, and, without uttering a syllable, fell back, stone dead . . . [while] four others sat for some time rooted apparently to the floor, the most pitiable objects of horror and utter despair my eyes ever encountered" (112). Pym explains that the sailors had no doubt "that the apparition of Rogers was indeed a revivification of his disgusting corpse, or at least its spiritual image." For them, the intrusion of Rogers amounts to a return of the repressed, a scandalous encounter with an image already forgotten, consigned to the deep (or so the mate believes) and thus figuratively hidden in the unconscious. Morin points out that the enclosure of the dead body in a shroud, coffin, vault, or mausoleum has always had the double function of protecting the living as well as the dead: "Les pierres funéraires sont-elles là pour protéger le mort des animaux, ou pour l'empêcher de revenir parmi les vivants?"[10] His question uncovers the anxiety of the return exploited by Pym and his companions. The mate expires precisely because reason cannot accommodate the threat embodied by the "disgusting corpse." The dead must stay buried, else we go mad with the anxieties they bring to full consciousness.

Pym's impersonation of a corpse places him in the singular position of being both a living subject and a dead object; for a moment (when seized by the "violent tremour") he experiences the alienation of the self from itself which—as Kafka figuratively suggests in "The Metamorphosis"—belongs to the phenomenology of dying. While the masquerade facilitates a violent revolt which leaves Pym physically unharmed, on the psychic level he has been unnerved by the glimpse of what he will himself become. Ineluctably he has begun to conceive of his own physical transformation, and subsequent encounters with putrefaction (as in the "Flying Dutchman" episode) activate the primal anxiety. Thus in a subsequent scene, Pym participates in a grisly attempt to forestall death through a paradoxical consuming of death's body.

This scene of cannibalism has been inspired (as noted earlier) by the gull gorging itself on the back of the dead sailor aboard the phantom ship. The unspeakable idea is broached just after Providence has again seemingly taunted the victims (at the end of chapter 11) with false hopes of deliverance. When Parker proposes a lottery to determine which man should die to preserve the lives of the others, he articulates a solution that is at once sane and mad, evincing a dispassionate logic about human sacrifice. Poe presents the scene as a crisis of civilized values; the survivors have reached a "horrible extremity" in which instinct has eclipsed reason, belief, and duty. Proximity to death has brought them face to face with their own craving for physical survival; yet while Pym remonstrates with Parker "in the name of everything which he [Parker] held sacred," the episode principally exhibits collective despair. Poe underscores this faithlessness through the ironic imagery of communion ritual; as Irwin has pointed out, the slaughter of Parker stands in telling contrast to the sacrificial death of Christ: "Unlike Parker's sacrifice in which the body that is eaten becomes part of the person who eats it, in Christ's sacrifice the person who eats the body becomes part of what is eaten: he is incorporated into the mystical body of Christ. By eating the dismembered parts of Christ's body, the disciples become members of that body; and after their own deaths when their physical bodies have decayed, that membership will be the means by which they are remembered by Christ and saved from everlasting destruction."[11] In Christian ritual, the devouring of the sacramental body serves precisely to insure the survival of the soul against the corruptibility of the flesh. The consuming of Parker, however, affords no spiritual nourishment; it parodies the Christian communion only to reveal the absence of faith and a concomitant anxiety about survival.

In various nature religions, the sacrifice of the scapegoat king secures a temporary postponement of death (often figured as a blight or curse) for participants willing to mark themselves with the victim's blood or to ingest a portion of the body. According to the logic of ritual, only through a metaphorical embracing of death can death be deferred. By virtue of his capacity to incarnate that which the community dreads, the scapegoat king inspires fear as a demigod; he is set apart, marked as different, despite his representative function. In some ways the killing of Parker replicates this archetypal practice: marked by fate and thus transformed into a living dead man, Parker takes upon himself the fear of death shared by the group; the eating of his body displays the desire to protect oneself from corporeal dissolution. But in actuality, Parker's death carries no talismanic or sacrificial force; the "fearful repast" mainly illustrates the condition of modern culture which René Girard calls "the sacrificial crisis," a symptom of social disorder in which the distinction between the pure and impure (or sacred and profane) has been effaced, precluding any purgation through sacrificial violence and thereby unleashing the contagion of reciprocal violence.[12] Girard's theory of "sacrificial crisis" elucidates the general problem of violence in Poe as well as the particular butchery heralded on the original title page of *Pym*. For Poe projects a world devoid of redemptive sacrifice and therefore helplessly exposed to the ultimate violence of death. Faced with the threat of mortality, his characters project their own sense of victimization as a violence toward others, as if blindly seeking a surrogate, a double whose death will have the effect of sacrificial ritual: to relieve one's own fear of death. The killing of Parker, which occurs between the violence of the mutiny and the massacre on Tsalal, manifests the insistence of reciprocal violence in a secular, death-haunted world.

Once again, Pym's encounter with death (he nearly loses the lottery himself) results from an inattentiveness which for Parker has fatal consequences. Two days after the last of the body has been consumed, Pym remembers leaving an axe in one of the larboard berths. With no awareness of his unfortunate timing, he remarks: "I now thought it possible that, by getting at this axe, we might cut through the deck over the storeroom, and thus readily supply ourselves with provisions" (136). The recovery of the axe soon yields provisions and later enables the castaways to cut up and preserve a sea turtle. Although Pym fails to register the irony of his belated recollection, its proximity to the "fearful repast" enables the reader to grasp the monstrous implication. Pym's forgetfulness reveals the importance of surface-depth relationships in *Pym*: the immediate, tangible "facts" of a situation mask an unseen and often contradictory set of conditions discoverable only through violence. As an instance of repression (which is less a misreading than a denial of the text), Pym's inability to remember the axe until after the bloodshed also discloses a more complicated meaning. On the one hand it seems to betray an unconscious longing for the kind of renewing, sacrificial violence described above—a motive contrary to Pym's conscious disgust with the idea of human sacrifice. The narrator's lapse insures the unfolding of the plan proposed by Parker. On the other hand, his forgetting also appears to signal Pym's own unconscious desire for the lasting forgetfulness of death. His psychic denial of the lifesaving tool manifests not an instinct for survival but an inchoate desire for oblivion, which (as we shall see) becomes more insistent as the narrator approaches the polar sea.

Like the killing of Parker, the subsequent death of Augustus seems charged with contradictory meanings. The sudden, ghastly manner of his demise calls attention to both the literal and metaphorical significance of decomposition. Pym writes that

> his death filled us with the most gloomy forebodings, and had so great an effect upon our spirits that we sat motionless by the corpse during the whole day, and never addressed each other except in a whisper. It was not until some time after dark that we took courage to get up and throw the body overboard. It was then loathsome beyond expression, and so far decayed that, as Peters attempted to lift it, an entire leg came off in his grasp. As the mass of putrefaction slipped over the vessel's side into the water, the glare of phosphoric light with which it was surrounded plainly discovered to us seven or eight large sharks, the clashing of whose horrible teeth, as their prey was torn to pieces among them, might have been heard at the distance of a mile. [142]

Within a few hours, Augustus is transformed from a living being to a putrid corpse, his fate anticipating the instantaneous decomposition of Monsieur Valdemar. For Pym, the spectacle represents another image of his own death, insofar as Augustus has been from the outset identified as Pym's alter ego. The narrator at one point affirms that the "intimate communion" between the two has "resulted in a partial interchange of character" (65). In the putrefaction of his friend's body, Pym sees the corruptibility of his own flesh; more importantly, he discovers the precarious and problematic nature of that which constitutes being. Augustus dies "without having spoken for several hours"; he leaves no verbal trace of essence as last words. There is no spiritualized scene of departure, and the physical falling apart of his body suggests that self is simply an effect of corporeal presence. This deconstruction of the human repeats an idea enacted in the cannibalism episode: prior to the "fearful repast," Parker's head, hands, and feet were removed, as if to efface his human identity. Reading the death of Augustus in this way, we perceive that decomposition implies the erasure of self.

In another sense, the decaying of Pym's friend occurs as a self-conscious irony and a portent of the narrator's own subsequent erasure by Poe. Augustus is written out of the novel in chapter 13 despite an explicit reference in chapter 5 to a conversation between Pym and his companion "many years" (94) after their adventure. Though this discrepancy may be attributed to authorial carelessness—Pollin dismisses it as a "relic of the first rough plan" for the novel (250)—the sudden disintegration of Augustus bears the mark of an intentional "quiz." For Poe dispatches the youth on the first of August, calling attention by this heavy-handed coincidence and the rapidity of his decay (itself a kind of visual pun) to the arbitrariness of his existence as a textual construct. Augustus is merely a product of writing; he can be de-composed as readily as he has been verbally embodied. As the author of a forged letter, the writer of the note scrawled in blood, and the copyist of business documents prior to the mutiny (85), the youth has already been identified with the act of inscription; hence the mortification of his right arm, said at the last to be "completely black from the wrist to the shoulder," serves to confirm his further uselessness in any project of writing. When Peters throws the corpse overboard, his gesture anticipates the maneuver by which Poe finally jettisons a narrator whose death is figured by a suspension of the text itself.

Like his encounter with the phantom ship, Pym's several rehearsals for death—his premature burial, his masquerade as a corpse, his consuming of death's body, and his witnessing the decomposition of Augustus—are all framed by delusions or deceptions which shift attention from the narrative to its problematic textuality. The narrator's misreading of the tall sailor on the bow of the Dutch brig becomes a model of the reader's relationship to the body of the novel. Pym's inability to see the "text" as a corpse corresponds to the modern inclination to read death in Poe as the sign of something else. More specifically, it exemplifies the way in which death disrupts the process of reading as it disrupts the semiotics of daily experience, imposing its blankness and silence upon the signs by which its presence-as-absence is known. Whenever Pym approaches death, he verges upon the limit of signification itself, thus repeating the dilemma in "MS. Found in a Bottle." The discontinuities of *Pym*, whether inscribed as narratorial misperceptions or authorial games of credibility, point to the radical uncertainty of reading itself within the zone of mortality. Death can only be misread; its signs produce a cognitive disturbance which not only thwarts our efforts to construe the text of mortality but which exposes the provisionality of all signs by which we read the terms of existence.

Having reached a narrative dead end in chapter 13, with Pym and Dirk Peters stranded in midocean on the floating hulk of the *Grampus*, Poe opens another adventure in misprision: "by the mercy of God" the *Jane Guy* arrives to rescue the survivors. Subsequent events cast doubt on this providential reading, however, as the ship's crew falls victim to a massacre; Pym and Peters escape the slaughter only to disappear into a milky vortex at the South Pole. In some respects, *Pym* becomes a different novel once the narrator has boarded the *Jane Guy*: geographical observations, cribbed from contemporary sources, mark a temporary escape from dread. But once the ship reaches Tsalal, an island inhabited by dark-skinned natives, Pym reenters the sphere of treachery and annihilation. This return to violence coincides with an increasing attention to cultural practice, speech, and hieroglyphs, as these phenomena pose problems of interpretation for Pym and his comrades. Juxtaposing death and hermeneutic crisis, Poe restates the problem of uncertainty as an effect of writing. For the ubiquitous opposition of black and white, which on one level issues in genocide, also stages (as Ricardou has remarked) "a dramatization of the ink-paper opposition," placing the concluding action of *Pym* within the metaphoricity of inscription. Pym's final voyage toward the vortex is in some sense a movement toward figurality itself, toward a trope of writing and textual closure.

Unlike his seemingly innocent rendering of adventures aboard the *Grampus*, Pym records his experiences on Tsalal with a reflective self-consciousness. A sudden passion for scientific discovery leads him to analyze details and to contemplate the meaning of observations. From the behavior of the black natives he surmises: "It was quite evident that they had never before seen any of the white race—from whose complexion, indeed, they appeared to recoil" (169). But Pym professes his inability to understand the natives' fear of "several very harmless objects—such as the schooner's sails, an egg, an open book, or a pan of flour." His mistake in classifying the objects as "harmless" rather than white has far-reaching consequences, for he thereby fails to perceive the principle of taboo which impels the natives to destroy their white visitors. This blatant misreading betrays the ethnocentricity of the narrator, who cannot conceive of whiteness as evil or deadly and thus cannot imagine himself as a mortal threat, an embodiment of death.

While alerting readers more attentive than Pym to the eventual massacre, Poe's insistence upon black-white oppositions also prefigures the end of the novel, in which Pym vanishes into the perfect whiteness of the polar region. Even those skeptical of Ricardou's theory that the text represents the "voyage to the end of the page" must grant that the description of Tsalal suggests an analogy between the physical terrain and inscription, between the site of death and the space of writing. As Pym and Peters explore the chasms amid the hills, they encounter hieroglyphs upon the walls and—as the concluding note explains—in the very configuration of the abyss. Rowe points out that "the relation between the irreducibly figurative landscape and the graphic nature of the narrative is made explicit in Pym's drawings of the shapes of the chasms themselves."[13] If we trust Poe's appended translations of the hieroglyphic writing, the markings on the walls—a human figure beside the phrases "to be white" and "the region of the south"—are inscribed within an abyss which spells out the "Ethiopian verbal root . . . 'to be shady.'" That is, "the inflections of shadow or darkness" contain and physically subsume "inflections of brilliancy and whiteness," thus forging a pre-scription of the recent massacre. But more broadly, the representation of a human form within the abyss of shadow or darkness refers to the universal fate of mortals. Pym and Peters find themselves literally within the valley of the shadow of death, in which the only vestige of human essence is the problematic inscription which portends their obliteration.

Curiously, Pym finds the graven text unreadable; indeed, he fails to perceive the markings as writing and convinces Peters that they are "the work of nature" rather than "alphabetical characters." As Irwin remarks, this refusal to see the inscriptions as man-made amounts to "a denial of human presence that is symbolic of that death of the self to itself in opposition to which self-conscious life is differentiated, a death that is not simply the external limit of self-consciousness but its internal limit as well, a death lying at the core of self-consciousness and inhabiting the objective otherness of the inscribed image."[14] Pym represses the reality embodied by the hieroglyphic markings, unable to accept consciously the fate already determined as a narrative inevitability. The human figure on the wall, said to be "standing erect" (there is indeed the suggestion of a tumescent phallus), incarnates in its cold fixity the principle of death as it simulates a priapic lust for life. Pym refuses to contemplate the mark as a pictographic representation of the fate of desire and so continues to resist the thought of his own perishability.

Yet in a subsequent scene, Poe implies that his narrator unconsciously yearns to complete his textual destiny—to become an inscribed figure, purely the "I" of writing and no longer the self who writes "I." When Pym and Peters attempt to escape the hill scored with chasms (Ethiopian letters), they discover that the promontory is ringed by cliffs; the "text" is itself defined by the abyss which encircles it. By dint of strength and agility Peters manages to descend the cliff, but Pym finds himself at the brink of the gulf overwhelmed by an "irrepressible desire," an irrational urge to fall:

The more earnestly I struggled *not to think*, the more intensely vivid became my conceptions, and the more horribly distinct. At length arrived that crisis of fancy, so fearful in all similar cases, the crisis in which we begin to anticipate the feelings with which we *shall* fall— to picture to ourselves the sickness, and dizziness, and the last struggle, and the half swoon, and the final bitterness of the rushing and headlong descent. And now I found these fancies creating their own realities, and all imagined horrors crowding upon me in fact. I felt my knees strike violently together, while my fingers were gradually yet certainly relaxing their grasp. There was a ringing in my ears, and I said, "This is my knell of death!" And now I was consumed with the irrepressible desire of looking below. I could not, I would not, confine my glances to the cliff; and, with a wild, indefinable emotion half of horror, half of a relieved oppression, I threw my vision far down into the abyss. For one moment my fingers clutched convulsively upon their hold, while, with the movement, the faintest possible idea of ultimate escape wandered, like a shadow, through my mind—in the next my whole soul was pervaded with *a longing to fall;* a desire, a yearning, a passion utterly uncontrollable. [197–98]

Pym momentarily surrenders to this urge and plunges into the void— directly into the arms of Dirk Peters.

This lengthy passage demands attention for it brings into the open Pym's fear of death, now experienced as that "oppression" which death alone can relieve. The desire to cast oneself into the abyss, which Poe later attributed to "perverseness," manifests here the burden of psychic experience in *Pym.* Irwin notes that Pym's swoon on the brow of the cliff marks his third fainting episode; these "symbolic deaths" all signal "the imaginative anticipation of death."[15] A witness to countless deaths and a survivor of two separate massacres, the narrator now feels for the first time a previously unconscious desire to die. Lifton's analysis of "survivor guilt" seems particularly apposite to the nature of Pym's ordeal:

> The survivor of disaster, and especially holocaust, faces several formidable problems concerning guilt. He has been witness not to death in appropriate sequence but random, absurd, grotesque, and in many cases man-made death; which, in turn, threatens his most basic commitments and images concerning life's reliability and significance; that is, radically threatens his centering and grounding. He is susceptible to the sense that it could or even should have been he, instead of the other, who died. . . . His debt to the dead can become permanent and unpayable.[16]

As Lifton suggests, the recurrence of gratuitous, violent death destabilizes the individual psyche by exposing the radical unreliability of suppositions about life's meaning. The horror of Pym's experience culminates in this suicidal impulse, which expresses at once the yearning to fall into oblivion or forgetfulness and the compulsion to pay his debt to the dead.

But this reading of the precipice scene takes into account only one of the metaphorical associations of the abyss. As we have seen, the landscape of Tsalal also defines a textual space, in which the chasms themselves are configured as archaic writing. When Pym tells us that "with a wild, indefinable emotion half of horror, half of a relieved oppression," he gazes "far down into the abyss," he also expresses the unconscious desire to fall into writing, to surrender his mortal being to the timelessness of the inscribed text. If we could imagine a rewriting of "The Oval Portrait" in which the painter destroyed himself in producing a self-portrait, the analogy would be exact. Pym's contemplated fall into writing entails the literal death of the writer while promising his symbolic survival as an inscribed presence. Poe thereby projects the notion that the deepest appeal of writing lies in its inherent fatality: it extracts life to perpetuate it; it emulates death to deny it. George Steiner remarks that "all great writing springs from *le dur désir de durer,* the hard contrivance of spirit against death, the hope to overreach time by the force of creation."[17] There is another sense, however, in which Pym's fascination with death in the abyss betrays the yearning not for immortality but for that confrontation with oblivion which makes writing possible. Blanchot quotes from the journal of Kafka (*"Write to be able to die—Die to be able to write"*) to elucidate the sense in which "art is a relation with death," a problem of mastery and self-possession which originates in the threat of annihilation. Not until one establishes an equality with death can writing occur: "If you lose face before death, if death is the limit of your self-possession, then it slips the words out from under the pen, it cuts in and interrupts. The writer no longer writes, he cries out—an awkward, confused cry which no one understands and which touches no one."[18] In this sense Pym's fall may be said to dramatize the beginning of writing: perhaps not until he has thrown himself into the abyss, plunged into the experience of his own death, can he inscribe the first word of his narrative.

To be sure, the scene on the cliff displays more abandon than self-possession. Not until the novel's final scene, in fact, does Pym appear to accept his mortal condition. As his canoe drifts further toward the brilliant whiteness of the pole, Pym, Peters, and their hostage Nu-Nu become increasingly listless. The approach of the polar winter inspires no terror; Pym writes, "I felt a *numbness* of body and mind—a dreaminess of sensation—but this was all" (204). The strange apathy of the voyagers increases with the velocity of their approach to the luminous but silent void. Like the narrator of "MS. Found in a Bottle," Pym finds himself approaching "a region of novelty and wonder"; on the verge of the abyss—a "limitless cataract"—he evinces no fear of annihilation: "And now we rushed into the embraces of the cataract, where a chasm threw itself open to receive us. But there arose in our pathway a shrouded human figure, very far larger in its proportions than any dweller among men. And the hue of the skin of the figure was of the perfect whiteness of the snow" (206). Drawing a connection between the chasms on Tsalal and the milky cataract, Irwin points out that "Pym's confrontation with the hieroglyphic human figure in the cavern *foreshadows* his final confrontation with the apotheosized human figure in the mist," and he speculates that the latter form is either an optical illusion, a projection of Pym's own shadow upon the white curtain, or an imagined "spectral illusion"— both symptomatic of a "veiled narcissism" associated with the psychic origins of language.[19]

One can discern a parallel between the two chasmic scenes, however, which leads to quite a different view of the "shrouded human figure." The fact that Pym's narrative breaks off dramatically as he approaches "the embraces of the cataract" reminds us again of the metaphoricity which associates the abyss with writing. Disappearing into the whiteness, he exchanges his putative historical existence for that of a purely textual entity. The "shrouded" form in Pym's pathway may be understood simply as an objectification of death, a defined representation of the indefinable and unknowable. But if we recall his prior misreading of the figure on the wall of the chasm, another possibility presents itself. Whereas he earlier mistook the written figure for a natural form, the narrator here conversely mistakes for a human presence the palpable body of the narrative rising before him to deliver him from silence. He is about to be gathered into the artifice of the text, to become an enduring subject caught in language like a fly in amber. The vortex scene enacts the process through which Pym is delivered from anxiety by the possibility of writing; he loses his fear by gazing upon the "perfect whiteness" of the textual space in which the life of writing unfolds. Only in this brilliance does the unreadable side of the letter from Augustus at last reveal its paradoxical signification: death's "dreary and unsatisfying blank," the source of terror and uncertainty, is also the necessary ground of inscription. The shrouded form speaks wordlessly, its blankness revealing that the space of death and the space of writing are one.

Beyond its difficult imagery, the ending raises an additional question: when did Pym compose the work attributed to him? The appended editorial note speaks of "the late sudden and distressing death of Mr. Pym," which has ostensibly prevented completion of the manuscript; reference is made to "the loss of the two or three final chapters" under revision at the time of Pym's fatal "accident." But this information seems more incredible than the novel's ending, insofar as it implies Pym's survival of the polar vortex. Through this strategy, the narrative projects three contradictory propositions: Pym surely died at the South Pole in the vastness of the cataract; he was delivered from certain death and ten years later wrote his marvelous narrative; he died during the writing of that story at the very juncture which narrates his own death. Each proposition entails an impossibility: if Pym died, his narrative could not exist; if he plunged into the cataract, he could not have survived; if he survived, his putative textual death could not coincide with his physical death. Late in the narrative Pym admits that he "kept no regular journal" (167n.) during the early portion of his adventure, thus implying that the logbook content of chapters 13 through 25 coincides with material inscribed at the time of the voyage. In portraying the configuration of the chasms on Tsalal, he comments: "I had luckily with me a pocketbook and pencil, which I preserved with great care through a long series of subsequent adventure, and to which I am indebted for memoranda of many subjects which would otherwise have been crowded from my remembrance" (193). He mentions this "pencil memoranda" again (203n.) in confessing the approximate nature of the dates assigned to his last recorded episode, the voyage into the cataract.

But these touches of verisimilitude expose the very problem they seek to conceal, for, like the narrative of premature burial, Pym's account seems to arrive from beyond the grave. The reader questions the survival not of the "pencil memoranda" but of its writer. The report of the author's recent "distressing" death places the whole story in yet another context: the writer of these words, manifestly alive in the representation of his adventure, is already dead. A living presence in the preface and a corpse in the postscript, Pym in effect dies during the time of reading. His literal fate thereby appears to corroborate his figurative itinerary. Indeed, it suggests again that the really hazardous adventure was not the excursion to the South Pole but the ordeal of writing. His reported decease renders entirely problematic both the site of death and the scene of writing. Like the inconceivable painting in "The Fall of the House of Usher," said to represent an underground vault without any visible source of light and yet suffused by a "flood of intense rays" producing a "ghastly and inappropriate splendor" (CW, 2:406), Poe produces in Pym a narrative which could not have been written.

It is likewise a book that does not permit itself to be read, if we understand reading to be the reconstruction of a coherence lodged in the text. Despite the patterning suggested by Pym's rehearsals for death, his encounters with living burial, putrefaction, murder, cannibalism, and suicidal fantasy only underscore the point that mortality cannot be naturalized, denied, comprehended, or indefinitely deferred. It disrupts the system of signs as it destabilizes contemporary metaphysics, posing the question of individual survival in the spectacle of decay. The unreadability of death deprives the natural order of a final intelligibility; unlike Emerson's vision of nature—that plenitude of transparent symbols affirming the connectedness of being— Poe imagines in Pym a world of deceptive and opaque surfaces which determine the isolation of the perceiving self. In the hermeneutic failures of the narrator, who learns nothing from his continuing bafflement and instead "enacts over and over again the same scenario without ever becoming aware of it," Poe represents the condition of uncertainty enforced by the modern crisis of death.[20]

As if to seal the narrative in an enveloping contradiction which would insure the book's unreadability, Poe, in the editorial appendix, not only disposes of his narrator but undermines his credibility through a series of tactics which lead back finally to the enigmatic complicity between death and writing. He first indicates that "the gentleman whose name is mentioned in the preface" ("Mr. Poe") has refused to complete the writing of Pym's tale, on account of the "general inaccuracy of the details afforded him" and—more tellingly—because of his "disbelief in the entire truth of the latter portions of the narration" (207). With this stratagem, "Mr. Poe" challenges the veracity of the work he has already endorsed in the preface, leaving the reader to puzzle out the contradiction as well as the issue of reliability which it raises. Poe thereby presents himself as a shrewder judge of narrative than the implied reader who has succumbed to Pym's blandishments about "fact" and "truth." But the supposed editor (Poe in another guise) imagines himself to be even more astute than "Mr. Poe." In glossing the hieroglyphs on Tsalal, he contradicts Pym's theory that the figures were the work of nature and then, as if to dismiss the skepticism of "Mr. Poe," exposes the latter's failure to construe the chasms themselves as writing: "The facts in question have, beyond doubt, escaped the attention of Mr. Poe." Through these supplemental disclosures, the editor leaves the whole matter of authority unclear, even as his exercise in "philological scrutiny" invites speculation on writing and the problem of meaning.

The riddle of Tsalal, the cry "Tekeli-li," and the polar oppositions of black and white may be traced, he implies, to the chasms or the figures "so mysteriously written in their windings." But whether the inscriptions portend racial massacre or refer more broadly to the yearning for escape from the shadow of death (the arm of the human form is "outstretched toward the south," toward "brilliancy and whiteness"), this commentary on writing within the abyss—or writing *as* abyss—calls attention to engravings which bear witness to the dilemma of mortality. In some primal scene, perhaps coeval with the formation of the chasms themselves, an unknown writer conscious of the ephemerality of speech and his own perishability as a speaking subject carved upon the wall those "alphabetical characters" by which he might continue to speak after his own decease.

Whatever their topical content, the ancient inscriptions on Tsalal thus refer to the genesis of writing, to an originary defiance of silence, which is of course the paradigm of all writing. In its most elemental form, inscription manifests a revolt against death, and this seems to be the implication of the unattributed final sentence in *Pym*: "*I have graven it within the hills, and my vengeance upon the dust within the rock*" (208). The postscript is cryptic because of its unknown provenance and because it posits an esoteric relationship between writing and vengeance. It is also cryptic in its allusion to the tomblike abyss on Tsalal and to the dust within the chasm. This dust may be understood both as a metaphor for mortality and as the detritus of writing; as it produces dust, inscription constitutes (in Irwin's words) man's "revenge against death, the revenge that man attempts to take, through art, against time, change, and mortality, against the things that threaten to obliterate all trace of his individual existence."[21] Interestingly, the "alphabetical characters" endure because they are "graven," scored deeply in stone, given over to the sepulchre. Though etymologically distinguishable, *grave* and *engrave* fuse in the word which implies the survival of writing. By assuming the conditions of death, language embarks upon a life of its own.

In this model of the relationship between writing and mortality, the fall into the abyss (the chasm or the cataract) suggests metaphorically that in a world claimed by death and divested of efficacious belief in salvation, inscription opens an alternative to oblivion, insuring the remembrance of the one who writes. Through writing, the word ostensibly preserves what the Word no longer redeems. At least such is the theoretical notion graven within the hills, written into the figurality of Pym's encounter with the catastrophe of death. As he approaches his own vanishing point, the narrator sees Nu-Nu stirring in the bottom of the boat, "but, upon touching him, we found his spirit departed." Death-in-life, Poe's recurrent image of existence without soul, epitomizes the prison house of materiality in which the denizen of the modern world must contend with his own fear and trembling. Pym's epistemological confusion is symptomatic of our metaphysical anxiety; the ubiquity and purposelessness of death throw in doubt the Providential design in which the narrator strives vainly to believe. Through the spectacle of violence and putrefaction and through the willed incoherence of the text itself, Poe achieves in *Pym* his most disturbing treatment of the new death.

7

Metamorphoses
of the Shadow

Much of the difficulty which attends a rereading of Poe derives from
the fact that his projections of dread have become so ingrained in
modern consciousness as to lose their singularity and prescience.
Collective fear in this "age of atrocity" (to borrow Lawrence Langer's
phrase) has moreover made Poe's texts continuous with our psychic
experience. In ways to be examined in this chapter, Poe anticipated
the ascendancy of death and produced a writing grounded in its
violent deformations. A recent fictional hero, Bellow's Moses
Herzog, has summed up the contemporary situation: "What is the
philosophy of this generation? Not God is dead, that point was passed
long ago. Perhaps it should be stated Death is God." A survivor of the
Holocaust, Herzog struggles against the memory of mass slaughter
while acknowledging its impact on contemporary "metaphysics":
"Look at these millions of dead. Can you pity them, feel for them?
You can nothing! There were too many. We burned them to ashes,
we buried them with bulldozers. History is the history of cruelty, not

love, as soft men think. We have experimented with every human capacity to see which is strong and admirable and have shown that none is. There is only practicality. If the old God exists he must be a murderer. But the one true god is Death."[1] Unable to escape the contagion of brutality, Herzog worries that the sheer volume of modern death, especially in the form of genocidal projects, has stripped individual existence of dignity and meaning. Through this debasement of life, death has become an insatiable deity against whose ravages religion and ethics seem impotent. As Bellow suggests, the concept of death's sovereignty betrays an essential nihilism: "This generation thinks—and this is its thought of thoughts—that nothing faithful, vulnerable, fragile can be durable or have any true power. Death waits for these things as a cement floor waits for a dropping light bulb."[2] Herzog resists such thinking but perceives that amid the contending beliefs and ideologies which define the horizon of philosophical relativism—that is, the locus of metaphysical uncertainty—death looms as an ineluctable presence, a virtual god. As Poe prophesied in "The City in the Sea," "Death has reared himself a throne," and through the atrocities which confirm his dominion, this deity has cast his shadow over the entire age.

The dark vision which Herzog associates with the present generation clearly has its roots in earlier experience. Just as the horrors of the Holocaust look ahead to Hiroshima and (on a different scale) to Vietnam, they look back to the unprecedented carnage of the Great War and to underlying attitudes which made such devastation possible. While participants on the western front were not literally interned and scheduled for death, they died ignominiously in trenches by the hundreds of thousands, destroyed by new technologies which made mass murder an utterly impersonal act. Something of the new conceptualization of death can be glimpsed in Hemingway's "A Natural History of the Dead" (1932), which depicts the physical decay of battlefield casualties. The narrator sardonically suggests that his work—which parodies the writings of Mungo Park, the Christian naturalist—seeks to determine "what inspiration we may derive from the dead." With mock detachment he notes mutations in corpses:

Until the dead are buried they change somewhat in appearance each day. The color change in Caucasian races is from white to yellow, to yellow-green, to black. If left long enough in the heat the flesh comes to resemble coal-tar, especially where it has been broken or torn, and it has quite a visible tarlike iridescence. The dead grow larger each day until sometimes they become quite too big for their uniforms, filling these until they seem blown tight enough to burst.[3]

This representation of battlefield decomposition surpasses its ostensible model—the "Chapel in the Pines" chapter of *The Red Badge of Courage*—both in scope and in nihilistic implication. Hemingway's narrator remarks that "most men die like animals," and this brute fact poses the essential horror of a naturalistic order which displays only the indifference or absence of a Creator. In "Natural History" the dead have become objects, data, mere scientific curiosities devoid of identity or personal dignity; the spectacle of carrion obliterates the meaning of individual lives and deaths. Through his insistent contemplation of fatal violence, Hemingway devised a code of heroism which finally (in *Death in the Afternoon*) cohered as a program of writing: "All stories, if continued far enough, end in death, and he is no true story teller who would keep that from you."

By insisting upon the real ending, Hemingway located in death both a rationale for narrative and a source of values. He sensed the same reciprocity explored by Heidegger in *Sein und Seit* (1927): the necessity of embracing the fact of death and the imminent possibility of one's own death to achieve authenticity as an individual. Anticipation of death becomes, for Heidegger, the principal source of truth; one achieves wholeness and "freedom toward death" only when *Dasein* (one's "Being-in-the-world") opens itself to authentic "Being-toward-death." Heidegger presents the richest, most profound elaboration of the crisis in metaphysics entailed by the new death and the void which it discloses. He valorizes anxiety precisely because it marks one's liberation from that "constant tranquillization about death" grounded in the illusion that only "they" (others) die. Demonstrating that the anticipation of one's own death is the origin and principle of individual Being, Heidegger's theory indirectly illuminates the narratorial perspective in such texts as "The Pit and the Pendulum" and "A Descent into the Maelström." In a curious way his thought also confirms Herzog's notion that "Death is God," for the affirmation of being once sought in God or Christ now arrives through the threat of death as an ontological event.

But the existential privileging of death, so apparent in Hemingway and Heidegger (not to mention such contemporaries as Rilke, Kafka, Sartre, and Camus), bears witness to conceptions and realities having their origins in the nineteenth century. Nietzsche's declaration of the death of God—a suspicion rampant in nineteenth-century poetry, as J. Hillis Miller has shown—foreclosed the possibility of an afterlife and thus reduced human death to a temporal problem, literally a question of timing. Nietzsche sponsored the concept of suicide and murder as essential manifestations of will; by flaunting his indifference to death and mastering the devices of cruelty, the *Ubermensch* could crush the fearful and tenderhearted. Death emerged as a source of power—not in the crude sense of physical domination practiced by tyrants from time immemorial, but as a daring derived from personal indifference to the problem of mortality. In *The Gay Science*, Nietzsche's madman exhorts listeners to accept God's death: "Gods too decompose. God is dead. God remains dead. And we have killed him." Such awareness, in Nietzsche's view, enables man to throw off the "slave mentality" imposed by the fear of death which he sees at the root of traditional faith. His Zarathustra urges followers to "live dangerously," to achieve the "free death" by dying victoriously through a conscious decision. But although Nietzsche postulates a mastery of death, we can readily construe the so-called "free death" as a tacit acknowledgment of its inexorability—capitulation masquerading as conquest. Despite an act of will (existential suicide or its equivalent) which creates the illusion of a free choice, death will always have its way. And so (as Bellow implies in *Herzog*) the effort to abolish God ends with the apotheosis of death; and this apotheosis in turn inspires and sanctions the politics of extermination.

While Nietzsche was developing his nihilistic theory of death as power, Tolstoy published a novella that established in different terms the crucial relationship between anxiety and insight. Through the modalities of realism, "The Death of Ivan Ilyich" (1886) renders the ordeal of dying in a way which figures the profound disparity between subjective experience and observed event. Its portrayal of the response to Ivan's disease, especially the avoidance practiced by his family, illustrates the condition of inauthenticity about which Heidegger (mindful of Tolstoy) would later write. In the affected behavior of his wife and children, Ivan "saw himself—and all that for which he had lived—and saw clearly that it was not real at all, but a terrible and huge deception which had hidden both life and death." In ways which scarcely need explanation, "The Death of Ivan Ilyich" exemplifies for Ariès the unmentionable "hidden" death, which in the twentieth century would conceal itself from public view in institutions of termination and disposal. This veiling of the moment of death seems a curious antithesis to the fascination with death as atrocity, recorded in prurient photographs and newsreels, but both the desire to conceal and the urge to peek bear witness to what Gorer has called the pornographic aspect of death. As a cultural (rather than a literary) text, this seems to be the crucial implication of "Ivan Ilyich": the drama of dying, still an important affirmation of faith in mid-nineteenth-century bourgeois society, has become in the bureaucratized "post-Christian" world of Tolstoy a source of embarrassment and humiliation. Without a mode of psychic or spiritual accommodation, death has become a revolting scandal.

In some respects Ivan's story also resembles the dilemma described by Kierkegaard in *The Sickness Unto Death* (1849)—that of the moribund who "struggles with death, and cannot die." When death is no longer a "transition unto life" in the Christian sense, Kierkegaard writes, "despair is the disconsolateness of not being able to die." Yet paradoxically, despair—the "sickness unto death"—does not consume the self as disease consumes the body; it intensifies the sense of self, makes one conscious of that which sickness cannot consume, and so discloses "the eternal in man." Through this ironic strategy Kierkegaard argues that despair, the condition of hopelessness before the problem of death, reveals that aspect of self which death cannot destroy. Acknowledgment of despair thus becomes the critical step toward selfhood and faith. By contemplating death, however, Kierkegaard uncovers the universality of despair, the pervasiveness in man of "a disquietude, a perturbation, a discord, an anxious dread of an unknown something . . . dread of a possibility of life, or dread of himself." While he contends that despair is finally "uplifting" because it gives evidence of the spirit, his critique has had the practical result (as evidenced in Nietzsche and Heidegger) of confirming the priority of death in any ontological scheme. Despite Kierkegaard's affirmation of spiritual inwardness, his writing bears witness to metaphysical anxiety and to the inability of organized Christendom to alleviate the soul's distress. "Official" religion no longer suffices; one must devise private, ironic schemes of reconciliation. As Kierkegaard perceived, the self now inhabits a solitary space, dispossessed of "secure communal ideologies of redemption" (to reappropriate Becker's phrase) which once enfolded the individual and endowed his death with collectively held meaning.

In *L'homme et la mort*, Edgar Morin credits Kierkegaard with establishing the crucial link between existential solitude and obsession with death. This connection marks a fateful transition, for Morin contends that about the middle of the nineteenth century, a "crisis of death" began to manifest itself, actually a "crisis of individuality in the face of death." He attributes this dilemma to a complex of phenomena: the rupture in Western thought after Kant and Hegel, in which the perception of truth as subjectivity emptied death of absolute metaphysical significance, calling into question the nature of reality itself; the individual's sense of despair and alienation within nineteenth-century bourgeois culture; the unsettling revelations of science, which reduced the individual to a minuscule creature in a vast, indifferent universe. On this last point Morin argues that the natural and human sciences had created a consciousness of voids opening upon voids: "Les civilisations sont mortelles. L'humanité est promise à la mort. La terre mourra. Et les mondes et les soleils. Et l'univers lui-même, gigantesque explosion lente. La mort humaine, déjà vide infini, se dilate sur tous les plans du cosmos, de plus en plus vide et infinie: elle est comme l'univers, en expansion. Tout renvoie donc l'individu solitaire à une solitude de plus en plus misérable au creux d'un néant sans limite."[4] Such discoveries have, in Morin's view, profoundly complicated our adaptation to the fact of death, since the results of scientific inquiry appear to contradict the theory (ingrained in Western culture since the Renaissance) of individual significance and uniqueness.

Though sustained at times by a tissue of reductive generalizations,

Morin's theory of a contemporary crisis of death resonates with too many literary and philosophical texts not to have explanatory validity. Obviously the sources of a modern attitude toward death defy the most comprehensive analysis. The pursuit of origins quickly transforms itself into an infinite regression along innumerable forking paths; as Borges suggests, time and history are not linear but labyrinthine. Nevertheless, the general sense—expressed variously by Tolstoy, Hemingway, and Heidegger—that death has become the crux of being in the modern world compels reflection. We need to understand how and when death achieved its sovereignty. For despite the presence of death in all ages and despite its occasional representation as a hideous threat, there is scant evidence that any prior epoch conceived of death itself as the only absolute truth governing human activity. At no time before Poe could we imagine a poem in which "Death looks gigantically down" as the unchallenged, reigning presence; in no century before our own could we imagine a fictional hero declaring that "Death is God."

If one were to construct a broad theory of death's modern ascendancy, it would have to account for the erosion of faith after the Enlightenment and the movement toward a secular, "post-Christian" mentality, in which residual religious practice seemed incapable of sustaining a vital mythos of resurrection and transcendence. It would have to consider as well the complex impact of Romanticism—the individuation of consciousness as well as the shift to a subjectively grounded theory of reality, which eventually exposed the solitude of the self and the uncertainty of the world beyond. It would have to assess the effect of anomie in mass culture, the breakdown of absolute structures of thought and belief into relative theories and into the psychic welter of relativity itself. It would have to gauge (as Morin suggests) the conceptual fallout of scientific discoveries, particularly those which impinge upon our assumptions about human individuality and our place in the cosmos. It would have to examine the ways in which Western capitalism has inculcated a materialist perception of human endeavor and thus conditioned an empirical view of life and death. It would have to take note as well of all ideologies which in revolutionizing the social order have denied the mystery of being and the yearning to surmount death. Such a comprehensive analysis of modern death (it needs scarcely be said) exceeds the scope of the present study.

But we can at least outline, in this way, the theoretical parameters of the problem which William Barrett has formulated in philosophical terms:

> With the modern period, man . . . has entered upon a secular phase of his history. He entered it with exuberance over the prospect of increased power he would have over the world around him. But in this world, in which his dreams of power were often more than fulfilled, he found himself for the first time *homeless*. Science stripped nature of its human forms and presented man with a universe that was neutral, alien, in its vastness and force, to his human purposes. Religion, before this phase set in, had been a structure that encompassed man's life, providing him with a system of images and symbols by which he could express his own aspirations toward psychic wholeness. With the loss of this containing framework man became not only a dispossessed but a fragmentary being. . . . Moreover, man's feeling of homelessness, of alienation has been intensified in the midst of a bureaucratized, impersonal mass society. He has come to feel himself an outsider even within his own human society. He is trebly alienated: a stranger to God, to nature, and to the gigantic social apparatus that supplies his material wants.[5]

Although Barrett here confronts the problem of alienation, his perspective has immediate relevance to the catastrophe of death, defining an implicit anxiety, a lost security and enclosure, and a vulnerability to fragmentation and annihilation. Death is not the only source of existential alienation, but it lies at the core of "homelessness," for it is our ultimate model of solitary banishment. It is moreover the nearest, most accessible experience of "nothingness," that "void of nonBeing" which according to Barrett "opens up within our own Being" and thus "makes itself present and felt as the object of our dread."[6]

In light of Barrett's characterization, we appreciate anew the early and discerning judgment of Sarah Helen Whitman, who observed of

Poe that the "unrest and faithlessness of the age culminated in him"; "sadder and lonelier" than any contemporary, he "came to sound the very depths of the abyss."[7] Yet Poe sounded the abyss not simply through existential motifs, through scenes of annihilation and expressions of dread. In less obvious ways he interiorized the void of meaninglessness as a problem of writing and explored through his own practice the emergent relationship between the new death and the act of inscription. In this regard Poe was largely ahead of his time, intuiting a previously unsuspected linkage between writing and mortality, language and truth. He sensed a momentous cultural transition and projected this awareness in texts which reflect the desperate situation of a subject striving through an always inadequate system of "mere words" to give coherence to unspeakable fears.

How this new, catastrophic death impinged upon the practice of writing merits serious attention, for it forms the broad cultural problem which the present discussion of Poe seeks to open up. Writing receives scant attention in Morin's study, which in amassing evidence for a crisis of death in the mid-nineteenth century has relatively little to say about its effects on the production of texts. Morin does note that "le spectre de la mort" now haunts literature: previously "enrobée sous les thèmes magiques qui l'exorcisaient, ou refoulée dans la participation esthétique, ou camouflée sous le voile de la décence, [la mort] apparaît nue." Oddly overlooking the early example of Poe, he speaks of entire canons—like those of Maeterlinck, Mallarmé, and Rilke—marked by death-obsession.[8] The perception of death's presence by these writers stands in contrast to the blindness or denial abroad in popular culture; yet Morin has nothing to say about language itself, nor does he pursue the question of how and when this specter began to enter into the space of writing. Such omissions are not surprising, given the absence (noted earlier) of a history of inscription in the modern sense; but to clarify the breakthrough achieved by Poe, we must construct at least a minimal concept of the transformation of writing and the emergence of *écriture*, drawing from time to time upon modern theorists who have contemplated the nexus of language and metaphysics.

To trace the effect of the crisis of death upon writing requires obvious qualification, for writing in the general sense involves a multiplicity of forms and purposes. Surely for literate persons in the nineteenth century, for ordinary folk who composed letters, notes, deeds, wills, contracts, reports, and other texts (including most kinds of book manuscripts), the practice of inscription underwent change only in the improvement of writing implements. Yet in other forms of writing—those "literary" gestures in which language constitutes an end in itself, a mode of creativity or self-expression or amusement—a new and menacing death had as early as the eighteenth century begun to intrude into the imaginative text and to change in subtle ways the writer's relationship to writing.

Here we approach a challenging frontier, for theory has not yet described with precision the juncture of language and mortality, much less placed that juncture within a diachronic scheme which takes account of evolving perceptions and models of death. And so we must resort to improvisation, constructing what is at best a tentative account of the process by which the crisis in metaphysics infiltrated and transformed the field of writing. From a historical perspective, there appear to be four distinct phases of change with certain obvious relationships, although resemblances seem to be more analogical than causal. On each level, the link between writing and death manifests itself in different terms; and as we approach the deepest level of intrusion—the concept of language as signification—we enter into the problem of modernist *écriture*.

In the most apparent sense, death enters literature in the mid-eighteenth century as a fetishized subject. As noted in the opening chapter, the graveyard poetry popularized in the 1740s by Young and Blair expressed more than a transient vogue for melancholy. Whatever differences might be observed among its practitioners, such poetry collectively betrays an emergent anxiety about dying, accompanied by deepening uncertainty about life after death. Whereas poets in earlier ages had composed elegies inspired by particular deaths, the graveyard poets began to produce lengthy elegiac poems without a subject in the usual sense; rather, they reflected on the universality of death, the terrors of the tomb, the weird ambience of the cemetery, and the experience of loss. Thomas Parnell's early "Night-Piece on Death" (1721) anticipated a curious trend: night became associated with a state of mind, a saturnine fearfulness quite unlike the pensive, Miltonic tone of such period pieces as Collins' "Ode to Evening." Death, burial, and doubt had seized the literary imagination. A later expression of this consciousness, the "Burials" section of George Crabbe's *Parish Register* (1807), enunciates with striking clarity the subsidence of faith and the onset of modern dread. Crabbe compares the new epoch of death with a time "when humble Christians died with views sublime":

> When lively Faith upheld the sinking Heart,
> And Friends assur'd to meet, prepar'd to part;
> When Love felt Hope, when Sorrow grew serene,
> And all was Comfort, in the Death-bed Scene.
> Alas! when now the gloomy King they wait,
> 'Tis Weakness yielding to resistless Fate;
> Like wretched Men upon the Ocean cast,
> They labour hard and struggle to the last;
> "Hope against Hope," and wildly gaze around,
> In search of Help, that never shall be found;
> Nor, till the last strong Billow stops the Breath,
> Will they believe them in the jaws of Death!
>
> . . . .
>
> What I behold, are feverish fits of Strife,
> 'Twixt Fears of Dying and Desire of Life;
> Those earthly Hopes, that to the last indure;
> Those Fears, that Hopes superior fail to cure;
> At best, a sad submission to the Doom,
> Which, turning from the Danger, lets it come.
>
> [11.5–16; 29–34]

It is hard to imagine a more explicit poetic acknowledgment of lost certitude. Through a mordant recasting of Gray's "Elegy," Crabbe devised his "simple Annals of the VILLAGE POOR" to show "how Death has triumph'd in so short a Space."

In a less contemplative fashion, death also insinuated itself into the Gothic novel, both figuratively—as ghosts, skeletons, or specters—and literally as a looming experiential possibility. Alone in a landscape of nightmare, the Gothic hero or heroine experienced the dark side of Romantic freedom: existential disorientation, wrought by the loss of defining structures. The Gothic paradigm enunciated the quintessential modern predicament of an alienated being whose skepticism has vitiated his capacity for belief, while paralyzing dread has exposed the insufficiency of science and logic. If this literature of terror presented a ratiocinative search for answers, its real force lay, as David Punter observes, in its capacity for "removing the illusory halo of certainty from the so-called 'natural' world."[9] Beyond the sociopolitical implications skillfully elaborated by Punter, what the Gothic chiefly depicts is the vulnerability of the human subject in a world of annihilating and unintelligible force. And in a work like Matthew G. Lewis's *The Monk,* we see through the lurid crimes of Ambrosio one of the most powerful assertions of the genre: that death has been not only desacralized but also appropriated by evil as its sign and seal.

In graveyard poetry and Gothic fiction, we thus observe the thematic incursion of death into the field of writing. A virtual presence in scenes of absence and desolation, mortality here presents itself as a conscious and conventionalized problem within a specific imaginative scheme. However, as narrative took its "inward turn" (in Erich Kahler's phrase) and Romanticism encouraged texts of a more introspective and autobiographical kind, death came to assume yet another relationship to writing. It may be, as Barrett John Mandel hints, that the new sense of death actually called the narrative of self into being: "Our own particular modern Western dread has done as much to bring about the present state of autobiography as any other influence."[10] In the most elemental way, autobiography involves the transposition of lived experience (or memories thereof) into written signs. But if its subject is *bios,* "the life" reduced to details, episodes, phases, turning points and the like, its fundamental energy derives from the prospect of death, the writer's awareness of his own finitude and his concomitant need to construct, while he can, a memorial to himself and to all that constitutes his world. As Thomas Couser remarks, the autobiographer seeks "a solution to the problem posed by his mortality" through writing which quite literally constitutes a "death-defying act."[11]

Just a year before the accident which took his life, Roland Barthes revealed in a series of lectures his intention to write an autobiographical novel patently inspired by Proust's A la recherche du temps perdu. He implied an analogy between the desire of writing (vouloir-écrire) and the situation of the poet at the beginning of The Divine Comedy; Barthes saw himself, like Dante, "in the middle of life's way"—not chronologically but experientially between life and death, able to foresee the end and impelled to write by the sense of its imminence.[12] Paradoxically, one's death is precisely the subject excluded by autobiography, except in the form of intimation or fictional projection. In this sense, the genre invariably fails to achieve its logical, formal closure; it cannot complete the trajectory between birth and death. Yet autobiography is nevertheless peculiarly haunted by death, insofar as it formulates in narrative terms the same questions which will be raised by the writer's death: who was this being who wrote and what was the nature of his existence? As a retrospective gesture, the writing of one's life expresses the desire to locate meanings and to insure that this self will not disappear into the void, anonymous and forgotten.

As the autobiographical mode began to assert itself in memoirs, poetry, and prose fiction, the connection between life and writing became increasingly self-conscious. Novels (and Tristram Shandy is a celebrated example) began to reflect on their origins and textual peculiarities; poems tracing the conditions of their inscription—one thinks of "Tintern Abbey," "Kubla Khan," and "Ode to a Nightingale"— proliferated under Romanticism. In works manifesting the experience of subjectivity, the act of inscription became—perhaps inevitably—its own subject, for the autobiographical mode implicitly carries the writer toward the present scene of writing, which is likewise the moment beyond which the narrative of one's experience cannot go. As the practice of writing became grounded in self-conscious inwardness, the text acquired a new metaphoricity: its boundedness became a sign of the writer's own finitude, and its reflexiveness marked both a preparation for and a resistance to death. Within the space of the text, mortality entered into the psychology of writing; about self-conscious novels, Robert Alter has observed: "Perhaps the most basic paradox of this mode of fiction which functions through the display of paradoxes is that as a kind of novel focusing on art and the artist it should prove to be, even in many of its characteristically comic embodiments, a long meditation on death."[13] A similar tendency surfaces in Keats's great poem, which posits a reciprocity between the beauty of the bird's song (figuratively, the poetic composition) and the zone of decomposition, "where palsy shakes a few, sad, last gray hairs, / Where youth grows pale, and spectre-thin, and dies; / Where but to think is to be full of sorrow / And leaden-eyed despairs." To be sure, earlier writers had meditated on the way in which poetry outlasts death; but by the nineteenth century, "leaden-eyed despairs" had closed off most other strategies of real or symbolic survival. Skeptical of the Beautiful Death which promised resurrection and reunion, deeper minds committed themselves to the written text and to the practice of writing as a quasi-religious activity. Self-consciousness about writing gradually produced an acute sense of analogies between lives and texts; between the experience of writing and the expenditure of being; between the end of inscription and the silence of death. These perceptions (so evident, for instance, in the letters and journals of Kafka) manifest a complicated, explicit awareness of the interchange between death and writing which characterizes the third stage of its unfolding.

If death entered writing first as a thematic fetish, then as a primal impulse for life writing, and then as the ground of self-conscious textuality, it ultimately penetrated to the level of language itself, as philosophy began to deconstruct its own linguistic premises in a radical rethinking of the way that verbal signs relate to truth. Whether the new death evoked a questioning of metaphysics, or whether this questioning itself contributed to the ascendancy of death, we can observe inchoately in Poe and manifestly in modern writers and theorists the impact of both phenomena: the sense of a language which has been emptied, hollowed out, encrypted. That which guaranteed the truth of language, an originary Logos, has been through the unfolding of time lost, obscured, or invalidated. This displacement has likewise forced the human subject to confront the problem of death nakedly, to live (as Sartre has said) without appeal. Through metaphorical association, the cleavage between speech and writing has become emblematic of the gap between life, being, or spiritual plenitude on the one hand and finite mortal existence on the other. In modern postmetaphysics, writing is merely the trace of a lost presence and wholeness; it is, Derrida remarks, a system of differences which would be inconceivable "without the nonpresense of the other inscribed within the sense of the present, without the relationship with death as the concrete structure of the living present."[14] At once more pervasive and more subtle than any other symptom of death's intrusion into writing, this abyss between the graphic sign and its referent, between word and world, discloses the provisionality of linguistic formulations purporting to convey truth.

Though the "fragmentation of language" has become a critical issue only in the last two decades, it too derives from the philosophical schism which divided the late eighteenth century. Foucault describes the process by which language lost its notational or representational function and underwent "dispersion":

The threshold between Classicism and modernity . . . had been definitively crossed when words ceased to intersect with representations and to provide a spontaneous grid for the knowledge of things. At the beginning of the nineteenth century, they rediscovered their ancient, enigmatic density; though not in order to restore the curve of the world which had harboured them during the Renaissance, nor in order to mingle with things in a circular system of signs. Once detached from representation, language has existed, right up to our own day, only in a dispersed way: for philologists, words are like so many objects formed and deposited by history; for those who wish to achieve a formalization, language must strip itself of its concrete content and leave nothing visible but those forms of discourse that are universally valid; if one's intent is to interpret, then words become a text to be broken down, so as to allow that other meaning hidden in them to emerge and become clearly visible; lastly, language may sometimes arise for its own sake in an act of writing that designates nothing other than itself.[15]

For both Foucault and Derrida, the spoken word is already a sign once removed from an archetypal inscription copresent with the thing it names; the system of letters, writing, thereby constitutes the trace of a trace. Derrida would argue that the fall from referentiality, the detachment of language from representation, occurred through the cultural superseding of speech by writing, presumably about the time that (according to Foucault) language underwent dispersion. Not until the later nineteenth century, however, when Nietzsche opened up the question of language in philosophical discourse, did thinking arrive at a perception of its place within the prison-house of language, within an order of depleted signs.

And not until Heidegger did philosophy come to understand the problem of language as a symptom of metaphysical crisis. In his "Letter on Humanism," Heidegger argued that the "devastation" of language separated man from Being itself: "Much bemoaned of late, and much too lately, the downfall of language is . . . not the grounds for, but already a consequence of, the state of affairs in which language under the dominance of the modern metaphysics of subjectivity almost irremediably falls out of its element. Language still denies us its essence: that it is the house of the truth of Being."[16] But whereas Heidegger contemplates a way back into the "house of Being" through the relationship to language epitomized by poetry, Derrida (after Rousseau) sees this yearning for plenitude as the desire for that which language perpetually defers and denies. Words are precisely the sign of an unbridgeable gap between man and the immanence or presence he dreams of recovering. Writing is the "dangerous supplement" to essence insofar as "representation there claims to be presence and the sign of the thing itself." In its supplementarity, writing constitutes a system of differences grounded in the fundamental *différance* of presence and absence, enabling Derrida to announce "the master-name of the supplementary series: death."[17] In redefining the metaphysics of self-presence, Derrida discloses a complicity between writing and death which reverses an originary relationship between Logos and life. Indeed, he describes writing as the "becoming-absent and the becoming-unconscious of the subject," a process constituted and made possible by "*the economy of death*": "All graphemes are of a testamentary essence. And the original absence of the subject of writing is also the absence of the thing or the referent."[18] At the risk of oversimplifying Derrida's intricate deconstruction of logocentrism, we might conclude that in moving from orality to writing, from living voice to silent mark, Western culture adopted as its model of discourse the corpse as signifier. By the nineteenth century, death had intruded so far into consciousness as to transform language, the house of Being, into a charnel house of written forms. The relationship between death and writing goes beyond analogy, for the dead body in fact became a signifying object and a source of signs (in the form of death masks and locks of hair) about the time that the authority of language shifted from the spoken word to inscription. Just as the traditional distinction between eternal soul and mortal flesh fell into desuetude or became colored by skepticism about the soul's very existence, the word became a grapheme and lost its living presence. Obviously, the eclipse of speech by writing occurred not through any deliberate contemplation of death's regnancy; yet as the corpse became dissociated from the soul (oddly, spiritualism and doubt had the same effect) the body assumed a semiotic function as the fetishized sign of the absent self. In its attachment to this silent form, one might speculate, culture endeavored to naturalize the increasingly disruptive difference between life and death which issued from metaphysical uncertainty. The encounter with absence—the absence epitomized by the body of death—became the recurrent, paradigmatic experience of modern consciousness, as Emily Dickinson and Henry James were among the earliest to realize.[19] Writing emerged, inevitably, as the appropriate notation of this absence, for the system of inscription doubles the action of death by replicating living speech as a network of encrypted signs. To borrow the phrase of Michael Davitt Bell, "the word . . . is the corpse of its origin."[20] In the paradoxical space of the text the writer foreshadows his own death by assuming the pronominal corpse, the "I" of writing.

Surrounded by the funereal sentimentality of popular culture and afflicted by melancholy attachments to the dead women who had loved him, Poe worked out a relationship to writing which assumed the domain of death as the very ground of experience. Mortality was not a "theme": it was for him the defining condition of being, the principle or force which impelled the act of inscription. Poe intuitively sensed the intrusion of death into writing and consciousness, the precarious situation of the writing self before the abyss of silence. And in the recurrent figures of his fictional and poetic texts, we perceive the struggle to articulate this premonition. Such a strategy manifests itself, for example, in "Shadow—A Parable" (1835) which comments upon the status of writing while it allegorizes the presence of death in the midst of life. Here, as in the more impressive sequel, "The Masque of the Red Death," Poe collapses the dialectic of inside and outside to reveal that the "shadow"—the personification of pestilence—is already within the place of sanctuary and has at the moment of composition already laid its hand upon the writer.

Yet the opening paragraph suggests another way of metaphorizing death: as a site of darkness which is implicitly elsewhere, distinguishable from the scene of writing. The narrator Oinos presents his parable as a communication from "the valley of the shadow of death," that destination he will have reached by the time a living successor attends to his discourse. He thereby invites us to contemplate the text as a sign of the metaphysical distance which finally separates every writer from living readers: "Ye who read are still among the living; but I who write shall have long since gone my way into the region of shadows. For indeed strange things shall happen, and secret things be known, and many centuries shall pass away, ere these memorials be seen of men. And, when seen, there will be some to disbelieve, and some to doubt, and yet a few who will find much to ponder upon in the characters here graven with a stylus of iron" (CW, 2:188–89). These "graven" characters tell of the "company of seven," victims whose fate represents that of the human species. According to this figurality, death is simultaneously immanent and remote, a proximate "shadow" and a foreign "region." The narrator's words constitute "memorials" to all of the departed, but they specifically register the individuality of the writer, who in the act of memorializing himself is both living and dead. Writing is both the proof of being and the acknowledgement of mortality; it points to a lost past and an unreachable future while inserting its own infinitely repeatable textuality into the succession of history. Even as it establishes its temporality and conceptual locus, however, writing unfolds "Out of Space—out of Time," contrived by one (the "I" of writing) who already declares himself to be a shadow.

This reflection on inscription and mortality brings into focus the tension or reciprocity which for Poe empowers the life of writing. Significantly, "Shadow" comments upon this relationship through a figuring of death's intrusion into the space of the text; that is, the narrative in some sense enacts the fate of Western discourse, not through any overt philosophizing but (as in "MS. Found in a Bottle") through a parabolic rendering of writing unto death. Poe portrays a chamber sealed off from contagion; the seven revelers drink and make merry, singing the songs of Anacreon. But the gaiety is contrived, for over the group hangs a "dead weight," a palpable depression imposed by an already thrice-present mortality glimpsed first in the pallid countenances of the seven ("those who are to die") reflected in the ebony table; then in the enshrouded corpse of Zoilus, whose unclosed eyes reveal a "bitterness"; and finally in the "dark and undefined shadow" that issues from the sable draperies and fixes itself upon the door. This terrifying and unintelligible shade signals the fate of the writer and his cohorts, and the unfinished condition of the text again manifests the dilemma of its inscription. Ironically, writing is here suspended by the return of speech; when the shadow announces his name and provenance, he speaks with the voice of the dead: "For the tones in the voice of the shadow were not the tones of any one being, but of a multitude of beings, and, varying in their cadences from syllable to syllable, fell duskily upon our ears in the well remembered and familiar accents of many thousand departed friends" (191). Here the text surrenders itself to silence, for the living presence of the spoken word, already doubled by the encrypted written sign, now returns from the grave as a horrifying articulation of absence. Writing, which derives its power of signification from the difference between the ephemeral living word and the fixed, deathlike grapheme, finds itself displaced by the speaking of death. Through this enigmatic break, this lapse at the end of "Shadow," Poe implies that the complicity of writing and death is rooted in the mortality of the speaking subject; if the dead could actually speak for themselves as they do in this fantasy, writing would have no function.

As Poe perceived almost from the outset, death had entered irrevocably into the life of writing, enthroning itself as the model and guarantor of inscription. Early and late, his texts display reformulations of the way in which death mediates and shapes our relationship to writing. Even a story like "The Gold-Bug" (1843)—on one level a gaudy exercise in mystification—contains amid its theatrical details a pointed figuring of the connection between the coded message and that which has been buried by the long-dead writer of the cryptogram. Significantly, Legrand makes the analytical breakthrough, discovers an effaced text when a "death's-head" emerges on a piece of parchment. The image appears on the reverse side immediately beneath Legrand's drawing of the beetle, producing a kind of gloss on the relation between "The Gold-Bug" and its concealed subject. After a series of operations (which recall Pym's efforts to read the note from Augustus) Legrand succeeds in restoring the once invisible text. The note situates a problem of decipherment between two signs: one is the figure of a goat or kid, the "punning or hieroglyphic signature" of Captain Kidd; the other is the image of the skull. Of the latter Poe writes, "The death's head at the corner diagonally opposite, had . . . the air of a stamp, or seal" (*CW*, 3:833). That is, the text occupies a space between the writing subject and death; the encrypting of the message—which itself refers to an encrypting of treasure—constitutes a defiance of death through an embracing of mortality. In devising the cryptograph, Kidd subjects language to the transformation which the "death's-head" prefigures; death seals the discourse against the fate of its living signatory by burying its meaning. Legrand's work involves a double exhumation, for he must uncover the enduring message within the inscribed text before he can dig up "the buried treasure still . . . entombed" (834). That he recovers the booty by dropping a weight (the gold bug) through the eye of a skull only renders more explicit the mediatory function of death in the economy of writing.[21] In a sense this discovery—that we communicate the buried secret, the enduring word, only through death—is the metaphorical treasure of "The Gold-Bug."

What Poe reveals, in the succession of tales and poems which constitute his literary corpus, is the enormous complexity, the imaginative fecundity, of this elemental insight. This is the problem to which he returns obsessively in his most striking enactments of the encounter with death. Hence, for example, the fatality of "The Fall of the House of Usher": at a crucial moment, the narrator attempts to calm his host by reading "the 'Mad Trist' of Sir Launcelot Canning" and in the correspondence between that narrative and underground noises, Poe suggests that the romance holds a clue to the curse upon the Ushers. At three separate points, events in the "Mad Trist" seem to evoke sounds within the mansion, as if the text possessed some preternatural agency which ultimately called forth Madeline from the burial vault. Although this "coincidence" may be dismissed as anticipatory anxiety—one can argue that the narrator unconsciously chooses a text which describes sounds like those he hears beneath the house—the details of the story indeed furnish a coded version of the problem of dread figured by Usher's relationship to his sister's corpse. And in a more important sense the "Mad Trist" exemplifies the way in which writing corresponds to the mortal condition which determines and authorizes it.

The episode supposedly read by the narrator (and then reproduced in the text of "Usher") depicts Ethelred's forcible entry into the dwelling of a "maliceful" hermit. Having battered down the door, the hero discovers no sign of the hermit; instead he confronts a scaly dragon which guards a golden palace ornamented by a brass shield bearing the inscription: "Who entereth herein, a conqueror hath bin; / Who slayeth the dragon, the shield he shall win" (CW, 2:414). Ethelred promptly dispatches the dragon, which dies hideously, "[giving] up his pesty breath, with a shriek so horrid and harsh, and withal so piercing, that Ethelred had fain to close his ears with his hands against the dreadful noise of it, the like whereof was never before heard." Wishing to complete "the breaking up of the enchantment," Ethelred "[removes] the carcass from out of the way before him" and approaches the shield. But as if unfastened by the removal of the carcass, the shield falls to the silver floor with a "great and terrible ringing sound." At this juncture the reading of the "Mad Trist" is interrupted by a "clangorous" reverberation within the House of Usher, followed by Roderick's hysterical interpretation of the romance as a figuring of Madeline's return: "And now—tonight—Ethelred—ha!ha!—the breaking of the hermit's door, and the death-cry of the dragon, and the clangor of the shield!—say, rather, the rending of her coffin, and the grating of the iron hinges of her prison, and her struggles within the coppered archway of the vault" (416). And indeed, the appearance of "the lofty and enshrouded figure of the lady Madeline of Usher" seems to validate this reading and imply an occult relationship between the "Mad Trist" and the fall of the Ushers.

But like the image of the house in the tarn, the analogy is reversed and inverted. For the ancient tale of Sir Launcelot Canning represents the dispelling of an enchantment, whereas the extinction of the Ushers marks the completion of a curse. And so the meaning of the last, horrific scene—the deadly embrace of Roderick by Madeline—becomes intelligible only through a consideration of the way in which it effects a reversal of the "Mad Trist." Reduced to constituent terms (the dragon, the palace, and the shield), the romance may be understood as a fantasy of psychic liberation; as such it corresponds closely to Poe's earlier insertion, "The Haunted Palace," and in some sense answers the despairing poem with a narrative of reclamation and recovery. Insofar as "The Haunted Palace" allegorizes the usurpation of reason by griefs and fears, the verses summarize the anxieties of Usher, who anticipates that he will "abandon life and reason together, in some struggle with the grim phantasm, FEAR" (403). Significantly, Ethelred too encounters a haunted palace and a frightening embodiment of that which holds the edifice in thrall; but he slays the monster, endures its dying shriek, disposes of the body, and thus gains the shield, which signifies both victory over the beast and entitlement to the palace. If we understand the palace in both texts as a metaphor for mind, we must then construe both the "evil things, in robes of sorrow" and the scaly dragon as versions of that phantasm which threatens life and reason together—that is, as figurations of the fate which Roderick dreads, the fate prefigured by the transformation of his twin sister. Poe underscores the analogy through the "death-cry" of the dragon, which anticipates Madeline's "moaning cry" as she falls upon her brother "in her violent and now final death-agonies." But whereas Ethelred destroys the dragon and lifts the enchantment, Usher falls to the floor "a corpse, and a victim to the terrors he had anticipated."

In the difference between Ethelred's story and Usher's, Poe inscribes the dilemma of the new death within the metaphysical void of the modern age. One key distinction lies in the relation of the hero to the body of death: whereas the knight removes "the carcass from out of the way before him" and so figuratively confronts and resolves the fear of mortality, Usher experiences a paralysis of will, cannot bring himself to bury his sister's body, and is at last driven mad by the uncertainty signaled by her "temporary entombment." His indecision derives not simply from the ambiguity of her demise (with the attendant symptoms of catalepsy) but from the tension between that which bonds him to Madeline—the "striking similitude" of the twins and the "sympathies of a scarcely intelligible nature"—and that which horrifies him, the signs of her moribund condition. With the apparent death of Madeline (she is said to be "no more"), Usher is caught between the desire to preserve the possibly still-living body and the need to protect himself from the contagion of death. In the decline of Madeline, the cadaverous Usher has perceived the image of his own disintegration; but in his desolate world, it is a fate too ghastly to be contemplated. Ultimately, his anxiety about the physical condition of Madeline betrays an unarticulated despair about her spiritual destiny. By refusing to consign his sister to the earth, Usher simultaneously denies death and condemns himself to a life of horror.

For, as the story of Ethelred suggests, it is only by confronting the dragon and disposing of the carcass—that is, by recognizing that death is paradoxically the end of the monster of death—that one can liberate the palace and live one's life. What Usher fears—what we all fear—is not so much death itself but the experience of dying, the last agony. Though he claims to have heard his sister's "first feeble movements in the hollow coffin," Usher has been unable to summon the moral energy to face the possible image of decay; in psychic terms, his velleity is itself the product of a refusal to confront death. Becker remarks that "the enemy of mankind is basic repression, the denial of throbbing physical life and the spectre of death."[22] To repress the specter is precisely to cut oneself off from "throbbing physical life." And so when Usher deposits the body of Madeline in the vault beneath the house, figuratively pushing into the unconscious that overwhelming reality which she incarnates, he condemns himself to a death-in-life. He has not faced the shadow; he has evaded it. And so its eruption, in the form of Madeline's enshrouded figure, marks the inevitable—and fatal—return of the repressed.

In this complex metaphorizing of the problem of death, Poe articulates both the nature of the crisis and a figurative solution to the paralysis of death anxiety. But that solution seems as remote as the world of the romance; our spiritual contemporary, Usher dwells literally and figuratively on the brink of the abyss and cannot escape the fatality of his situation. Nor in fact does the putative narrator, who flees "aghast" from the crumbling mansion to record his tale and thus (like the Ancient Mariner) to signify the continuing hold of the experience upon his consciousness. But the writing of "Usher" may be construed as a modern effort to confront the dragon, to extract from the romance a principle of survival. In this sense the text of the "Mad Trist" presents a model of the complicity between inscription and mortality, for the surface action replicates the resistance to death which is the agon of writing. Poe attributes the romance to Canning, the same imaginary author to whom he later ascribed the motto for the *Stylus*: "—unbending that all men / Of thy firm TRUTH may say—'Lo! this is writ / With the antique *iron pen*'" (*CW*, 1:328). The idea of a writing whose truth outlasts death occurs in the "Mad Trist" as the legend "enwritten" on the magical brass shield: one who enters into writing "a conqueror hath bin." Ethelred's adventure enacts the ordeal undergone by both Canning and the narrator: that confrontation with death which impels writing by foreshadowing the silence of nonbeing.

To perceive "Usher" as a fable of dread and avoidance is to understand more clearly its centrality within the Poe canon. If the text signifies the survival of the writer, it also implies the impossibility of writing within the house of Usher—that is, in a condition of paralyzing denial. The narrator inscribes his account from an unspecified place on the opposite side of "the old causeway," at some geographical and psychic distance from the tarn into which the house disappears. Only elsewhere can he record Usher's struggle to preserve life and reason against the consciousness of impending annihilation. That struggle, objectified in the relationship of Usher to his dying sister, defines a fundamental opposition, a quintessential version of the deep structure which may be said to inform most of those texts Poe described as tales of effect.

For as we move from "Metzengerstein" to "The Light-House," tracing the itinerary of writing, we observe the obsessive recurrence of a particular figure, the protagonist's threatening encounter with avatars of mortality. In its various metamorphoses, this presence assumes the form of persons, animals, apparitions, or natural phenomena. For Baron von Metzengerstein, it is the phantasmic horse with its "sepulchral and disgusting teeth"; the protagonist's "perverse attachment" to the unnamable beast implies a self-destructive fascination with the immemorial curse of death. For the Norwegian fisherman, it is the maelström of "liquid ebony," an abyss which excites the desire to know the never-to-be-imparted secret: "I positively felt a *wish* to explore its depths, even at the sacrifice I was going to make; and my principal grief was that I should never be able to tell my old companions on the shore about the mysteries I should see" (*CW*, 2:588–89). But the survival instinct prevails, and the sailor returns to tell the story of his near-encounter with extinction. For the mesmerist Templeton (in "A Tale of the Ragged Mountains") it is the cadaverous Augustus Bedloe, whose eyes are said to be "so totally vapid, filmy, and dull, as to convey the idea of the eyes of a long-interred corpse" (*CW*, 3:940). Through a mystical experience, Bedloe reenacts his death in a previous life and contemplates his own "swollen and disfigured" corpse. Interested in "psychal discoveries," Templeton seems to construe the resemblance between Bedloe's story and the earlier death of a friend named Oldeb as an instance of metempsychosis. But there is also the suggestion of telepathy, for Bedloe has his vision at the very moment that Templeton has been inscribing an account of Oldeb's demise. And so the tale teases us with the question of spiritual survival while furnishing another example of death's insistent relationship to writing.

In "The Masque of the Red Death," Poe's most lavish evocation of fatality, Prince Prospero and his guests endeavor to isolate themselves from contagion. The seclusion metaphorizes a denial of sorrow and death: within the abbey "it was folly to grieve, or to think" (*CW*, 2:671). Yet mortality cannot be forgotten or excluded from the human scene, and so immurement functions as self-entombment. Death's arrival is only a matter of time, and Poe's attention to the ebony clock with its disquieting chiming places the action within the framework of temporality and mutability, thus promoting a broadly symbolic reading of the masquerade and the spectral intruder. It is, as Joseph Patrick Roppolo has noted, "a parable of the inevitability and the universality of death." Death cannot be barred from the palace, he points out, because it is in the blood, part and parcel of our humanity, not an extrinsic force. Hence, according to Roppolo, the spectral figure is not a representation of mortality (which is already present) but a figment of the imagination, man's "self-aroused and self-developed fear of his own mistaken concept of death."[23]

This approach has a certain validity—death is indeed in our blood, coded in our genes—and it leads to the interesting hypothesis that Prospero succumbs to his own terror, to the "mistaken concept" that death is a tangible enemy. But it also collapses the supernaturalism of the tale and reduces the intriguing figure to a mere delusion, thus distorting the allegorical signification of his effect upon the masquerade. The notion of the specter as hallucination loses credibility when we realize that all of the revelers observe "the presence of a masked figure" (674); either everyone deludes himself in precisely the same way, or else there *is* a figure. Poe's careful description of the "spectral image," as he is seen by "the whole company," supports the latter thesis:

> The figure was tall and gaunt, and shrouded from head to foot in the habiliments of the grave. The mask which concealed the visage was made so nearly to resemble the countenance of a stiffened corpse that the closest scrutiny must have had difficulty in detecting the cheat. And yet all this might have been endured, if not approved, by the mad revelers around. But the mummer had gone so far as to assume the type of the Red Death. His vesture was dabbled in *blood*—and his broad brow, with all the features of the face, was besprinkled with the scarlet horror. [675]

In symbolizing the unmentionable, the mummer has violated a taboo and brought death into the open. But why does Poe insist upon the particularity of the Red Death imagery? In the first paragraph he describes the plague as extraordinarily fatal and hideous: "There were sharp pains, and sudden dizziness, and then profuse bleeding at the pores, with dissolution." Even more terrible, "the whole seizure, progress and termination of the disease, were the incidents of half an hour." That is, the disease produces disfigurement and instantaneous decomposition, transforming a vibrant person into a loathsome object. There is no talk of the soul's deliverance; human carrion raises the question at the core of naturalistic thought: are we nothing more than the biological organization of our perishable flesh? When Prospero falls dead on the threshold of the seventh chamber, the black apartment, the masqueraders fall upon the intruder, only to discover an emptiness behind the corpselike mask: "Then, summoning the wild courage of despair, a throng of the revellers at once threw themselves into the black apartment, and, seizing the mummer, whose tall figure stood erect and motionless within the shadow of the ebony clock, gasped in unutterable horror at finding the grave cerements and corpselike mask which they handled with so violent a rudeness, untenanted by any tangible form" (676). This is surely one of the most intriguing moments in Poe's fiction: before the clock and within the black apartment—the zone of mortality—the maskers attempt to unmask death, literally to deconstruct the representation of death. But the cerements and mask are signs without a proper referent; they mark the semiotic impasse in which writing has begun to locate its own activity. The discovery of the revelers enacts the nineteenth-century perception of death as "pure negativity," a nothingness resulting from "the separation of the body and soul."[24] Paradoxically, Poe's portrayal of pure absence signifies "the presence of the Red Death"; the revelers fall, the clock stops, and the flames of the tripods expire. Death itself has no essence; it cannot be seized, known, destroyed, or avoided. It is a presence-as-absence whose meaning is forever denied to presence and already accomplished in absence.

Persistently in his fiction Poe draws upon an ur-narrative: an enervated and spiritually isolated protagonist confronts a form whose mysterious origin or nature obsesses him and whose physical features signify the threat of death. Yet this fundamental dilemma generates a multiplicity of outcomes, ranging from murder and suicidal capitulation to physical evasion, rational demystification, or symbolic transformation. If one were to work out a grammar of narrative in Poe, these would be the modalities of articulation. To identify the deep structure, however, amounts to a restatement of the crisis defining Poe's relationship to writing; to explore differences of resolution is to perceive the uncertainties which attended the act of inscription.

Poe's thanatopsis did not culminate in any definitive projection of mortal circumstance. Beset by visions of transcendence and annihilation, separation and self-destruction, Poe represented his metaphysical quandary in two tales of hypnotic influence, "Mesmeric Revelation" (1844) and "The Facts in the Case of M. Valdemar" (1845). The former frames a conversation between a mesmerist long "sceptical . . . on the topic of the soul's immortality" and a dying man, Mr. Vankirk. In a mesmeric trance Vankirk describes God as "unparticled matter" and man as an incarnate portion of "the divine mind." What humans experience as death, he relates, is "the painful metamorphosis" from the "rudimental" corporeal form to the completed "ultimate body" which participates in the "unorganized life" of unparticled matter (CW, 3:1037). Immediately after this revelation, Vankirk expires "with a bright smile irradiating all his features" and illuminating the only easeful death in Poe's fiction.[25] But as if to cast doubt upon that deathbed scene, Poe, four months after "Mesmeric Revelation," asked in his "Marginalia": "Who ever *really* saw anything but horror in the smile of the dead?" Vankirk's smile is more precisely a suppression of horror, disclosing the incongruity of Poe's attempt to transpose the dialogic format of "The Conversation of Eiros and Charmion" and "The Colloquy of Monos and Una" (both derived from the tradition of the Platonic dialogue of spirits) into a verisimilar transcript. To paraphrase Poe's 1847 review of *Twice-Told Tales,* if the story establishes a fact about the soul's immortality, it is by dint of overturning a fiction. Approaching death as a matter of intellectual perplexity rather than visceral experience, Poe nearly empties the discourse of narrative content; the effort to explain dying as a "painful metamorphosis" occurs within a text devoid of pain, devoid of that essential opposition between life and death which makes Poe's narratives—perhaps all narratives—possible. In another sense, the dialogue betrays the desire to escape the problem of writing by returning to the immediacy of speech; writing here duplicates verbal utterance in an act so perfunctory that the role of narrator slides into that of amanuensis. His response to the episode is minimal, for unlike the narrator of "Usher" he remains detached, insulated by theory from the death that he witnesses.

At the end of "Mesmeric Revelation," the narrator speculates that the last words of the dying man may have arrived "from out the region of the shadows." Poe seems to have been intent upon enabling the dead to speak: between the stories of Vankirk and Valdemar, he published "Thou Art the Man," in which a "bruised, bloody and nearly putrid corpse" appears to accuse his murderer, and "Some Words with a Mummy," wherein a galvanic charge permits the mummified Count Allamistakeo to deliver satirical observations on progress and democracy. The same ventriloquistic fantasy can be traced to such earlier burlesques as "Loss of Breath" and "A Predicament." Whatever hilarity Poe may have found in the banter of a mutilated or decaying corpse, we can recognize the psychosymbolic appeal of this linguistic transcendence of death. Through an ironic, farcical inversion of the relation between language and silence, he exposed the core of his own writerly anxiety while indulging in imaginative denial. G. R. Thompson appositely remarks: "Irony was the device that allowed [Poe] both to contemplate his obsession with death, murder, torture, insanity, guilt, loss, and fear of total annihilation in a meaningless universe, and also to detach and protect himself from the obsession."[26]

As we have seen, however, not all of the speaking dead present themselves as ludicrous figures. The last of Poe's spiritualized dialogues, "The Power of Words," appeared shortly before "Valdemar" and reveals an apparently serious notion of both the survival of the soul and the creative power of language. Oinos and Agathos inhabit a dimension defined by the words they speak, and the latter explains creation itself as a product of the motion of speech, that "impulse on the air." It may be that Poe conceived of Aidenn (Heaven) as a site of infinite, disembodied speech acts; yet such projections could not dispose of the problem of dread. Indeed, the fascination of "Valdemar" seems grounded in the obstinate relationship between language and the body of death. The narrative concerns itself with the effect of death upon language as implied by two sources of horror: the emanation of speech from an apparently lifeless subject and the repulsive action of decay.

As in "Mesmeric Revelation," the narrator of "Valdemar" doubles as a hypnotist, and the opening paragraphs seek to establish both his reliability as an observer and the factuality of the narrative itself, which is meant to correct "a garbled or exaggerated account" said to be in circulation. That is, Poe adopts the tactics of pseudo-documentation employed in *Pym* and "The Premature Burial," and on one level his motive again seems to be that of public mystification. Yet beneath its seemingly veridical surface, the self-confessed hoax once more reveals embedded anxieties and ambiguities.[27] And as in *Pym* the text calls attention to its own inscription, for we learn at one point that the narrative is based upon the notes of a medical student, Mr. L____l: "It is from his memoranda that what I now have to relate is, for the most part, either condensed or copied *verbatim*" (*CW*, 3:1236). Yet L____l does not witness the first examination of Valdemar, and during the second visit, he swoons and loses consciousness for nearly an hour upon hearing the sepulchral voice. Thus, working from incomplete notes and from his own skewed recollections, the narrator vows to "give the *facts*—as far as I comprehend them myself." But he too is brought up short, especially when faced with the problem of representing the intonation of the sleep-waker: "There issued from the distended and motionless jaws a voice—such as it would be madness in me to attempt describing" (1240). Determined to convey "some idea of its unearthly peculiarity," the narrator again faces the insufficiency of language: "I fear, indeed, that it will be impossible to make myself comprehended."

The connection between the "broken and hollow" voice and the speechlessness of the onlookers becomes clear when Valdemar makes his impossible declaration, "I *have been* sleeping—and now—now— *I am dead*":

> No person present even affected to deny, or attempted to repress, the unutterable, shuddering horror which these few words, thus uttered, were so well calculated to convey. Mr. L____l (the student) swooned. The nurses immediately left the chamber, and could not be induced to return. My own impressions I would not pretend to render intelligible to the reader. For nearly an hour, we busied ourselves, silently—without the utterance of a word—in endeavors to revive Mr. L____l. [1240–41]

The dumbness induced by Valdemar's claim is more than a sign of terror; for language has been appropriated by the dead, reducing the living to deathlike silence. What Valdemar says, as Roland Barthes has pointed out, is both grammatically and semantically unspeakable: the "I" designates a speaking presence which is no longer present, and the adjective "dead" signals a scandalous "turning of the metaphoric back into the literal."[28] But equally curious is the speechlessness of the living, in a reciprocity implied by Poe's play on variants of the word "utter": the "unutterable" horror of what Valdemar has "uttered" makes "utterance" impossible for the narrator. The point of this reiteration lies in the double sense of "utterance," which is both an articulation and, in an earlier sense, "the last extremity, the bitter end." Valdemar's statement "*I am dead*" is thus an utterance in both senses, alluding to an originary bond between language and death. For the narrator, however, this utterance constitutes a terrifying erasure of the difference between life and death, a breakdown, as Jean Baudrillard might say, of the barriers by which we segregate the dead from the symbolic exchange of the living.[29] The narrator's inability to render intelligible his impressions of the scene replicates the lapse of language which the incident itself produced. His failure suggests that the speaking of the dead subverts language by disrupting the function of the signifier: presence and absence have lost their dialectic relation.

For seven months, we are asked to believe, Valdemar remains suspended in a trance, technically dead but still (impossibly) possessed of and by language. Significantly, the only sign of "mesmeric influence" is "the vibratory movement of the tongue" whenever a question is posed. Self has been reduced to voice; through Valdemar, *die Sprache spricht* in virtual detachment from everything except its own rhetorical field. What responds is the tongue, literally a *langue vivante*, which outlasts even breath. This persistence of language in the body of death forms the principal interest of the final, ghastly experiment, in which the narrator attempts to awaken Valdemar. The effort causes the tongue to quiver and articulate a contradictory command: "For God's sake!—quick!—quick!—put me to sleep— or, quick!—waken me!—quick!—*I say to you that I am dead!* (1242). Now caught between sleeping and waking, between speech and silence, between utterance and utterance, language manifests its doubleness, being both a performative phenomenon, the product of an individual tongue, and an extrinsic system, a tongue which one acquires and then surrenders. Language inhabits the body and ceases with death; or rather it forsakes the dead and perpetuates itself through living speakers and through the embodiment of writing. What we witness at the end of "Valdemar" is the evacuation of language from the body of death: "Amid ejaculations of 'dead! dead!' absolutely *bursting* from the tongue and not from the lips of the sufferer, his whole frame at once—within the space of a single minute, or even less, shrunk—crumbled—absolutely *rotted* away beneath my hands" (1242–43). Unable to "re-compose the patient," the narrator can only watch as Valdemar rots. The decomposition of the subject coincides with the loss of the word.

About this attenuated discourse, Daniel Hoffman has asked, "If the body was held from decomposition for seven months by the passes of a Mesmerist, what then was speaking if not the soul?"[30] Surely what speaks is not the soul but language itself, divested of metaphysical possibility. For the horror of "Valdemar" is precisely its secular reductiveness, its rigorous denial of the spiritual. When the hollow voice, speaking as if "from a vast distance," enunciates the stunning words, "*I am dead,*" the text brings us to the verge of exciting knowledge; but no disclosure follows. Valdemar never experiences the illuminations of Vankirk: from him we obtain no "mesmeric revelations." Instead, Poe stages the calamity of modern death, a revolting spectacle mediated by two voices, one detached, confining itself to "facts" and physiological details, the other intoning words emptied of human content. We receive no hint of an "ultimate life," no intimation of a "complete body," only observations of putrefaction. As far as we can determine, the closing sentence records Valdemar's ultimate metamorphosis: "Upon the bed, before that whole company, there lay a nearly liquid mass of loathsome—of detestable putridity."

Even so, the narrator-mesmerist's scheme to arrest "the encroachments of Death" provides a suggestive figure for the author's own intermittent desire to abolish or surmount mortality. Poe's efforts to envision a world without death led, for example, to two late landscape pieces, "The Domain of Arnheim" and "Landor's Cottage," in which the previously fatal images of the chasm and vortex have been domesticated into picturesque vales and streams that compose scenes of Edenic harmony. In *Eureka*—that late exercise in transcendental logic—Poe confects a happy, Emersonian vision of a ubiquitous Divine Being, whose presence subsumes "individual identity" and guarantees "Life within Life." This purely cerebral prose-poem advances a concept of entropy in which the cosmos disintegrates to nothingness or oneness, which are, in Poe's metaphysics, identical. His theory of attraction and repulsion, which sees all matter returning to "Material Nihility," explains the existent universe as a diffusion and concretion of Spirit; yet the argument that our "Inexorable Fate" (death) is but "the re-constitution of the *purely Spiritual* and Individual God" disposes of dread and decomposition by ignoring altogether the problem of dying. Poe's "Book of Truths" amounts to a rationale for death in which the word "death" is studiously suppressed. As Hoffman notes, "Here is a long, coherent, rational work from which *pain is banished.*"[31] In the most literal sense *Eureka* displays the mechanism of sublimation; Poe fastens upon lofty themes and vast perspectives to avoid immediate anxiety. Yet a "note of urgency" enters the writing: voicing a presentiment, Poe wrote in the preface: "It is as a Poem only that I wish this work to be judged after I am dead."

As we have seen, Poe's letters indicate that near the end of his life, an inveterate sense of foreboding opened into a graphic premonition of death. In his last, unfinished composition, Poe sketched in diary form the ruminations of a lighthouse keeper, a writer conscious of his own vulnerability: "As regularly as I *can* keep the journal, I will—but there is no telling what may happen to a man all alone as I am—I may get sick, or worse." This implicit calculation of the end of writing recalls "MS. Found in a Bottle" and the project of exploration therein adumbrated. As if by some imperative of figurality, Poe returned in "The Light-House" to the encircling sea and the task of inscription. A self-described "noble of the realm," the narrator has renounced society to gratify a "passion for solitude" and to write a book. He expresses relief that he has come unaccompanied by Orndoff, whose "intolerable gossip" would have interrupted his writing. Yet he also acknowledges disquietude: "It is strange that I never observed, until this moment, how dreary a sound that word has— 'alone'! I could half fancy there was some peculiarity in the echo of these cylindrical walls—but oh, no!—this is all nonsense. I do believe I am going to get nervous about my insulation" (CW, 3:1390–91). The narrator chides himself for nervousness: "*That* will never do. I have not forgotten De Grät's prophecy." Did De Grät predict a crisis occasioned by solitude? Is this why the narrator maintains a diary "as agreed on with De Grät"? Is this diary, like the flight recorder of a modern airliner, conceived to register potential last words, last thoughts? Much of the fascination of "The Light-House" lies in its incompletion, its refusal to answer questions raised by its own cryptic referentiality. Like his comment on the peculiar echo of the word "alone," the narrator's reflections on the safety of the lighthouse inject a hint of danger. Whether he will be overwhelmed by high seas or irrational fears, his writing betrays an undercurrent of existential anxiety. No cosmic visions of unity illumine his psychic horizon; this lighthouse keeper has only a foreshortened view: "Now for a scramble to the lantern and a good look around to 'see what I can see'. . . . To see what I can see indeed!—not very much." In this condition of uncertainty and isolation he waits to learn the outcome of his story, perhaps already anticipating the fate he will share with Poe (and all writers)—to leave behind a truncated manuscript, to disappear within an ellipsis, to reach that lacuna which terminates the life of writing.

From the outset Poe perceived the impossibility of completing the final text, of delivering the "exciting knowledge" beyond mortality. Yet he engaged in a relentless contemplation of the one experience about which one cannot write in the preterite, devising instead vicarious episodes of destruction and transcendence. To be sure, he occasionally escaped dread in fantasies of rebirth, thus evincing an essential ambivalence to death which confirms Yeats's observation that "a man awaits his end / Dreading and hoping all." If Poe probed the origins of despair more insistently than any of his contemporaries, he also longed to believe in the ultimate translation or transformation of the self. But the displacement of faith, the erosion of traditional values, and the decentering of culture itself undermined such notions about mortality. It is a mark of Poe's genius that he perceived the gigantic centrality of the problem of death, locating in his own dubiety the themes of modern ontological confusion. To a great extent he resisted the tendency of his age to mask anxiety with the illusion of funereal beauty. However, he achieved insight at a heavy price; Becker comments that the exposure of the psyche to "the terror of one's condition" entails a continual struggle with despair: "To see the world as it really is is devastating and terrifying. It achieves the very result that the child has painfully built his character over the years in order to avoid: it *makes routine, automatic, secure, self-confident activity impossible.* It makes thoughtless living in the world of men an impossibility. It places a trembling animal at the mercy of the entire cosmos and the problem of the meaning of it."[32] While Poe could construct visions of a benign spirit world to calm the "trembling animal," he was finally too much the victim of our own crisis of death to exorcise its dread. Indeed, he confronted the shadow with remarkable tenacity and acuity, producing a literature that seems, in our age of atrocity, more than ever disturbing and menacing. As Terence Martin has remarked, Poe remains in some ways "too much for us, his latter-day contemporaries": "We continue, after all, to be self-protective; and thus our judgment of Poe as excessive testifies to what we have to think of a hero of the imagination who imagines our death as his way of life."[33]

The contemporaneity of Poe's writing lies not in his evocation of violence, alienation, or solitude—although all of these elements inhere in a modernist vision of life. Rather it comes from the perception of death as an absolute horizon of existence; though he invented dialogues between spirits and worked variations on the motif of resurrection, the essential horror of his writing resides in blankness and silence, in the perception of emptiness at the core of being. For all of the phantasms, revenants, and specters who intrude into the world of Poe's imagining, his protagonists seem inescapably trapped by materiality, confined within coffins, vaults, dungeons, chambers, houses, and ships, which are in some sense figures for the prison of corporality itself. Glossing a letter from Poe to Lowell, Michael Davitt Bell concludes: "There is no 'other' realm, no 'spiritual' world into which to have 'mystic' insight. There is only matter, and our terms for the 'other' realm are 'mere words'"[34] In Poe (again to quote Yeats) the sentient, imagining self is "fastened to a dying animal," incapable of evading the Conqueror Worm and   despite contrary speculation in

"Mesmeric Revelation"—unable to sustain belief in the soul's survival. Allen Tate once argued that Poe perceived the "great subject" of modern literature, "the disintegration of the personality," because he anticipated the disappearance of God and the reign of death: "If Poe must at last 'yield himself unto Death utterly,' there is a lurid sublimity in the spectacle of his taking God along with him into a grave which is not smaller than the universe."[35] Much as Poe's writing traffics in otherworldliness, his supernaturalism implies no access to a redemptive order of being.

But beyond his apprehension of an enfolding "Universe of Vacancy" (in the suggestive language of *Eureka*), Poe anticipated modernism in his recognition of the burden placed upon writing by the catastrophe of death. As faith in an afterlife dwindled, so too did the possibility of spiritual discourse (such as that imagined in "The Colloquy of Monos and Una"), which thus foreclosed the idea of an eternally speaking self, a consciousness capable of infinite, incorporeal expression. The perception of death as complete cessation generated not only the dread characteristic of the modern age but the anxiety of remembrance and the acutely felt need to "speak" after death through inscription. Having arrived at a metaphysical degree zero, the writer turned to the text and the act of writing as a way of translating his isolation into coherence, of recovering through his own creative gesture a purpose and significance no longer apparent in the universal scheme, and he conferred upon writing itself a quasi-mystical power derived largely from its capacity to resist death— miraculously—through lifeless graphic marks and to create an alternative, parallel life for the one who writes. Intuitively, Poe sensed the complicity between death and writing, devising tales and poems which bodied forth the predicament of modernity through a self-conscious textuality.

Poe's paradoxical relationship to writing, impelled by the attraction and repulsion of death, brought him in 1849 to the verge of the never-to-be-imparted secret. Unable to complete "The Light-House" (and thus doubling the fate of his textual counterpart), he was likewise prevented by his fatal seizure from composing a culminating, autobiographical narrative of the end of consciousness. Instead, the narration of his death fell to John J. Moran, whose *Defense of*

Edgar Allan Poe (1885) provides an ironic epilogue to Poe's engagement with the life of writing. According to an unsigned preface (probably also by Moran), the physician was uniquely qualified to engage in thanatography, having treated Poe "in his last hours" during which time he "received from the expiring poet his dying declarations, with a brief history of his life."[36] But his reconstruction of the deathbed scene reveals, more than anything else, Moran's own craving for remembrance and the persistence of the Beautiful Death as an occasion for religious sentimentality.

In the *Defense,* composed thirty-six years after Poe's death, he sketched the last days, the hour of death, and the funeral in amazing detail, assigning to the dying Poe orotund poetic utterances apparently recalled verbatim. Interspersed with excerpts from Poe's verses, the narrative suggests that Moran's memories had become hopelessly intermingled with scenes from the poetry. Recalling the patient's gazing at a window, the physician writes: "Did he hear a 'gentle tapping at the window lattice,' and was his heart still a moment, 'this mystery to explore'? Did he see that stately raven 'perched upon his chamber door?'" Elsewhere he attributes to Poe conventional deathbed sentiments in which poetry and biography converge; the writer yearns, we are told, to be reunited in the spirit world with his wife: "How long, oh! how long . . . before I can see my dear Virginia, my dear Lenore!" And Moran quotes Poe's ostensible premonition of the end: "'Doctor,' said he, 'Death's dark angel has done his work. Language cannot express the terrific tempest that sweeps over me, and signals the alarm of death. Oh, God! the terrible strait I am in.'" Moran's account of Poe's last words reaches the nadir of implausibility:

At length he exclaimed: "O God! is there no ransom for the deathless spirit?"

I said, "Yes, look to your Saviour; there is mercy for you and all mankind. God is love and the gift is free."

The dying man then said impressively, "He who arched the heavens and upholds the universe, has His decrees legibly written upon the frontlet of every human being, and upon demons incarnate."[37]

Even in his blatant effort to show that "Poe did recognize the one Supreme Being, who holds in His merciful hand the destiny of all," Moran betrays Poe's uncertainty about redemption, perhaps the better to cast himself in the role of spiritual counselor. But the supposed final utterance seems as vacuous as it is implausible. Poe's dying cry for "Reynolds" has no place in the doctor's account, which cannot accommodate the cryptic.

Moran concludes his narrative with a description of Poe's burial clothes, coffin, and funeral. He notes that during the period in which Poe's body lay in state, "at least fifty ladies received a lock of his hair, the attendants waiting upon them." Whether the detail is accurate or not, we see Moran evoking the cult of remembrance, suggesting that the poet's locks became to a coterie of mourners signs of devotion later transformed into memorial pins, rings, and bracelets. Poe would have been amused by the doctor's conventionalized description of a smiling corpse: "The appearance of the dead poet had not materially changed; his face was calm and placid; a smile seemed to play around his mouth, and all who gazed upon him remarked how natural he looked; so much so, indeed, that it seemed as though he only slept."[38] How much of Moran's adulatory reminiscence corresponds to the facts we cannot determine; as a cultural gesture, however, his monograph displays an imperative to produce, from the fallible resources of memory, a sanitized version of the writer's demise as a serene passage to the spirit world. That Poe's writing embodied dread and radical disbelief escaped the notice of Moran, whose principal concern was to reaffirm orthodox pieties and to glorify his role at the deathbed of a famous author. Yet in his rendering of the putative details, the physician bore witness to the implicit threat of meaningless or unintelligible death. For all its preposterous dialogue, A Defense of Edgar Allan Poe manifests the need to recuperate death as a sacred event, to deny its opacity, and to disguise its physiological horrors. And in its perpetuation of the Beautiful Death, Moran's account anticipates the modern concealment of dying and our own reluctance to face the conditions of being inscribed in Poe's uncompromising texts.

Notes

Chapter 1

1 John R. Reed, *Victorian Conventions* (Athens, Ohio: Ohio University Press, 1975), 171.

2 Ann Douglas, *The Feminization of American Culture* (New York: Alfred A. Knopf, 1977; New York: Avon Books, 1978), 1. Deathbed scenes in Dickens, Charlotte Brontë, and others come under discussion in Garrett Stewart, *Death Sentences: Styles of Dying in British Fiction* (Cambridge: Harvard University Press, 1984), 55–138.

3 Edgar Allan Poe, *Collected Works of Edgar Allan Poe*, ed. Thomas Ollive Mabbott (Cambridge: Harvard University Press, 1978), 2:318. Unless otherwise indicated, all subsequent references to Poe's works will be to the Mabbott edition, hereafter cited as *CW*. Poe's first version of "Ligeia" (1838) contained only a brief paragraph on the heroine's death. In 1845 he expanded the scene to three paragraphs which included "The Conqueror Worm," a lyric Poe had published separately in 1843.

4 See especially the chapter "Writing Restructures Consciousness" in Walter J. Ong, *Orality and Literacy: The Technologizing of the Word* (London: Methuen, 1982), 78–116.

5 Edward H. Davidson, *Poe: A Critical Study* (Cambridge: Harvard University Press, 1957), 106, 113.

215

6 Robert Jay Lifton and Eric Olson, *Living and Dying* (New York: Bantam, 1974), 3–21; Ernest Becker, *The Denial of Death* (New York: The Free Press, 1973), 11–24.

7 Philippe Ariès, *The Hour of Our Death,* trans. Helen Weaver (New York: Alfred A. Knopf, 1981), 473.

8 Lawrence Stone, *The Family, Sex and Marriage in England 1500–1800* (New York: Harper and Row, 1977), 249.

9 Ibid., 68.

10 Ibid., 70.

11 *The Hour of Our Death,* 405.

12 *Family, Sex and Marriage,* 247.

13 John McManners, *Death and the Enlightenment: Changing Attitudes to Death among Christians and Unbelievers in Eighteenth-Century France* (New York: Oxford University Press, 1981), 92, 93.

14 *Family, Sex and Marriage,* 251.

15 Ibid., 248.

16 Philippe Ariès, *Western Attitudes toward* DEATH: *From the Middle Ages to the Present* (Baltimore: The Johns Hopkins University Press, 1974), 72.

17 Stanley French, "The Cemetery as Cultural Institution: The Establishment of Mount Auburn and the 'Rural Cemetery' Movement," in *Death in America,* ed. David E. Stannard (Philadelphia: University of Pennsylvania Press, 1975), 78–79.

18 *Death and the Enlightenment,* 349.

19 *Family, Sex and Marriage,* 247.

20 See the exhibition catalogue by Anita Schorsch, *Mourning Becomes America: Mourning Art in the New Nation* (Harrisburg, Pa.: Pennsylvania Historical and Museum Commission, 1976).

21 *Victorian Conventions,* 157–58.

22 James Stevens Curl, *The Victorian Celebration of Death* (Devon, England: David & Charles, 1972), 1–26. See also John Morley, *Death, Heaven and the Victorians* (Pittsburgh: University of Pittsburgh Press, 1971), 19–31.

23 *The Feminization of American Culture,* 242.

24 I have characterized the modern age as "post-Christian" in the sense defined by Alan D. Gilbert: "A post-Christian society is not one from which Christianity has departed, but one in which it has become marginal. It is a society where to be irreligious is to be normal, where to think and act in secular terms is to be conventional, where neither status nor respectability depends upon the practice or profession of religious faith." See *The Making of Post-Christian Britain: A History of the Secularization of Modern Society* (London: Longman, 1980), ix.

25 David E. Stannard, *The Puritan Way of Death* (New York: Oxford University Press, 1977), 185.

26 Washington Irving, *The Sketch Book,* in *History, Tales and Sketches,* ed. James W. Tuttleton (New York: Library of America, 1983), 1047.

27 James Fenimore Cooper, *The Prairie* (1827; reprint, New York: Holt, Rinehart and Winston, 1950), 446.

28 Ibid., 451.

29 Nathaniel Hawthorne, *Tales and Sketches*, ed. Roy Harvey Pearce (New York: Library of America, 1982), 95.
30 Lydia Huntley Sigourney, *Poems* (New York: George A. Leavitt, 1841), 127–28.
31 *The Feminization of American Culture*, 17–93.
32 Edgar Allan Poe, *Essays and Reviews*, ed. G. R. Thompson (New York: Library of America, 1984), 1342.
33 See Claude Richard, "Les Contes du Folio Club et la Vocation Humoristique d'Edgar Allan Poe," in *Configuration Critique d'Edgar Allan Poe*, ed. Claude Richard (Paris: Minard, 1969), 79–96; Alexander Hammond, "Edgar Allan Poe's *Tales of the Folio Club*: The Evolution of a Lost Book," *Library Chronicle* 41 (1976): 13–43.
34 A. H. Quinn, *Edgar Allan Poe: A Critical Biography* (New York: Appleton-Century, 1941), 215.
35 *Poe: A Critical Study*, 115.
36 Walter J. Ong, *Interfaces of the Word: Studies in the Evolution of Consciousness and Culture* (Ithaca: Cornell University Press, 1977), 235.
37 *Orality and Literacy*, 81.
38 Maurice Blanchot, *The Space of Literature*, trans. Ann Smock (Lincoln: University of Nebraska Press, 1982), 26, 30.
39 David Halliburton, *Edgar Allan Poe: A Phenomenological View* (Princeton: Princeton University Press, 1973), 251–52.
40 John T. Irwin, *American Hieroglyphics* (New Haven: Yale University Press, 1980), 69.
41 Ibid., 235.
42 *The Denial of Death*, ix, 96. Becker would seem to argue that all cultures, in all ages, have been built upon dread and the repression of death. Yet his focus is clearly upon the modern period, with Kierkegaard and Freud as prototypical figures.
43 Focusing upon the tactics of Scheherazade, Wendy B. Faris discusses the effort in modern texts to "simulate the postponement of human death through the prolongation of fictional life," in "1001 Words: Fiction Against Death," *Georgia Review* 36 (Winter 1982): 811–30.
44 Roland Barthes, "Textual Analysis of a Tale by Edgar Poe," trans. Donald G. Marshall, *Poe Studies* 10 (June 1977): 10.
45 Roland Barthes, *Writing Degree Zero and Elements of Semiology*, trans. Annette Lavers and Colin Smith (Boston: Beacon Press, 1970), 9.
46 Joseph N. Riddel, "The 'Crypt' of Edgar Poe," *Boundary 2* 7 (Spring 1979): 120, 124.
47 Jacques Derrida, *Of Grammatology*, trans. Gayatri Chakravorty Spivak (Baltimore: The Johns Hopkins University Press, 1976), 25.
48 *Interfaces of the Word*, 238.

Chapter 2

1 Daniel Hoffman, *Poe Poe Poe Poe Poe Poe Poe* (Garden City, N.Y.: Doubleday, 1972), 221.

2 Marie Bonaparte, *The Life and Works of Edgar Allan Poe: A Psycho-Analytic Interpretation*, trans. John Rodker (London: Imago, 1949), 586.

3 D. H. Lawrence, *Studies in Classic American Literature* (1923; reprint, New York: Viking, 1964), 79. G. R. Thompson, *Poe's Fiction: Romantic Irony in the Gothic Tales* (Madison: University of Wisconsin Press, 1973), 182.

4 *The Hour of Our Death*, 397.

5 J. H. Powell, *Bring Out Your Dead: The Great Plague of Yellow Fever in Philadelphia in 1793* (1949; reprint, New York: Time-Life Books, 1965), 67–119.

6 *The Hour of Our Death*, 397–98, 402.

7 A. M. Lassek, *Human Dissection: Its Drama and Struggle* (Springfield, Ill.: Charles C. Thomas, 1958), 115–26.

8 Charles Kite, *An Essay on the Recovery of the Apparently Dead* (London: C. Dilly, 1787), 122–26.

9 *The Hour of Our Death*, 354–59.

10 *Quarterly Review* 85 (1849): 362, 363.

11 *Family, Sex and Marriage*, 78; "The Cemetery as Cultural Institution," 74.

12 George H. Walker, *Gatherings from Grave Yards; Particularly those of London: with a concise history of the Modes of Interment among different nations* (London: Longman and Co., 1839), 188–89.

13 Ibid., 191.

14 *Quarterly Review* 73 (1844): 458.

15 James Stevens Curl, *A Celebration of Death: An introduction to some of the buildings, monuments, and settings of funerary architecture in the Western European tradition* (London: Constable, 1980), 157.

16 See W. T. Bandy, "A Source for Poe's 'The Premature Burial,'" *American Literature* 19 (April 1947): 167.

17 *The Casket* 9 (October 1834): 379.

18 *The Letters of Edgar Allan Poe*, ed. John Ward Ostrom (1949; reprint, New York: Gordian Press, 1966), 1:84. Subsequent references to Poe's correspondence will be to the 1966 edition with supplement, hereafter cited in the text as *L*.

19 Michael Allen, *Poe and the British Magazine Tradition* (New York: Oxford University Press, 1969), 22–23, 30.

20 Lassek, *Human Dissection*, 226–27.

21 *The Casket* 1 (September 1826): 257.

22 See Raymond Moody, Jr., *Life After Life* (Covington, Ga.: Mockingbird Books, 1975); Kenneth Ring, *Life at Death: A scientific investigation of the near-death experience* (New York: Coward, McCann and Geoghegan, 1980); and especially Michael Sabom, *Recollections of Death: A Medical Investigation* (New York: Simon and Schuster, 1982), 39–54.

23 *The Denial of Death*, 26.

24 Thomas O. Mabbott points out that Poe culled the expression from *The Proud Ladye* (1840) by the little-known poet Spencer Wallace Cone. See *CW*, 1:323.

25 *The Denial of Death*, 12.

26 *Collected Writings of Edgar Allan Poe*, ed. Burton R. Pollin (Boston: Twayne,

1981), 1:75–76. Subsequent references to *Pym* will correspond to Pollin's edition of *The Imaginary Voyages*, hereafter cited as *IV*.

27 *Poe's Fiction*, 15, 16.

28 As pointed out by Mabbott, *CW*, 3:971n16.

Chapter 3

1 Mary Ann Caws also discusses translation in "The Oval Portrait" in "Insertion in an Oval Frame: Poe Circumscribed by Baudelaire (Part I)," *French Review* 56 (April 1983): 679, 682.

2 Roland Barthes, *La chambre claire: Note sur la photographie* (Paris: Gallimard Seuil, 1980), 131; J. Gerald Kennedy, "Roland Barthes, Autobiography, and the End of Writing," *Georgia Review* 35 (Summer 1981): 381–98.

3 Mario Praz, *The Romantic Agony*, trans. Angus Davidson (1933; reprint, London: Oxford University Press, 1970), 31.

4 Barton Levi St. Armand, *Emily Dickinson and Her Culture: The Soul's Society* (Cambridge: Cambridge University Press, 1984), 63.

5 Washington Irving, *Biography and Poetical Remains of the late Margaret Miller Davidson* (1841; reprint, Philadelphia: Lea and Blanchard, 1845), 18.

6 Ibid., 112.

7 *Emily Dickinson and Her Culture*, 57.

8 Moses Waddel, *Memoirs of Miss Caroline E. Smelt* (Philadelphia: Henry Perkins, 1836), 124.

9 Rufus W. Griswold, *The Cypress Wreath: A Book of Consolation for Those who Mourn* (Boston: Gould and Lincoln, 1844), iv.

10 Karen Halttunen, *Confidence Men and Painted Women: A Study of Middle-class Culture in America, 1830–1870* (New Haven: Yale University Press, 1982), 148–49.

11 *The Hour of Our Death*, 453.

12 Ibid., 422.

13 Nicolas Abraham and Maria Torok, *Cryptonomie: Le verbier de l'Homme aux loups* (Paris: Aubier-Flammarion, 1976).

14 Jacques Derrida, "Fors," trans. Barbara Johnson, *Georgia Review* 31 (Spring 1977): 71–72.

15 Ibid., 78, 80.

16 Michael Davitt Bell, *The Development of American Romance: The Sacrifice of Relation* (Chicago: University of Chicago Press, 1980), 92, 99, 100.

17 *The Denial of Death*, 146.

18 Ibid., 167.

19 Geoffrey Gorer, *Death, Grief, and Mourning* (Garden City, N.Y.: Doubleday, 1965), 192–99.

20 *The Denial of Death*, 35.

21 Roy P. Basler, "The Interpretation of 'Ligeia,'" in *Poe: A Collection of Critical Essays*, ed. Robert Regan (Englewood Cliffs, N.J.: Prentice-Hall, 1967), 58.

22 "The Poetic Principle," in *Literary Criticism of Edgar Allan Poe*, ed. Robert L. Hough (Lincoln: University of Nebraska Press, 1965), 56.

Chapter 4

1 Eugenio Donato, "Who Signs 'Flaubert'?" *MLN* 99 (September 1984): 712–13, 722.
2 Robert Jay Lifton, *The Broken Connection: Death and the Continuity of Life* (New York: Simon and Schuster, 1980), 68, 69.
3 Ibid., 57.
4 Ibid.
5 See *Essays and Reviews*, 1377–78, 1414–15.
6 Lewis P. Simpson, *The Man of Letters in New England and the South: Essays on the History of the Literary Vocation in America* (Baton Rouge: Louisiana State University Press, 1973), 133.
7 Ibid., 143.
8 *Letters*, 1:74–75n.
9 "The Domain of Arnheim" first saw print in March 1847, while "Landor's Cottage" (a "pendant" to the earlier work) appeared in June 1849.
10 *Poe: A Critical Biography*, 640.

Chapter 5

1 Sidney P. Moss, *Poe's Literary Battles* (1963; reprint, Carbondale, Ill.: Southern Illinois University Press, 1969).
2 Geoffrey Hartman, *Saving the Text: Literature/Derrida/Philosophy* (Baltimore: Johns Hopkins University Press, 1981), 119, 122.
3 *Essays and Reviews*, 1370.
4 J. Gerald Kennedy, "The Limits of Reason: Poe's Deluded Detectives," *American Literature* 47 (May 1975): 184–96.
5 Patrick F. Quinn, *The French Face of Edgar Poe* (Carbondale, Ill.: Southern Illinois University Press, 1957), 230.
6 Barbara Johnson, "The Frame of Reference: Poe, Lacan, Derrida," in *Literature and Psychoanalysis: The Question of Reading: Otherwise*, ed. Shoshana Felman (Baltimore: The Johns Hopkins University Press, 1982), 470.
7 See Derrida's critique of Lacan's "phallogocentric" reading in "The Purveyor of Truth," *Yale French Studies* 52: 59–64, 94–100.
8 Jacques Lacan, "Seminar on the Purloined Letter," *Yale French Studies* 48 (1972): 41–45.
9 "The Frame of Reference," 487.
10 Max Bird, "The Detective Detected: From Sophocles to Ross Macdonald," *Yale Review* 64 (October 1974): 76.
11 *The French Face of Edgar Poe*, 226, 227.
12 Ibid., 221.
13 *The Broken Connection*, 223.
14 Robert Con Davis, "Lacan, Poe, and Narrative Repression," *MLN* 98 (December 1983): 996–97.
15 *The Broken Connection*, 224.
16 *The Denial of Death*, 98.

17 "Psychoanalytic Aspects of Suicide," in *A Psychiatrist's World: Selected Papers of Karl Menninger* (New York: Viking, 1959), 338.
18 See Joseph J. Moldenhauer, "Murder as a Fine Art: Basic Connections between Poe's Aesthetics, Psychology, and Moral Vision," *PMLA* 83 (1968): 284–97.
19 See, for example, Francis B. Dedmond, " 'The Cask of Amontillado' and the War of the Literati," *Modern Language Quarterly* 15 (June 1954): 137–46.
20 As late as January 4, 1848, Poe was crowing about his "reply" to English, whom he referred to as "the Autocrat of all the Asses." See *Letters*, 2:355.
21 *The Development of American Romance*, 99.
22 Allen Tate, "The Angelic Imagination," in *The Recognition of Edgar Allan Poe*, ed. Eric W. Carlson (Ann Arbor: University of Michigan Press, 1966), 242.

Chapter 6

1 For a helpful survey of critical responses to *Pym* see Douglas Robinson, "Reading Poe's Novel: A Speculative Review of *Pym* Criticism, 1950–1980," *Poe Studies* 15 (December 1982): 47–54. For an earlier discussion of Poe's covert strategy see J. Gerald Kennedy, "The Preface as a Key to the Satire in *Pym*," *Studies in the Novel* 5 (Summer 1973): 191–96.
2 *The French Face of Edgar Poe*, 176–77, 181, 188.
3 *Poe: A Critical Study*, 168, 169.
4 Jean Ricardou, "Le Caractère singulier de cette eau," *Critique* 243–44 (August-September 1967): 729–30; John Carlos Rowe, *Through the Custom-House: Nineteenth-Century American Fiction and Modern Theory* (Baltimore: The Johns Hopkins University Press, 1982), 95, 99; John T. Irwin, *American Hieroglyphics: The Symbol of the Egyptian Hieroglyphics in the American Renaissance* (New Haven: Yale University Press, 1980), 117.
5 *Poe Poe Poe Poe Poe Poe Poe*, 192.
6 J. Gerald Kennedy, "The 'Infernal Twoness' of *Arthur Gordon Pym*," *Topic* 30 (Fall 1976): 53.
7 *Through the Custom-House*, 102. Rowe's chapter on *Pym* is a revision of his essay in *Glyph* 2 (1977): 102–21.
8 Michel Ragon, *The Space of Death: A Study of Funerary Architecture, Decoration, and Urbanism*, trans. Alan Sheridan (Charlottesville: University of Virginia Press, 1983).
9 Edgar Morin, *L'homme et la mort* (Paris: Editions de Seuil, 1970), 41.
10 Ibid., 33.
11 *American Hieroglyphics*, 139.
12 René Girard, *Violence and the Sacred*, trans. Patrick Gregory (Baltimore: The Johns Hopkins University Press, 1977), 49.
13 *Through the Custom-House*, 105.
14 *American Hieroglyphics*, 170.
15 Ibid., 186.
16 *The Broken Connection*, 145.

17 George Steiner, *Language and Silence: Essays on Language, Literature, and the Inhuman* (New York: Atheneum, 1976), 3.

18 *The Space of Literature*, 91, 94.

19 *American Hieroglyphics*, 213. Douglas Robinson has recently argued that the white figure may be "an iconic dream-body that will permit a visionary habitation of the gap" between presence and absence. This icon compels interpretation, he claims, precisely to reveal the "uncertainty of interpretation" which is the novel's "rhetorical focus." See *American Apocalypses* (Baltimore: The John Hopkins University Press, 1985), 119, 121.

20 Ibid., 183.

21 Ibid., 230.

Chapter 7

1 Saul Bellow, *Herzog* (New York: Fawcett Crest, 1970), 353.

2 Ibid.

3 "A Natural History of the Dead," *The Short Stories of Ernest Hemingway* (New York: Scribners, 1938), 443.

4 *L'homme et la mort*, 305.

5 William Barrett, *Irrational Man* (Garden City, N.Y.: Doubleday Anchor, 1962), 35–36.

6 Ibid., 226.

7 Sarah Helen Whitman, *Edgar Poe and His Critics* (New York: Rudd and Carleton, 1860), 6.

8 *L'homme et la mort*, 304.

9 David Punter, *The Literature of Terror: A History of Gothic Fictions from 1765 to the Present Day* (London: Longman, 1980), 404.

10 Barrett John Mandel, " 'Basting the Image with a Certain Liquor': Death in Autobiography," *Soundings* 57 (1974): 186.

11 G. Thomas Couser, "The Shape of Death in American Autobiography," *Hudson Review* 31 (1978): 66.

12 See J. Gerald Kennedy, "Roland Barthes, Autobiography, and the End of Writing," *Georgia Review* 35 (Summer 1981): 381–98.

13 Robert Alter, *Partial Magic: The Novel as a Self-Conscious Genre* (Berkeley: University of California Press, 1975), 243.

14 *Of Grammatology*, 71.

15 Michel Foucault, *The Order of Things: An Archeology of the Human Sciences* (New York: Vintage Books, 1973), 304.

16 Martin Heidegger, "Letter on Humanism," in *Basic Writings*, ed. David Farrell Krell (New York: Harper and Row, 1977), 199. For a suggestive discussion of Heidegger, language, and contemporary writing, see Allen Thiher, *Words in Reflection: Modern Language Theory and Postmodern Fiction* (Chicago: University of Chicago Press, 1984), 35–62.

17 *Of Grammatology*, 144, 183.

18 Ibid., 69.

19 See especially Inder Nath Kher, *The Landscape of Absence: Emily Dickinson's*

Poetry (New Haven: Yale University Press, 1974), and Tzvetan Todorov, "The Secret of Narrative," in *The Poetics of Prose*, trans. Richard Howard (Ithaca: Cornell University Press, 1977). Todorov argues that the Jamesian narrative "is always based on *the quest for an absolute and absent cause*, producing a poetics in which "the essential is absent, the absence is essential" (145).

20 *The Development of American Romance*, 121.

21 The metatextuality of "The Gold-Bug" is discussed by Jean Ricardou, "L'Or du scarabée," in *Théorie d'ensemble* (Paris: Editions du Seuil, 1968), 363–83.

22 *The Denial of Death*, 261.

23 Joseph Patrick Roppolo, "Meaning and 'The Masque of the Red Death,'" in *Poe: A Collection of Critical Essays*, ed. Robert Regan (Englewood Cliffs, N.J.: Prentice-Hall, 1967), 142, 144.

24 *The Hour of Our Death*, 360.

25 Poe also depicts Eleonora as "tranquilly dying," but only after she has "very bitterly wept" over her fate (*CW*, 2:642).

26 *Poe's Fiction*, 9.

27 *Letters*, 2:337.

28 Roland Barthes, "Textual Analysis of a Tale by Edgar Poe," trans. Donald G. Marshall, *Poe Studies* 10 (June 1977): 9–10.

29 Jean Baudrillard, *L'échange symbolique et la mort* (Paris: Gallimard, 1976), 196.

30 *Poe Poe Poe Poe Poe Poe Poe*, 167.

31 Ibid., 295–96.

32 *The Denial of Death*, 60.

33 Terence Martin, "The Imagination at Play: Edgar Allan Poe," in *The Naiad Voice: Essays on Poe's Satiric Hoaxing*, ed. Dennis W. Eddings (Port Washington, N.Y.: Associate Faculty Press, 1983), 40.

34 *The Development of American Romance*, 94.

35 "The Angelic Imagination," 241, 252.

36 John J. Moran, *A Defense of Edgar Allan Poe* (Washington: William F. Boogher, 1885), n.p.

37 Ibid., 72.

38 Ibid., 82.

Index

Alienation, 12, 80, 82–83, 87, 162, 182, 184, 188
Allan, Frances Valentine, 95
Allan, John, 92–97
Autobiography, 188–89

Blackwood's Magazine, 33, 40–41, 46
Blair, Robert, 186; The Grave, 9, 49
Bloom, Harold, viii
Borges, Jorge Luis, 146, 183
Broadway Journal, 100
Brontë, Charlotte: Jane Eyre, 1
Bryant, William Cullen: "Thanatopsis," 9
Burial, 37, 162, 187, 199; premature, 18, 32–59, 75, 87, 142, 152, 158–59, 174
"Buried Alive, The," 33, 45–47, 49, 57
Burton's Gentleman's Magazine, 97
"Burying Alive," 59

Camus, Albert, 180
Cannibalism, 162–65
Cemeteries, 5; relocation of, 8; rural, 9;

38; urban, 37; Père-Lachaise, 38; visitation, 108, 109
Christian ritual, 37, 163
Clemm, Maria, 101–03, 110–13
Coleridge, Samuel Taylor: "Kubla Khan," 189
Collins, William: "Ode to Evening," 187
Conrad, Joseph: Heart of Darkness, 127
Consolation literature, 5–6, 11, 16–17, 64–67, 70, 82
Cooke, Philip Pendleton, 119
Cooper, James Fenimore: The Prairie, 13–14
Crabbe, George: The Parish Register, 187
Crane, Stephen: The Red Badge of Courage, 179
Crébillon, Prosper-Jolyot de, 126

Dante: The Divine Comedy, 189
Davidson, Margaret Miller, 64–65, 82
"Dead Alive," 39
Death: crisis of, viii, 3, 77, 91, 174, 179,

Death (*continued*)
182–83, 185, 198, 211; denial of, viii,
4, 25, 72, 81–82, 86, 134, 160, 169,
185, 199–201, 214; deathbed scene, 1,
2, 10, 13, 14, 64, 65, 204, 213–14;
anxiety, 2, 6, 7, 15, 25, 47, 50, 53,
80, 82–83, 84, 86, 116, 130, 133,
137, 143, 144, 153, 158, 162, 170,
176, 181–82, 184, 186, 188, 197–200,
209–11; decomposition, 2, 25, 68, 83–
86, 155–57, 160–62, 165–66, 174,
179, 190, 202, 208; the Beautiful, 5–
6, 10–11, 21, 64, 67, 69, 81, 190,
211, 213, 214; history of, 5–17, 35;
demographic aspects, 6–7, 10; religious
attitudes toward, 7–9, 11, 12, 65–66,
180, 182, 187, 193, 210; corpse, 7, 11,
15, 35–36, 38, 41–45, 66, 68, 77, 85,
90–91, 133, 155–57, 159, 160–62,
166, 178, 193, 195, 197, 198, 201,
205; secularizing of, 8, 12, 208;
reunion in, 10, 12, 13, 52, 69–71, 77,
81, 87, 108–10, 113; longing for, 26,
135, 156, 164–65, 169–71; ascendancy of, 31, 177–78, 180, 183–84, 185,
190, 195, 212; apparent, 36, 39, 41,
45, 84, 86, 199; as contagion, 41, 78,
81, 87, 201–03; and rebirth, 47, 204–
05, 209, 210, 212; phenomenology of,
51–53, 85–86, 146, 158, 204; concealment of, 81, 161, 181, 214; in-
comprehensibility of, 153, 155, 157–
59, 161, 166–67, 174, 203; space of,
158, 173; sacrificial, 163–64; of God,
177, 180
De Quincey, Thomas, 137
Dickens, Charles: *Our Mutual Friend,* 1
Dickinson, Emily, 49, 133, 160, 193
Dissection, 35–36, 41–42, 47
Donne, John, 74

Ellet, Mrs. E. F., 17
Emerson, Ralph Waldo, 18, 174, 209
English, Thomas Dunn, 138, 143
Evelith, George, 103–04

Flaubert, Gustave, 89–90
Fontenelle (Julia de), Jean-Sebastien Eu-
géne: *On the Signs of Death,* 36, 39, 56
Freud, Sigmund, 72–73, 157–58
Fuller, Hiram, 138, 143
Funeral customs, 5, 7, 11, 37, 64

Genocide, 167, 178, 180
Gothic conventions, 4, 17, 48–49, 187–
88
Gould, Mrs. H. F., 17, 66
Graham's Magazine, 17
Graveyard poetry, 8–9, 36, 55, 56, 186–
88
Gray, Thomas: "Elegy Written in a
Country Church-Yard," 8, 187
Griswold, Rev. Rufus W., 66–67
Guilt, survivor, 15, 83, 142, 170–71

Hawthorne, Nathaniel, 18; "Roger Malvin's Burial," 14–15; "The Birthmark," 60; "Young Goodman Brown,"
129; "Ethan Brand," 135
Heidegger, Martin, 182; *Sein und Seit,*
179–80; "Letter on Humanism,"
192–93
Hemans, Felicia, 66
Hemingway, Ernest, 180; "A Natural
History of the Dead," 178–79

Irving, Washington: *The Sketch Book,*
12–13; biography of Margaret Miller
Davidson, 64–65

James, Henry, 193; "The Altar of the
Dead," vii

Kafka, Franz, 162, 171, 180, 190
Kahler, Erich, 188
Keats, John, 61, 114; "Ode to a Night-
ingale," 189–90
Kennedy, John Pendleton, 99, 103
Kierkegaard, Søren, 31, 82; *The Sickness
Unto Death,* 181–82

Langer, Lawrence, 177
Language: and death, 3, 18, 20, 27, 29,
42–44, 156, 190, 205, 206–08; loss of,
42–43, 116, 120, 121, 123, 125, 140,
142, 144, 155, 207; origin of, 43, 147,
172
Lewis, Matthew G.: *The Monk,* 188
"Living Inhumation," 47–49
Lovecraft, H. P., 95
Lowell, James Russell, 99–100

Maeterlinck, Maurice, 185
Magazine writing, 4, 6, 33, 39–41, 55,
97, 99, 115

Mallarmé, Stephane, 185
Maryland, University of: School of Medicine, 42
Melville, Herman, 18
Miller, J. Hillis, 180
Moran, John J.: *A Defense of Edgar Allan Poe*, 212–14
Mourning, vii, ix, 8, 10, 12, 66–69, 72, 77, 111, 214
Mourning art, 5, 6, 10, 64
Murder, 18, 120, 128, 131–38, 143, 144, 164, 178, 180, 203

Nietzsche, Friedrich, 180, 192

Parnell, Thomas: "Night-Piece on Death," 186–87
Patrick, Mrs. M. A.: *The Mourner's Gift*, 66
Patterson, Edward H. N., 100–101
Plato, 115
Poe, Edgar Allan: conceptions of death, 3–4, 18, 28, 57, 63–64, 94–95, 193, 200–212; relationship to writing, 17–18, 29, 104–07, 109, 111, 193, 203, 210, 212; and death of a beautiful woman, 18, 60–88; correspondence, 89–113; sense of dread, 90–93, 96, 98, 100–101, 105, 109, 111, 112, 185, 209; separation anxiety, 91, 94–96, 98, 101–03, 112; quest for fame, 97–101, 109; on revenge, 97, 114–44; *Stylus*, 98–101, 112; attraction to death, 101, 108–09, 113; reliance on Virginia Clemm Poe, 103–05; courtship of Sarah Helen Whitman, 105–10; suicide attempt, 109, 111; courtship of Annie Richmond, 110–12; death of, 113, 212–14; literary battles, 114–15, 138, 143; on mystification, 116–19, 124–26, 145, 206; tale of ratiocination, 118, 119–28; attitude toward reading public, 149
—cosmology: *Eureka*, 209, 212
—criticism: "Marginalia," 99, 116, 204; "The Philosophy of Composition," 18, 63–64, 67, 75; "The Poetic Principle," 88; review of *Twice-Told Tales* (1847), 204
—fiction: "Berenice," 34, 50, 77–80, 104, 128; "The Black Cat," 32, 34, 132, 135–37; "The Cask of Amon-

tillado," 58, 138–43, 144; "The Colloquy of Monos and Una," 34, 51–53, 204, 212; "The Conversation of Eiros and Charmion," 204; "A Descent into the Maelström," 158, 179, 201; "The Domain of Arnheim," 111, 208; "The Duc de L'Omelette," 115; "Eleonora," 78; "The Facts in the Case of M. Valdemar," 26, 47, 79, 165, 204, 205–08; "The Fall of the House of Usher," 25, 33, 34, 40, 50, 77, 86–88, 109, 111, 174, 196–200; "The Gold Bug," 195–96; "Hop-Frog," 79, 143; "How to Write a Blackwood Article," 33, 45, 57; "The Imp of the Perverse," 132, 135, 137–38; "King Pest," 50; "Landor's Cottage," 111, 208; "Ligeia," 1–3, 18, 33, 34, 50, 77, 82–86, 88, 104–05, 108; "The Light-House," 27, 200, 209–10; "Lionizing," 40; "The Literary Life of Thingum Bob, Esq.," 115–16; "Loss of Breath," 33, 34, 40, 49–50, 57, 205; "The Man of the Crowd," 118–19; "The Man that was Used Up," 115; "MS. Found in a Bottle," 23–29, 32, 42, 92–93, 146, 167, 172, 209; "The Masque of the Red Death," 28, 194, 201–03; "Mesmeric Revelation," 204–05, 212; "Metzengerstein," 79, 200–201; "Morella," 34, 40, 77, 80, 88, 104–05; "The Murders in the Rue Morgue," 119–20, 125; "The Mystery of Marie Rogêt," 120, 125; "Mystification," 116–18, 125, 139, 144–45; *The Narrative of Arthur Gordon Pym*, 23, 24, 34, 51, 54, 57–58, 116, 145–76, 196, 206; "The Oblong Box," 41, 127; "The Oval Portrait," 60–63, 171; "The Pit and the Pendulum," 32, 34, 53–54, 57, 179; "The Power of Words," 115, 205; "A Predicament," 40–41, 205; "The Premature Burial," 34, 55–59, 206; "The Purloined Letter," 119, 120–28, 139; "Shadow—A Parable," 194–95; "Silence—A Fable," 19–21; "Some Words with a Mummy," 58, 205; "A Tale of the Ragged Mountains," 201; "Tales of the Folio Club," 18–19, 23, 28; *Tales of the Grotesque and Arabesque*, 21, 49; "The Tell-Tale Heart," 130, 132–35, 139, 144; "Thou Art the

Poe, Edgar Allan (*continued*)
Man," 127, 205; "William Wilson,"
33, 128–32
—poems: "Al Aaraaf," 82; "Annabel
Lee," 67, 70, 75, 110; "The City in
the Sea," 19, 178; "The Conqueror
Worm," 2–3, 82, 88; "The Haunted
Palace," 86; "To Helen" (*1831*),
106–07; "To Helen" (*1848*), 107;
"Lenore," 67, 69, 75, 88; "To One in
Paradise," 75; "The Raven," 67–69,
88; "The Sleeper," 73–75; "Sonnet—
Silence," 20–21; *Tamerlane and Other
Poems*, 97; "Ulalume," 71, 88, 111;
"The Valley of Unrest," 19
Poe, Elizabeth, 91
Poe, Neilson, 101, 102, 103
Poe, Virginia Clemm, 100, 101–05, 110,
111
Poe, William, 98
Proust, Marcel: *A la recherche du temps
perdu*, 189

Repression, 25, 55, 73, 79, 81, 83, 86,
134, 162, 164–65, 199
Revivification, 18, 39, 47, 78, 80, 84–
86, 105, 162
Reynolds, Jeremiah, 113
Richmond (Va.), 101, 103, 112
Richmond, Annie, 105, 110–12
Rilke, Rainer Maria, 180, 185
Rivalry, 117, 118, 120, 121–22, 126–27,
129–32, 138, 142–43
Royster, Sarah Elmira, 112

Sartre, Jean-Paul, 180, 190
Schizophrenia, 134, 136–37
Sentimentalism, 12, 15–17, 64, 66–68,
193
Shakespeare, William, 25, 55
Shew, Marie Louise, 105
Sigourney, Lydia Huntley, 17, 66; "Boy's
Last Request," 15–16
Smelt, Caroline E., 65
Snodgrass, Joseph Evans, 98
Sophocles: *Oedipus Rex*, 127
Southern Literary Messenger, 17, 97, 101,
103, 149–50
Stannard, Helen Stith, 106
Sterne, Lawrence: *Tristram Shandy*, 189

Stowe, Harriet Beecher: *Uncle Tom's
Cabin*, 1
Suicide, 103, 132, 134–35, 136–38,
143–44, 170, 180, 203

Taylor, Joseph: *The Dangers of Premature
Burial*, 36
Tennyson, Alfred, Lord, 10
Thoreau, Henry David, 18
Thousand and One Nights, The, 26
Tolstoy, Leo: "The Death of Ivan
Ilyich," 180–81
Tomb visitation, 8–10, 13–14, 70–73
Transference, 79–81, 135
Twain, Mark (Samuel Clemens): *The
Adventures of Huckleberry Finn*, 17, 159

Unreadability, 145–46, 148, 153–54,
157–58, 167, 173–75

Vidocq, François Eugène, 118
Vigne, J. B.: *Mémoire sur les inhumations
précipitées*, 36
Virginia, University of, 96

Waddel, Rev. Moses: *Memoirs of Miss
Caroline E. Smelt*, 65
White, Thomas (publisher of the *Southern Literary Messenger*), 103
Whitman, Sarah Helen, 100, 105–10,
111, 184
Wolf Man, 72–73
Wordsworth, William: "Lines Composed
a Few Miles Above Tintern Abbey,"
189
Writing: decentered, viii, 29, 30, 117,
122–23, 147, 185, 190–93; relation to
death, 3, 21–27, 30–31, 46, 59, 75–
77, 89, 93, 116, 146, 152, 168, 171–
73, 175–76, 185–200, 212; origins of,
3, 23, 171, 175–76; as violence, 114–
16, 122, 144; activity of, 19, 22–24,
173, 206; scene of, 32–33, 173–74,
189; as representation of truth, 148–
51, 154, 191–92, 206; survival of, 176

Yeats, William Butler, 210, 211
Young, Edward, 186; *The Complaint, or
Night Thoughts on Life, Death, and Im-
mortality*, 9, 54, 56